Religion
and Revolution
in Peru, 1824–1976

INTERNATIONAL STUDIES OF THE

COMMITTEE ON INTERNATIONAL RELATIONS

UNIVERSITY OF NOTRE DAME

Coexistence: Communism and Its Practice in Bologna, 1945-1965. Robert H. Evans.

Marx and the Western World. Nicholas Lobkowicz, ed.

Argentina's Foreign Policy 1930-1962. Alberto A. Conil Paz and Gustavo E. Ferrari.

Italy after Fascism, A Political History, 1943-1965. Giuseppe Mammerella.

The Volunteer Army and Allied Intervention in South Russia, 1917-1921. George A. Brinkley.

Peru and the United States, 1900-1962. James C. Carey.

Empire by Treaty: Britain and the Middle East in the Twentieth Century. M. A. Fitzsimons.

The USSR and the UN's Economic and Social Activities. Harold Karan Jacobson.

Death in the Forest: The Story of the Katyn Forest Massacre. J. K. Zawodny.

Chile and the United States: 1880-1962. Fredrick B. Pike.

Bolshevism: An Introduction to Soviet Communism, 2nd ed. Waldemar Gurian.

German Protestants Face the Social Question. William O. Shanahan.

Soviet Policy Toward International Control of Atomic Energy. Joseph L. Nogee.

The Russian Revolution and Religion, 1917-1925. Edited and translated by Boleslaw Szcześniak.

Introduction to Modern Politics. Ferdinand Hermens.

Freedom and Reform in Latin America. Fredrick B. Pike, ed.

What America Stands For. Stephen D. Kertesz and M. A. Fitzsimons, eds.

Theoretical Aspects of International Relations. William T. R. Fox, ed.

Catholicism, Nationalism and Democracy in Argentina. John J. Kennedy.

The Catholic Church in World Affairs. Waldemar Gurian and M. A. Fitzsimons, eds.

East Central Europe and the World: Developments in the Post-Stalin Era. Stephen D. Kertesz, ed.

Religion
and Revolution
in Peru, 1824–1976

JEFFREY L. KLAIBER, S.J.

UNIVERSITY OF NOTRE DAME PRESS
NOTRE DAME   LONDON

Library of Congress Cataloging in Publication Data

Klaiber, Jeffrey L
  Religion and revolution in Peru, 1824–1976.

  1. Peru—Politics and government—1829-
2. Catholic Church in Peru. 3. Church and state—Peru.
4. Poor—Peru. I. Title.
F3446.5.K55   322'.1'0985   76-51616
ISBN 0-268-01599-6

To

Antonine Tibesar, O.F.M.

CONTENTS

PREFACE

In his famous letter from Jamaica, Simón Bolívar expressed
wonder at the great attraction that the image of Our Lady of
Guadalupe had for Mexico's lower classes, who rose in rebellion
under that banner against the Spanish in 1810. "Political enthusiasm," said the Liberator, "has mixed with religion and produced
a vehement desire for the cause of liberty." Bolívar affirmed
what other astute political leaders before and since have observed
about the potential use of religion for political purposes among
Latin America's lower classes. All too often, however, students of
Latin America have treated these two forces in isolation, relegat-
ing politics to the political historian and religion to the anthropologist or church historian.

Religion and politics are so deeply intertwined in Peru that
government officials automatically seek the support of the church
in order to win religious legitimacy, without which their political
influence would be seriously limited. University professors and
students, who belong to a select intellectual elite, may criticize
the church and deride some of the religious customs of the lower
classes, but few public figures would dare risk losing popular support by engaging in such criticism, at least publicly. As in most
other Latin American countries, especially those with large Indian
and mestizo populations, anticlericalism in Peru may be fashionable
in some circles, but expressions of antireligious sentiment are not
popularly received by the majority of Peruvians.

As a Jesuit missionary who has studied and worked in Peru at
different times since 1963, I have had the opportunity to witness
this intimate and at times highly subtle interplay between religion and politics. In 1967 I undertook a study of the university
origins of the Aprista party, and in the course of that study I
grew increasingly fascinated by the way old-fashioned liberal anticlericalism and simple traditional Catholicism had mixed and
eventually made their peace in that tempestuous and controversial

movement. I decided then to set aside for special consideration the interaction between liberalism and popular religiosity, not only in the Aprista party but throughout all of Peru's modern history. In the summer of 1974 I had the privilege of serving under the bishop of Huaraz in the north-central Andes. From that vantage point I was able to observe the enormous prestige which the church enjoys among the Indians and lower-class mestizos in Peru. On other occasions I have witnessed and participated in the great religious processions in Peru such as the Lord of Miracles in Lima, Our Lady of Chapi in Arequipa, and the Lord of Solitude in Huaraz. These and many other experiences have convinced me of the strength of popular religiosity in Peru and of the need to view religion and politics as integral realities of Peruvian social and political history.

Most of the research for this work was done in Lima in the summer of 1972 and throughout most of 1975. In Lima I made extensive use of the National Library and the private collection of Rubén Vargas, S.J., which was especially helpful for materials relating to the nineteenth century. I also complemented my work in Lima by visiting the municipal libraries and certain private collections in Cuzco, Puno, Arequipa, Ayacucho, Trujillo, and Huaraz. I am grateful to many Peruvians who permitted me to make use of materials in their private collections and who also shared with me their own experiences and opinions, particularly Dr. Manuel Reina Loli in Lima, Sra. Julia Philipps in Caraz, and Father Alfonso Ponte, the director of the Cathedral Library in Lima. Also, on many different occasions since 1967 I have had interviews with Víctor Raúl Haya de la Torre, the leader of the Aprista party. Many other Apristas whom I also interviewed have graciously lent me materials that survived the political persecutions of the thirties and forties on the history of their movement. I also wish to express gratitude to Thomas West and James Riley, both professors at Catholic University, who read the completed manuscript and offered valuable, constructive criticism. Most of all, I wish to thank my dissertation director, Antonine Tibesar, O.F.M., whose vast knowledge of Peru and extensive contacts there proved invaluable for carrying out the research and composing this work. Finally, I am indebted to the great many Peruvians, students, teachers, professionals, and fellow Jesuits, who helped me directly or indirectly with this work. Each of them exemplified in distinctive ways the gracious courteousness and attentive hospitality characteristic of all Peruvians.

INTRODUCTION

Like Heraclitus, who announced that he had gone in search of himself, Peru is a nation in search of an identity. Peru contains a multitude of different cultures, racial mixtures, and social classes that have only begun in the twentieth century to forge a shared identity and common purpose. The fundamental cultural and social division of Peru from the sixteenth century on has been between the white Spanish ruling elite and its white creole successors on the one hand and, on the other, the Indians, mestizos, and Negroes who made up the bulk of the population. According to an estimate in 1812, out of a total population of 1,509,551 inhabitants, there were some 178,025 Spaniards, 954,799 Indians, 287,486 mestizos, and 89,241 Negro slaves in Peru.[1]

In spite of its size, the white population, which included many mestizos who passed for "white," constituted the cultural and social elite of the country. After the final defeat of the Spanish armies in 1824, the control of the government, the church, the army, education, and commerce, as well as ownership of most of the land, passed to the creole elite, which shared most of the conservative attitudes of the very Spaniards whom it had ousted. Within this elite, however, there was an even smaller group of enlightened statesmen, churchmen, lawyers, and soldiers who aspired to liberate Peru from the negative elements of its Spanish-colonial past and bring into existence a unified, progressive nation. Most of the men who belonged to this reformist elite had been indoctrinated in the ideas of the Enlightenment and, toward the end of the nineteenth century, the tenets of positivism and rationalism. The ideological formation of this elite and its attempts to influence public opinion and national policy is an important chapter in the history of Peru.

But the history of Peru is incomplete without a complementary study of the attitudes and intellectual formation of the lower classes, which the reformers intended to integrate into the new

1

national culture. The most significant drama in the modern social and intellectual history of Peru has been the encounter and confrontation between these two groups and their joint search for a common identity. In this encounter both the elite and the masses were challenged to question, readjust, or discard many of the prejudices and attitudes that they entertained with respect to each other.

In a land where the Spanish had deliberately fostered a separation between the white Spanish settlers and the native Indian communities, it was difficult to find unifying elements. Peru's beautiful but hostile natural environment, especially the massive phalanx of Andes mountains that rise up out of the coast and descend gradually into the Amazon basin in eastern Peru, contributed greatly to the fragmentation of Peru into cultural islands separated by great distances and diverse traditions. Even the Quechua language that the Incas used to unify their empire was so blended into the pre-Inca local languages that Quechua speakers from Cuzco hardly understood Quechua speakers from Ancash.

POPULAR CATHOLICISM

Nevertheless, there was a common heritage that all Peruvians shared, and that was the Roman Catholic religion which the sixteenth-century missionaries preached and fairly successfully implanted even in the most remote regions of the country. From the Spanish cities on the coast to the most primitive Indian communities in the bleak *altiplano* the same signs and symbols of the Christian faith were recognized and revered, pointing to a unity of religious belief that cut across steep economic, social, and linguistic barriers.

Yet, many have observed that even this unity of religious faith was more apparent than real. The highland Indians practiced a syncretic fusion of animism, mother-earth worship, and sixteenth-century Spanish Catholicism, which at times hardly seemed to be the same religion as that practiced in Lima or Arequipa. Even the more urbanized and hispanized mestizos and zamboes developed their own religious practices and traditions, which, though less obviously pagan than those of the highland Indians, formed a distinct cultural subworld within the orthodox Roman Catholicism professed in republican Peru. This religious subculture, which continues to flourish throughout all of Latin America in the twentieth century, has been commonly termed "popular religiosity" or "popular Catholicism."

One anthropologist describes popular religiosity as the religious expression of the economically and socially marginal sectors of society, which may, as in the case of Latin America, make up the majority of the population. Popular religiosity exists alongside and at times in opposition to the norms and orthodox practices laid down by the "officials" of the religion, the priests, bishops, and laymen, who are committed to the support and protection of the established religion. Popular religiosity is transmitted informally from generation to generation and forms an important part of a marginal group's "subculture." Nevertheless, even though it may exist without the approval of church officials, popular religiosity is never totally divorced from the orthodox faith. Very often many practices and beliefs of popular religiosity are the result of the people's attempts to redefine and reinterpret the more abstract ideas of the official religion in terms and symbols with which they are more familiar. The most common manifestations of popular religiosity in Latin America are the feasts in honor of patron saints, the cults surrounding places where the Virgin or a saint are believed to have appeared, funeral rites, devotions to sacred images, certain sacraments, the use of religious symbols such as holy cards, medals, relics, habits, and candles, and, finally, the creation of special social institutions such as the confraternity or special roles such as the *mayordomo* of the village feast.[2]

CELEBRATION AND RESIGNATION

The two fundamental moods that pervade most public displays of popular religiosity in the Andean highlands are those of joyful celebration and fatalistic resignation. Although these moods seem to be contradictory, in reality they represent two related modes of relief from the miserable living conditions of the Indians in the highlands. The Masses and the processions in honor of the village patron saint throughout most of the Andes are traditionally very somber affairs during which the people intone long, plaintive litanies calling upon God or a favorite saint to hear them and ease the burdens of life. Immediately following the religious rituals, the people begin dancing and singing—activities that will continue for hours. The heavy drinking that accompanies most of these religious feasts underlies the mood of fatalistic escapism that permeates them.

In this regard it is instructive to note the pastoral difficulty which churchmen encountered after Vatican II in fostering a devotion to the resurrected Christ among the lower classes in many parts of Latin America. Partially because they were deeply influ-

enced by sixteenth-century Spanish piety, with its heavy emphasis on the Passion and Good Friday, but more importantly because they live in conditions of dehumanizing exploitation, many
lower-class Latin Americans have much more readily identified
with the crucified Christ or the sorrowful Virgin than with the
resurrected Christ.[3]

Almost all of the major devotions and processions in Peru
center around an image of the suffering Christ or the sorrowing
Mother of God. In Huaraz it is the devotion to Our Lord of
Solitude; in Arequipa it is the devotion to Our Lady of Chapi;
and in Cuzco the principal procession is held in honor of the
Lord of Tremors. But by far the most important manifestation
of popular religiosity in Peru is the great annual Lord of Miracles
procession held in October in Lima. This procession was originated
in the late seventeenth century after one of Lima's great earth-
quakes by a Negro confraternity in thanksgiving to God for pre-
serving intact a wall with an image of the crucified Christ painted
on it. Over the years the lower classes of Lima attributed miraculous powers to the image, which they appropriately named *the
Lord of Miracles*. By the end of colonial times the Lord of Miracles had become the most popular devotion among Lima's
Negroes and mestizos. [4]

When the image of the Lord of Miracles is taken out in procession each year, thousands of Limanians pour out into the streets
to accompany it. Dressed in purple garbs to symbolize the peni-
tential attitude that is the motif of the procession, they form a
purple sea extending for seemingly endless blocks through Lima's
narrow streets. The slow, solemn cadence of the music and the
melancholic wails of grief arising from the pressing crowds suggest
a people in mourning awaiting some type of liberation.

In spite of all its grandiose plans to pose as the liberator of the
lower classes, the reformist elite was often far less sympathetic to
the culture of lower-class mestizos and Indians than the conservative churchmen who worked among these classes and who were
often the brunt of the reformer's attack. Overly influenced by a
paternalistic attitude that came with their elitist station in life
and by their own untested reformist theories, the reformers at
times actually widened the gap that separated them from the
lower class that they intended to "redeem." Nowhere is the
distance of the reformist elite from the lower classes better illustrated than in its disdain for popular religiosity. In 1909 the
leading spokesman for social reform in Peru and its principal

anticlerical, Manuel González Prada, penned these verses mocking the Lord of Miracles procession:

> Bearing on their shoulders the Lord of Miracles
> Prayerful worshippers and tattered children file by;
> Sweating, gasping and worn out,
> They move at the pace of a turtle.
>
> . . . .
>
> Suddenly, the rebellious waves
> Of the mob begin to seethe and overflow;
> The platform veers clumsily from side to side
> And threatens to crash into the crowd below.
>
> One of the weary faithful staggers
> And cries out in a voice full of desperation:
> "Give me a hand, brothers, give me a hand!
> This devil of a Christ is crushing me!"[5]

RELIGION AND REFORM

The aim of this study has been to examine the interaction between the religious world views of the reformist elite and the Peruvian lower classes from the period of independence in 1824 up to and including the reformist military government that took power in 1968. One of the principal conclusions of this overview is that the spokesmen for social and political reform, many of whom tended to be anticlerical and even prejudiced against popular religiosity, ended up adopting the religious symbols held in reverence by lower-class Peruvians in order to gain adherence to their cause. Conversely, as a result of their contact with the reformist elite, lower-class Peruvians reinterpreted their traditional religiosity by identifying it with the cause of social justice and by infusing their religious symbols with a new, revolutionary sense.

The first reformist elite that successfully identified itself with the interests of the lower classes was the Peruvian Aprista party in the twentieth century. The Aprista party, which became a populist forum in which anticlerical liberalism and popular Catholicism were brought into direct confrontation, is a model of the cultural transformation that resulted from the encounter between the reformist elite and the lower classes. Although originally inspired by the tenets of anticlerical liberalism, the Aprista party was converted into a quasi-religious crusade during the period of persecution from

1931 to 1945 as a result of the blending of political radicalism and popular Catholicism within the party.

After the Second World War, new groups and elites competed for the attention of the lower classes. But only three of these elite groups really made a significant impact nationally: the Aprista party, which continued to be the only perdurable mass-based movement; the armed forces; and the Catholic church. Although the Aprista party maintained its monopoly over the lower-middle classes on the coast, it failed to make significant inroads among the peasantry or to attract newcomers from among the waves of migrants from the Andean region who flocked to the squatter settlements ringing the major coastal cities. The task of expressing the political and social aspirations of these groups fell to the armed forces, which took power in 1968, and the newly socially awakened church.

Inspired by a Christian humanism, the new military regime aimed to set into motion the revolution heralded so long by Peruvian reformers. Although the military have been successful in eradicating many social injustices in Peru, they have been far less successful in penetrating the reserves of the newly politicized lower classes and inspiring enthusiasm for the revolution. By way of contrast, the church, Peru's oldest elite group, has been far more successful in entering the life situation of the marginal classes and bridging the gap between tradition and revolution. In the church, the symbols of tradition and revolution have become fused together. The mixing and blending of politics and religion among the lower classes today is giving form to a new national identity for millions of marginal Peruvians who are destined to inherit the land tomorrow.

Most of the works in English or Spanish to date on Peru have either emphasized the aspect of church-state relations or the strictly political formation of modern Peru. Few have attempted to bridge the gap between religion and politics on a popular level and to trace the formation of the modern political and religious consciousness of lower- and middle-class Peruvians. This is not a study, therefore, either of popular religiosity or of Peruvian politics in general—rather, it is an interpretative overview of the process by which these two realities, reformist politics and popular religiosity, have interacted and altered the world view of many Peruvians in their modern history. It is hoped that this study may contribute in some small way to a better understanding of one Latin American nation's search for identity.

1: THE GREAT TEMPLE OF THE LAW: THE NINETEENTH-CENTURY ORIGINS OF ANTICLERICALISM

LIBERALISM AND ANTICLERICALISM

The nineteenth-century Latin American liberal is frequently hailed as a prophet of contemporary social change. In the case of Peru, for example, Francisco de Paula González Vigil and Manuel González Prada are viewed as precursors of modern populist and socialist movements. Benito Laso's tract on the triumph of law over force and Vigil's essays calling for popular education and the creation of public associations in Peru are but a couple of examples of the crusading manifestos that inspired later generations of social reformers. In their war against caudillistic militarism, despotism, and a privileged church, the liberals sought to sever Peru from the bondage of its colonial past. In so doing they also cleared the way for the construction of a new society. What is overlooked at times, however, is that the last-century liberal also harbored certain very conservative notions, especially in religion. While much attention has been paid to the liberal's campaign against the church as an institution, relatively little has been given to the liberal's concept of religion itself and its role in society.

Karl Mannheim's distinction between ideology and utopia provides a helpful frame of reference for analyzing the liberal's concept of religion. For Mannheim, ideology involved whatever set of ideas or attitudes that tends to justify the status quo. Hence, ideology is essentially conservative. Utopia, on the other hand, is a cluster of ideas and attitudes that envisions a new order not yet in existence. By actually attempting to live according to their visionary expectation in the present, utopians naturally threaten the stability of the reigning order. Mannheim cautions, however, that ideas that transcend the existing order are not necessarily in themselves utopian or "revolutionary." The idea in the Middle Ages of an other-wordly paradise for example, not

7

only did not challenge the status quo but actually served to strengthen it. On the other hand, the Christian doctrine of brotherly love was utopian because it undermined the principle upon which medieval serfdom rested.[1] The case to be argued here is that although in many areas the liberals were utopian in their thinking, in the area of religion they were strictly ideological, that is, conservative.

In comparison with that of other Latin American countries, liberal anticlericalism in Peru was relatively mild and never a popular issue. This was true, in part, because of the strength of Spanish culture and tradition among the landowning upper class and, in part, because of the strength of Roman Catholicism among the lower-class mestizos and Indians. At the first congress, in 1822, the vast majority of the delegates voted to uphold the Catholic church as the established church. Only a handful of delegates voted in favor of granting religious toleration to other denominations. Among those who voted for toleration were the priest-delegates, Francisco Luna Pizarro, later the conservative archbishop of Lima, and Toribio Rodríguez de Mendoza, the former liberal rector of San Carlos College.[2] Optimistic liberalism in the wake of the collapse of the Spanish empire was shared by clergy and laity alike. It was only after this initial liberalism took on anticlerical tones in the decades of the thirties and forties that most churchmen openly aligned themselves with the conservatives.[3]

The liberals who concerned themselves the most with the church question won many significant but relatively minor victories for their cause during the first several decades after independence. Legislators and jurists like Manuel Lorenzo de Vidaurre, Francisco Javier Mariátegui, and Benito Laso managed to close down many convents and reduce the number of priests and nuns in the first decade after independence. In the liberal constitution of 1856, the ecclesiastical *fuero* and tithes were abolished. In the liberal congress of 1867, however, new anticlerical proposals were greeted by jeers from hostile crowds. Most liberals heeded that and other public outbursts as a warning that the politically expedient limit to anticlerical liberalism had been reached, at least for the time being. In the liberal constitution of 1867, religious toleration was again rejected, although this time by a narrow margin, and the majority of the delegates who forged the constitution voted to retain Roman Catholicism as the official religion of the state.[4] Although they fell considerably short of their legislative objectives, the anticlericals, a vocal minority among the liberals in general, labored incessantly to sway public opinion to their point of view. As a result of their propagandistic zeal, their opinions and attitudes, though not always popularly received at the time, gradually became the dogmas that undergirded later reform movements.

Although the target of their attack was the socially influential native church, the anticlerical liberals drew most of their inspiration from the same sources that motivated reformers in Europe: the Enlightenment; Gallicanism, or its Spanish counterpart, regalism; and some aspects of Jansenism.[5] A few years after independence, the archdeacon of the cathedral, José Ignacio Moreno, warned against all these evils which he believed were invading the newly emancipated republic. In his *Ensayo sobre la Supremacía del Papa,* he lamented the attacks by atheists, Jansenists, and Protestants against the spiritual power of the pope. He singled out as particularly pernicious the ideas of the liberal French bishop, the Abbé de Pradt, who urged Americans to complete their emancipation by breaking with Rome, and Pietro Tamburini, the Jansenist theologian who publicized the decrees of the Synod of Pistoia which called for the restoration of the primitive, nonpapal church. He also inveighed against the Gallican bishop, Jacques Bossuet; the church historian, Claude Fleury; the Louvain professor, Zeger Bernhard Van Espen; and the bishop of Trier, Johann Nikolaus Von Hontheim, better known under his pseudonym of Justinius Febronius. All of these authors advocated curbing the power of the Holy See and augmenting the power of the local bishops. Finally, Moreno attacked the Portuguese regalist, Antonio Pereira, and the Spanish theologian, Joaquín Villanueva, both of whom called for subjecting the laws and external discipline of the church to princes and secular governments. Warning that these doctrines might undermine the newly won unity of the Latin American church with the Holy See, Moreno exhorted the new republics to look to the pope as their common center.[6]

MANUEL LORENZO DE VIDAURRE

Even as Moreno wrote, however, the ideas of one of the first Peruvians to espouse these doctrines, Manuel Lorenzo de Vidaurre, were already decisively influencing legislation dealing with the Peruvian church. A student of both canon and civil law at San Carlos, Vidaurre was a professed *fidelista* when he composed his *Plan del Perú* in 1810. Appointed as an *oidor* of the royal audience of Cuzco in 1811, he was later deposed for remaining neutral during Pumacahua's revolt. After that he underwent a self-imposed exile, during which he visited France, England, Spain, and the United States. He also served briefly as an *oidor* of the royal audiences of Puerto Príncipe in 1821 and later in Galicia. In 1823 he dedicated the revised edition of his *Plan del Perú* to Bolívar, thus indicating his allegiance to the cause of independence. From the time he returned to Peru in 1823 until his death in 1841, he served at different times as president of the Supreme Court, minister of government, president of congress, and dean of the College of Lawyers in Lima.[7]

In the words of Alberto Tauro, Vidaurre was a man "formed in the discipline of the Enlightenment, who saw in the law the most efficient instrument for achieving happiness in the Republic."[8] In or out of power, Vidaurre spent most of his life composing ideal legal charters for Peru or attempting to implement his theories through court rulings or parliamentary legislation. In many ways, Vidaurre's experiments in legislation, especially as regards religion, reflected not only his own personal crises, but the transitional crisis of Peru itself as it emerged from colonial status. It was Vidaurre's task to shelve the old *Patronato Real Indiano* and devise a new nationalistic formula. Although his proposals rarely pleased churchmen, from Vidaurre's point of view, they represented his best efforts to compromise the demands of the new nation with his personal faith.

In his suggestions for church reform, Vidaurre pointed to the Sermon on the Mount as the model for Christianity. Like most of the Jansenist and Gallican reformers, Vidaurre wanted simplicity and order to reign in the church. His twenty reform proposals for the clergy in his *Plan del Perú* included limiting the amount of stipends which the clergy could accept, restricting clerical involvement in financial matters, reducing the number of visits that rural clergymen could make to the capital, and raising the standards of training and personal conduct of the clergy.[9] His proposed norms for religious women fell into the same genre: He lamented the lack of chastity among the religious orders of women in Peru, their ostentatious ways, and lack of proper religious decorum. According to Vidaurre, Gomorrah was but a shadow compared to the great convents in Lima.[10] Lest his numerous reform proposals appear to be overly burdensome, however, Vidaurre insisted that he had no intention of limiting the power of the church. On the contrary, he stated that he wished to join his voice with that of Montesquieu in praising the clergy as the chain and brake holding back bad rulers.[11]

In his *Proyecto del Código Eclesiástico* (1830), Vidaurre cited Montesquieu again, but this time to argue for stringent state supervision of the church. By his proposed code, the state would set the norms for the training of priests, the selection of bishops, and the external discipline by which public worship, sermons, church synods and councils would be conducted. In his lengthy dissertation on celibacy, Vidaurre argued that celibacy was an unnatural state and that priests should be allowed to marry. Furthermore, Vidaurre noted, priestly celibacy was not an early church practice. Voicing the sentiments of many Gallicans and Jansenists, Vidaurre declared that the state should not recognize any powers of the bishop of Rome that were not clearly founded in the first three centuries of the church. Among the norms for naming bishops, Vidaurre mentioned that of "not having had previous relations with the Church of Rome."[12]

In general, however, although Vidaurre sought to adopt many of the reform measures of Gallicanism and regalism, he did not wish to subscribe to the entire philosophy behind these doctrines. In the chapter entitled, "Nota muy Extensa," added in 1823 to the *Plan del Perú,* Vidaurre describes a *tertulia* in which he, an Englishman, and an enlightened Frenchman, compare opinions on the subject of religion. During the conversation the Frenchman takes all of the advanced anti-Christian positions of the French Enlightenment, among which he rejects Scripture in favor of a religion of reason. The Englishman accepts Scripture but not the Church of Rome. Vidaurre assumes the offensive against both. Declaring himself an "Apostolic Roman Catholic," he responds to the Frenchman that reason alone is a poor guide to come to know the mysteries of God. To the Englishman he answers that though he does not want the pope to exercise any temporal power or to be a sovereign of Europe, there should be a pope.[13] In his last work, *Vidaurre contra Vidaurre,* he rejected the charge that he was a follower of Febronius, Tamburini, Villanueva, or Pereira. On the other hand, he also rejected as equally unacceptable the ultramontanist positions of De Maistre, Bolgeni, and Moreno.[14] On another occasion, he attacked Bellarmine and the Jesuits for trying to make a "semi-God" of the pope.[15] Yet to the end of his life he held that the pope was the "common center" for all Christians.

In his *Proyecto de un Código Penal,* begun while he was an *oidor* in Cuzco and finished during his exile to the United States in 1828,

Vidaurre reveals considerably more clearly his ideas on religion. In the section, "Crimes Against Religion," Vidaurre assails as social evils blasphemy, heresy, and atheism. Vidaurre felt so strongly about blasphemy that he believed that a habitual blasphemer should be deprived of his rights of citizenship until he reforms. Another Draconian measure stated that anyone who should violently impede a public act of worship should be condemned to four years of prison and deprived of a tenth part of his wealth. In one area, however, Vidaurre displayed a liberality not present in the first publication of the *Plan del Perú*. In 1823 he declared that he was more amenable to toleration as a result of having witnessed the harmony among the sects in the United States. In his penal code he proposed that anyone who opposed toleration should be suspended of his rights of citizenship for two years.[16]

The area in which Vidaurre admitted of no compromise, however, was that of atheism. He declared that while he had once believed religious and superstitious fanatics to be worse than the individual atheist because at least the latter did not sacrifice victims in the name of religion, he had come to fear the atheist more "than a wild beast in the mountains." Atheism, said Vidaurre, was a public act against society because "I find no crime of which one who denies the power of a Supreme Being is not capable." For this crime Vidaurre reserved his strictest censure: "Whoever teaches atheistic or materialistic doctrines and fails to desist in spreading his errors after three warnings should be exiled."[17]

Vidaurre's remarks on atheism are consonant with his general view of religion as a principle of order in society. In his *Cartas Americanas,* written while he was still a monarchist, Vidaurre argued that religion has always been the basis of government. Both Lycurgus in Greece and Manco Capac in Peru spoke to their respective peoples in the name of their gods. Vidaurre rejected the belief held by Bayle and Rousseau that Catholicism impeded the growth of nations. The Christian, he said, is a good soldier because he does not fear death. He is a good citizen because he respects the rights of others. And he is a good subject because he believes in legitimate authority. The real problem, explained Vidaurre, are those bad priests who teach "superstition and fanaticism" to the people.[18] When Peru established relations with the Holy See, Vidaurre, then a convinced republican, wrote an open letter to the pope. In it he again attacked Rousseau's concept of the social contract, instead asserting that good government depends on a commonly accepted public morality, which in turn depends on an established religion.[19]

In his final work, *Vidaurre contra Vidaurre* (1839), intended to be a manual for a course on canon law, the ailing jurist also attempted to repudiate some of his earlier liberalism. In light of his rather moralistic and even pious religious views, his "retraction" of 1839 hardly represented a sweeping reconversion back to the church, in spite of the fact that he compared himself to St. Augustine. Nor is it entirely clear why his stated desire of rectifying past errors should take the form of a new polemic on the nature of power within the church. It could be, as Vidaurre claimed, that he did not want to "run to the opposite pole" by accepting everything then commonly held by Rome on the nature of the papacy. Whatever his intentions may have been, he called, among other things, for a type of popular sovereignty within the church according to which the pope would be subject to all general councils. The general councils would operate very much as parliaments do in the political order—as checks on the executive branch. Vidaurre praised the Council of Constance (1414–18), repudiated by later popes, which affirmed the principle of conciliar supremacy over the pope.[20]

. Obedient to the end to his pious instincts and spirit of reform, Vidaurre followed a path between two extremes. On the one hand, he warned against "spiritual fanatics" who wanted to give the pope too much power over the church in America. On the other hand, he feared an influx of liberal ideas that would destroy the "Holy Foundation of Religion."[21] Although his intentions were conciliatory, Vidaurre's last word as a liberal managed to touch off the first of many heated public debates between liberals and conservatives on the church. The archbishop of Lima condemned the book as heretical, while Francisco Javier Mariátegui wrote a vigorous polemical tract in Vidaurre's defense.[22]

FRANCISCO DE PAULA GONZALEZ VIGIL

If churchmen frowned on Vidaurre's vacillating forays against the church, they were unprepared for the veritable onslaught that followed during the next three decades in the works of Francisco de Paula González Vigil. A priest from Tacna, Vigil studied and taught at San Jerónimo Seminary in Arequipa. In 1826 he entered public life as the delegate-elect from Arica. In 1832, as the delegate from Tacna, he won national prestige for his defiant " ¡Yo debo acusar! ¡Yo acuso! " speech directed against President Agustín Gamarra. Disillusioned by the politics

of militaristic caudillism, Vigil retreated somewhat from the public forum and dedicated the next three decades of his life to
writing on religious and church questions. From the National
Library in Lima where he served as director for many years, Vigil
became the main spokesman in Latin America for national supervision of the church.[23]

Like Vidaurre, Vigil focused on reform within the church as a
means of securing greater freedom within both the church and
society. For him, however, the real obstacle to freedom within
the church was not so much intransigent popes who dominated
church councils but rather the clique of determined bureaucratic
cardinals and bishops who surrounded the person of the pope
and virtually made him a victim of their political designs. This
clique was the Roman curia, or curialists, whose "pretensions"
threatened to suppress the pope as shepherd of the church in
favor of the pope as a temporal prince. With the clarion call for
"Peter to be Peter," Vigil affirmed the supremacy of the pope to
the end of his life. He believed that the pope, once liberated from
the curia, would be bound to the churches of America in a new
and fraternal manner.

In his massive, multivolume work, *Defensa de la Autoridad
de los Gobiernos y de los Obispos contra las Pretensiones de la
Curia Romana,* Vigil developed his case with painstaking and
tedious attention to early church history, church councils, and
conflicts between crown and pope. In the first of fourteen dissertations, he laid down the cardinal principle of his entire work—
Jesus Christ had definitively separated the two orders, kingdom
and priesthood, secular and spiritual authority. Religion and politics should not mix, Vigil categorically asserted that the church
and the popes enjoy only that power conferred on them by Jesus
Christ and that does not include temporal power.[24]

Somewhat inconsistantly with this principle of separation,
however, Vigil went on to introduce the notion of the "Protector-
Government," which has the right and duty to regulate affairs
related to the church. Vigil, of course, held that the newly liberated republics of Latin America had inherited the right of
patronage over the church. As a clergyman conscious of the dual
nature of the church, Vigil declared that governments may regulate only those church affairs which do not involve its spiritual
nature. Concretely, this meant that the government could regulate presumed intrusions of the church into the temporal order
such as excessive feast days, the clerical *fuero,* the *recurso de*

fuerza, high funeral costs, and the ringing of church bells. Furthermore, the government could give or withhold the *pase* on papal
bulls or briefs, fix the number of ecclesiastics, convoke church
councils, nominate and present bishops, regulate episcopal elections,
and establish dioceses.[25]

Vigil, like Vidaurre, believed religion to be the foundation of
a well-ordered society. "Religion," said Vigil, "according to the
will of its divine author, is a powerful element of order and tranquility, ineffable stimulus to love and justice, respect for the
highest authorities, and the fulfilling of all types of obligations."[26]
This concept of religion is, in effect, Vigil's underlying justification for the state's regulation of church affairs. If the church pro-
motes order and stability in society, then the state, which is also
fundamentally concerned with procuring these objectives, should
see that the church fulfills that function.

In his dissertations on bishops, Vigil argued that the new Latin
American nations inherited the right to nominate and present
bishops and establish new dioceses. He justified this claim on
the grounds that independence did not effect a radical change
in the right of the state to exercise patronage and that it is im-
plicit in the right of patronage for the state to watch over the
church for the general good of its citizens. Governments may,
for example, regulate episcopal elections because such elections
ultimately affect the public good. This same principle also calls
upon the state to demand that bishops perform their spiritual
functions properly.

Vigil's attitude on the function of religion in society becomes
most clear in his last dissertation, "On Freedom of Thought and
the Inviolability of Conscience." He defined conscience as the
religious sentiment in the heart of every individual by which he
is led to know the laws of the moral order set down by the
Creator. Influenced by the Enlightenment's emphasis on science
and order, Vigil compared the laws of the moral order to those
of the physical universe.[27]

The state should respect the rights of conscience, argued Vigil,
because it should be pleased that its citizens have religious sentiments. Religion, he explained, is the "only brake capable of re-
straining a man when he acts or thinks evil in private." A man's
conscience, moreover, is his private domain beyond the legitimate
reach of the state. Even the church, though it may be more
properly constituted to deal with men's conscience, may never
use any coaction to influence the conscience. There is one justifi-

cation alone for restricting the rights of conscience, Vigil quali-
fied, and that is if the exercise of this liberty of conscience in-
fringes on the rights of others or defeats the ends for which society exists.[28]

Praising religion as the cornerstone of order and peace in
society, Vigil pointed out that these benefits of religion could
be obtained without an established religion. The state, said Vigil,
should be interested in curbing only those religious groups that
do not adhere to the Gospel. Arguing that any Christian confession conduces to good public order as long as it respects the
rights of others, Vigil capitalized on the ill effects of religious
intolerance in society. Intolerance breeds contempt for the individual's true religious convictions and consequently weakens the
general esteem for religion itself. Religious intolerance, concluded
Vigil, is counterproductive because it weakens the basis of order
and respect for law upon which the state and society rest.[29] Anticipating scandalized protests from his less-enlightened contemporaries, Vigil added that toleration of a non-Catholic cult did
not necessarily imply official approval.

Vigil argued assiduously against the concept of an established
religion. With impeccable logic, Vigil pointed out that only individuals, not a government or a state, can have a religion. Vigil
praised what he termed, somewhat infelicitously, the "political
atheism" of the United States where the intolerance of submit-
ting to a "national God" was avoided.[30] He appealed to all men
of good will to use whatever peaceful means available to combat
intolerance and to fight for the rights of man, especially that of
freedom of conscience. In his concluding remarks, Vigil addressed
himself to the problem of the atheist. Unlike Vidaurre who showed
little toleration for this anomalous type, Vigil exhorted Christians to reach out in compassion to the atheist.[31]

Most of the themes elaborated by Vigil in his master work appeared again in his later writings. Undeterred by repeated papal
condemnations of his works, Vigil forged ahead in his campaign
to liberate the pope from a narrow-minded curia and the Peruvian
church from ultramontanism.[32] In his polemic against the Jesuits
(1861), he castigated them for aligning themselves with absolut-
ism and for mixing in secular affairs.[33] Lamenting the antinational
doctrines taught in some schools and in the pulpit, Vigil outlined
a program of strict state supervision of all church activities in his
Manual de Derecho Público-Eclesiástico.[34] Upon hearing of the

loss of the papal lands, Vigil fired off an essay, *Roma* (1871), in which he attacked the notion that the papal lands were a loss to the church. In poetical language foreshadowing the biblical metaphors of Vatican II, Vigil declared that all Christians are pilgrims on the earth and in this spirit the temporal losses should be seen.[35]

In other writings dealing more directly with religion itself, Vigil continued to affirm religion as a universal value for men. In his catechism on the existence of God, designed to bolster faith through the use of reason alone, he concurred with Vidaurre on the essentially antisocial nature of atheism. Only the idea of God and of a future life, argued Vigil, can inhibit rational beings from committing bad actions and thinking bad thoughts in all situations in life.[36] In an unpublished work entitled, "La Religión Natural," Vigil called for a purified natural religion, free of all the stains with which men have tainted religion. If all men followed their conscience and obeyed the law of God as revealed in nature, Vigil reasoned, there would be no discord or disunity among men. Vigil looked to a day when neither priests nor politicians would impede mankind from arriving at a higher faith. Praising work and marriage as the two foundations of public morality, Vigil denied that armed revolution is an effective solution to social problems. Recognizing the social roots of poverty, however, Vigil called for the creation of public self-help associations for the benefit of all citizens. Finally, Vigil expressed his hope that as men progress toward a world of peace and concord, so also will they come to worship the same God revealed in nature.[37]

In his later years Vigil accentuated the theme of peace and progress as he turned away from exclusive attention to the church back to more directly political questions. Increasingly he related religious toleration to industrial progress. In one of his essays on toleration, Vigil urged legislators to clear the way for "intelligent and industrious foreigners" to come to Peru.[38] Vigil warned that foreigners would "take their capital and industry" to other places if they could not practice their own religion in Peru.[39]

In his essay on education, Vigil championed popular education as the most effective defense of the people against the "pretensions" of the curia. Popular education, claimed Vigil, would inculcate in the people a love of work and self-discipline. Above all else, popular education would inspire the people to fulfill their duties as citizens and to acquire "virtuous habits" beneficial for an orderly society.[40] In his social and political essays, Vigil advocated the unity of Latin America and assailed the endemic scourges of the American republics—war and militarism.[41]

FRANCISCO JAVIER MARIATEGUI

Even while Vigil was turning to more vital social and political questions of the day, his lifelong friend, Francisco Javier Mariátegui, continued to resurrect the specter of papal intervention in America. Born in 1793, one year after Vigil, Mariátegui studied law at San Marcos. After fighting for independence, he was elected to the first congress. He served briefly as minister of foreign affairs and as representative to Ecuador. Like Vidaurre, he was for many years a member of the Supreme Court and on a number of occasions president of that body. One of the founders of Masonry in Peru, he was perhaps even more vehement than Vigil, if not more prolific, in the campaign against ultramontanism. In 1831 he composed a rebuttal to José Ignacio Moreno's works. Calling himself a "true Catholic," he took Moreno to task for equating the pope with the church.[42] In 1840 he issued a "Catholic Defense" of Vidaurre's last work.[43]

Fear of papal concordats motivated him to compose a treatise on the ill effects that such agreements have on the sovereignty of secular states. Mariátegui's immediate concern was that a concordat celebrated between Bolivia and the Holy See in 1851 would become a model for a concordat with Peru. At the time that he wrote, 1852, President Echenique's ambassador, the ultramontanist churchman Bartolomé Herrera, was already in Rome drawing up just such a concordat. Mariátegui excoriated the Bolivian concordat for three reasons: firstly, it "degraded" Bolivia; secondly, it was "against the liberties of the American churches"; and thirdly, it was "against the structure of the primitive Church."[44] Like Vigil, Mariátegui declared that he believed the pope to be Peter's true successor. Unlike Vigil, however, he did not distinguish between the pope and his curia: both were blind to the advances of the modern age.

In 1873, two years before Vigil's death, Mariátegui published his *Manual del Regalista*. As a justification for writing a new work on church-state relations, he pointed to the great ignorance which the youth had of their national patrimony. Mariátegui defined six fundamental rights inherent in national sovereignty: to present bishops; to erect bishoprics; to protect (supervise) the church; to suppress religious houses; to nationalize excessive church wealth; and to give the *pase* to papal documents.[45] Although it contained little that was new on the subject, the work serves as an example of a motif of Gallicanism and the new national liberalism—the myth of the early church. Vidaurre, Vigil, Mariátegui, and nearly all the other liberals had continual recourse to the "primitive" church to justify their reform measures. In many ways, however, they used that image in a somewhat arbitrary fashion to secure their own ideological positions.

Mariátegui justified the state's right to name bishops, for example, by referring to the early church. According to Mariátegui, there was no precedent for naming successors to the apostles. Soon it became customary for each diocese to elect its own bishop. In time, however, to prevent corruption in the elections, the clergy alone voted for the bishop. Finally, after the Edict of Milan, the post of bishop became such an attractive political position that it became necessary for the emperors to name bishops lest narrow vested interests dominate episcopal elections. After the collapse of the Roman Empire, the different national kings assumed the right to nominate bishops in the name of the people. At no point did Peter or his successors interfere in this process. Arguing that this system of naming bishops should continue, Mariátegui noted that the kings were positively interested in appointing only those ecclesiastical functionaries who would be "instruments of morality and order" and not "instruments of bad customs or disturbances."[46]

The state may regulate the external discipline of the church, Mariátegui asserted, because the proper domain of the church is the strictly spiritual. Jesus Christ, Mariátegui asserted, came to save souls and He never intended for his followers to become involved in temporal or political affairs. Christianity grew rapidly because it preached liberty and equality for all men. Mariátegui cautioned, however, that this liberty and equality refers to the reign of Christ in Heaven, not on Earth. As a result of an unfortunate literalism, Mariátegui explained, the "ignorant masses" interpreted these concepts in the earthly sense. From time to time these unlearned Christians challenged civil authority and broke laws. The persecutions were brought on in part, Mariátegui concluded, by the antisocial actions of these early Christians.[47]

In another section, Mariátegui observed that though Jesus Christ preached liberty and equality, He always respected and obeyed the civil authorities and He positively enjoined his disciples to obey the "powers of the earth."[48] Mariátegui blamed the bishops of the post-Constantinian era for failing to heed this teaching of Christ and involving themselves in the political affairs of the people.

The myth of the early church assumed different nuances from author to author. Vidaurre, for example, looked upon the first six centuries as the golden age of pristine Christianity. Only after the fall of Rome and the rise of barbarism and ignorance did bishops become warriors and politicians. It was Charlemagne, according to Vidaurre, who made princes out of bishops and made the church an instrument of his imperial designs.[49] Vigil, who praised the church for its work of civilizing the barbarians, lamented the intolerance which characterized Christians after they themselves received the benefits of toleration. Once protected by "Caesar," Vigil noted, the church began to view as "rights" the privileges which the state had conceded to it. An example of a usurpation of a right was the ecclesiastical *fuero*. Originally, Christians went to the bishops to resolve their problems. Though civil judges accepted this practice because it was effective, the bishops never had a proper title to adjudicate in civil matters. Once the ministers of the church stepped inside Caesar's palace, Vigil concluded, they remained there, "secularized exteriorly, and many of them in their hearts."[50]

Another myth that fascinated liberals was the deist belief in natural religion. Vigil associated the advance of humanity with the universal acceptance of a single religion grounded in the natural law. An exponent of this concept was Mariano Amezaga, who of all the liberals came the closest to denying the doctrines of Christianity itself. Amezaga, a professor at the liberal Colegio de Guadalupe, summarized his creed in the cryptic statement: "Religion is a great truth, but religions are a solemn lie."[51] Amezaga believed that the originally good religious impulse in the hearts of all men had been vitiated historically by the different religions with their superstitious beliefs and priestly domination. He praised Christ for his good example but criticized Him for placing before men moral standards which only God could obey. In particular, Amezaga singled out the doctrine of hell as not worthy of a merciful God. Though he praised religion as the most noble instinct in man, Amezaga nevertheless pointed out the need for religion to purify itself and conform itself to human progress.[52]

The liberal spokesman from Puno, Benito Laso, identified the natural religion of man with Christianity itself. In his essay on the triumph of law over force (1858), Laso declared that Christianity is the religion of charity, equality, and liberty that will one day be the religion of all men. Somewhat lyrically, Laso exhorted his fellow citizens to erect a great temple to the law. In this temple all men will respect and even adore the law as the very will of the Supreme Being.[53]

The liberal's great faith in law, order, reason, and the natural goodness of man was both his strength and his weakness. Liberalism, as Basadre observed, was an illusion that sought to bring about reform and change by the strength of ideas alone.[54] The liberals were little prepared to understand or to deal with the complicated and deep-rooted social inequalities that bound Peru to its colonial past. In their critique of Peruvian Catholicism, for example, they made several important distinctions but stopped short of making the key distinction that would have invested the notion of religion with a more positive meaning for later generations of social reformers. All of the liberals distinguished, for example, between the simple church founded by Jesus Christ and the sophisticated church-state that Roman Catholicism had become. Vigil's call for a simpler church and his eloquent plea for "Peter to be Peter" anticipated the spirit of Vatican II. Although his defense of the rights of bishops was really an apology for national patronage and control of the bishops, it did foreshadow another dominant theme of Vatican II—episcopal collegiality.

The liberals also distinguished, although with less clarity, between institutionalized religion and the religious instinct itself. Most of Vigil's pleas for religious toleration, for example, rested on his assumption that any religious man, although preferably of a Christian persuasion, would be a law-abiding and useful citizen of the republic. Finally, the liberals insisted upon a distinction between the temporal and the spiritual orders. Perhaps because they were so accustomed to a privileged and established church, however, few of the liberals could conceive of religion as anything else but a conservative and stabilizing force in society. From their perspective, conditioned by three centuries of the *Patronato Real*, the intrusion of the church into the temporal sphere had had only one negative consequence—the religious legitimization of monarchical and repressive political regimes.

Throughout all of his works, Vigil reiterated the theme of religion as an "element of order and tranquility" in society. Nowhere did he suggest that religion, and Christianity in particular, might have any influence in society other than that of conducing to public order. Vigil hoped, as most of the liberals did, that the church would continue to help maintain order and peace in republican Peru as it had under the monarchy. He did not seem to entertain as a serious possibility that the liberal republican state might ever impede the very national and social progress to which he was committed. He certainly did not envision the state as creating or maintaining a social order in contradiction to a Christian social order. If any breach of peace were to occur, it would be due to the church's encroaching on the temporal-political order. Vidaurre, of course, looked upon a reformed, seminational church as a mainstay of the new society.

The model for the liberal-republican church was, of course, the liberal's version of the primitive church. In his biblical exegeses and historical analyses, Mariátegui emphasized the early Christian virtues of obedience, respect for authority, and noninterference in political affairs. At the same time, however, he selectively ignored biblical passages and incidents of early Christianity that suggest that the Gospels and Christianity also leveled a harsh indictment against the social and political injustices of the period. He glossed over the political implications of Christianity by attributing certain acts of civil disobedience of early Christians to "ignorance." A religion which encouraged political nonconformism was not part of the experience of Mariátegui or the other liberals.

In conclusion, neither Vidaurre, Vigil, nor Mariátegui conceived of the day when Catholic Christianity might, in Mannheim's terms, cease to be an ideology, legitimizing the established order, and become a utopia, heralding a new social order while the old order is still dominant. Vidaurre with his censorious piety, Vigil with his encyclopedic assault on curial claims, and Mariátegui with his strident admonitions against papal concordats all championed a liberalism that presumed religion to be the handmaiden of order. In this belief, the liberals of the nineteenth century shared the same world view as the conservatives.

It would not be until the advent of José Carlos Mariátegui and the *indigenistas* in the twentieth century that reformers began to discover a dynamic and positive element in religion. In the meantime, many of the negative attitudes of Manuel González Prada and other social thinkers toward religion, and Catholic Christianity in particular, were responses to the liberal's notion of religion as a stabilizing, and hence conservative, force in society. Furthermore, by emphasizing the need for a purer, more rational, and less "superstitious" religion, the liberals created another intellectual barrier to a sympathetic understanding of the popular Catholicism of the Indians and lower-class mestizos who made up the majority of the country.[55] In many of their proposals for institutional reform in both the church and society, the liberals were forward-looking visionaries. But in their view of the religious element in man and society as well as their understanding of the role of religion among the lower classes of Peru, they were captive students of dusty encyclopedias.

2: GONZALEZ PRADA'S ANTI-CATHOLIC KNEE:
THE RISE OF RADICAL ANTICLERICALISM

Manuel González Prada once stated in ironic jest that even if he wanted to he could not have become a Catholic. When asked why, the grandmaster of Peruvian anticlericalism replied that because of a peculiar deformation, his left knee would not bend. "I have," he explained, "an anti-Catholic knee."[1] This anecdote sums up in many ways the nonconformist spirit and stoic resistance of González Prada to all established powers, whether in Heaven or on earth. Partially because he was a proud individualist and partially because the social conditions of the country were not ripe, González Prada produced no lasting political movement of his own or left as a legacy any concrete program of action for future reformers. A militant reformer who distrusted his own reform party, González Prada was a humanist who detested the narrowness of some of the ideologies he championed. Admired by freethinkers and Masons, he mocked masonic ritual and hierarchy. Sought out by intellectuals, he scoffed at academic solutions to Peru's problems. Hailed as a prophet by radical workers' groups, he shied away from personal involvement in union politics. A bit of a maverick and a Don Quixote, González Prada eludes simple analysis. What remains clear, however, is that from the end of the War of the Pacific (1879–84) until his death in 1918, he became the social conscience of Peru through his many essays, poems, and public addresses. Indeed, his spirit of protest made a major impact on the educated youth and growing workers' movement in Peru.[2]

Furthermore, González Prada became the major link between the nineteenth-century liberal reformers and the social movements of the twentieth century. In many ways he complemented the prewar liberal's positive critique of the church and religion with his negative critique. Where Vigil and Mariátegui fought against ultramontanist doctrines in favor of a nationalist church, González Prada called for the liberation of the state, education, and all society from all church influence whatsoever. Where Vigil saw Christianity as a source of order in a progressive society, González Prada condemned Catholic Christianity as one of the main brakes on progress in Peru. Finally, where Vigil saw religion as an element which moralized and civilized men, González Prada indicted religion as a cluster of superstitious beliefs that held Indians, women, and children back from attaining the full use of their liberty and reason. Although the liberals called for the reform of church institutions, they viewed religion itself as a necessary good for society. González Prada, however, saw religion, and Catholicism in particular, as both unnecessary and pernicious. By the time the full cycle of criticism had been completed with the death of González Prada, there were few new negative things left to be said either about religion or the church in Peru.

Frequently accused of being a prophet of doom because he produced no grand scheme for the future, González Prada did, however, contribute positively to a new evaluation of social and religious ideas in Peru. The liberals had all been lawyers or priests who had great faith in legal and juridical solutions to the problems of the country. Profoundly skeptical of the efficacy of laws and constitutions, not to mention the integrity and good will of politicians, González Prada called for social solutions to what he believed were basically social problems. He awakened reformers to the idea that religion was not a mere church-state problem but an integral phenomenon of all of society. Furthermore, the liberals had been optimistic propagandists of a new nation. In their zeal they frequently entertained illusions about the nature of man and about the ease with which Peru would progress as a nation. Most of them had died or were old men when the Chilean invasion of 1881 plunged the country into ruin and despair. González Prada's merciless attack on Peruvian history, customs, and institutions was intended to destroy the myths that had blinded Peruvians before the war to the real problems of their country. In many ways, his criticism of organized religion was the necessary Cartesian denial that cleared the way for a fresher and more realistic inquiry into the role of religion in Peruvian society.

Some of González Prada's antireligious attitudes have been explained as a reaction to the conservative and religious family atmosphere in which he was raised. With characteristic candor,

González Prada himself concurred in part with this interpretation. On one occasion, his French-born wife, Adriana de Verneuil, pointed out to him that her father too was anticlerical but that he did not flee from priests. González Prada objected that her father had not been raised in the same atmosphere of "stale Spanish Catholicism" in which he had been. With a touch of humor and some bitterness, he added that in his house, "I ate monks for breakfast; I had monks for lunch; I breathed monks; they dominated everything."[3] On another occasion he noted that while his sisters prayed the rosary daily, he remained aloof from these practices. Concerned over his precocious nonconformism, his parents sent him to Santo Toribio Seminary against his wishes. While there he discovered his "anti-Catholic knee," and at the age of thirteen he fled the seminary and enrolled in the more liberal Colegio de San Carlos.[4]

EARLY LITERATURE

He set out to study law but stopped short of a degree because the Latin reminded him too much of the seminary. From Lima he traveled through the interior of the country and then established himself as a planter in the valley of Mala south of Lima. For the next eight years he raised crops and steeped himself in the interior solitude that would characterize the rest of his life. His solitude and new acquaintance with Indian Peru inspired him to produce some of his first literary productions, *Baladas Peruanas*.

The ballads all treated of the Peruvian Indian in his past glory during the Inca empire as well as his current misery under white rule. González Prada's anti-Spanish and antichurch feelings as well as his concern for justice for the Indians were already clearly pronounced at this stage of his life. In one particularly caustic ballad entitled "Valverde's Charity," González Prada suggests how Valverde, Pizarro's chaplain, might have responded to Pizarro's indecision in meting out the death sentence to Atahualpa. Exclaims the impatient Dominican:

> Muerte al Inca, muerte al Inca!
> Y, si temes y flaqueas,
> Apercíbeme la pluma:
> Yo firmaré la sentencia.[5]

In another imaginative vignette, González Prada describes a priest and a king's official conspiring to rob an Indian of his gold.

Though the priest prefers a "peaceful" solution, he admits other means may be necessary. Thus encouraged the official kills the Indian, and the priest kneels over the corpse of the Indian to ease his conscience:

> Mas el Cura, ante el cadáver,
> Se arrodilla en santa paz,
> Y el oficio de difuntos
> Empieza humilde a rezar.[6]

In another poem González Prada evoked the pathos of the Indian woman whose husband is dragged off to fight in a white man's war:

> ¡Adiós, oh mi choza!
> ¡Adiós, oh mis campos!
> ¡Adiós! que me alejo
> Siguiendo al Amado.
> . . . .
> Tú callas, oh Esposo,
> Tú marchas callando . . .
> ¡Maldita la guerra!
> ¡Malditos los Blancos! [7]

It was in just such a war that González Prada's vocation as a social protester was born. Soon after hostilities broke out between Chile and Peru in 1879, he volunteered for the army and as the Chilean forces advanced on Lima he was named a captain of a company. After the disastrous debacle of the Peruvian armies at Chorrillos and Miraflores in 1881, an embittered González Prada retreated to his house in Lima where he remained for the duration of the war.[8] The country that he beheld when he emerged from his self-imposed reclusion in 1884 was a ravaged vestige of prewar Peru. The proud nation that most foreign analysts predicted would easily win the war found its cities burnt, its fields devastated, and its economy wrecked. Most of all, its inhabitants were thoroughly demoralized. If military defeat and four years of occupation were not enough, the postwar years were characterized by struggles between factions of the army to control the government, by rampant inflation, and by humiliating "deals" with foreign companies to attract capital to Peru and pay for the war. In 1887 the government granted the William R. Grace Company the rights for sixty-six years to own, control, and expand most of the railroads of the country and many of the mines and oil fields.[9]

FROM LITERATURE TO POLITICS

Shortly after the war, González Prada married and began participating more actively in the Club Literario, to which he had belonged several years before the war. Within a short period, he was
elected president of the club, which included most of the leading
advanced thinkers, writers, and poets among the youth of Lima.
His star as a literary and social critic had already been rising when
he delivered his famous speech in the Politeama theater in Lima
in 1888. As part of a campaign to ransom back Tacna and Arica
from Chile, the Club Literario sponsored a literary-musical per-
formance in the theater that included the reading of González
Prada's speech. In listening to the speech, the somewhat startled
cultured upper-class audience, which included President Andrés
Cáceres, heard what Basadre termed "the most energetic condemnation of Republican history." Blaming "our ignorance and our
spirit of servility" as the real causes of Peru's defeat in the war,
González Prada called on Peruvians to look to science as the key
to future progress. He warned that only when the Indian is liberated from the "brutalizing trinity" of the justice of the peace,
the governor, and the priest will he become truly civilized. Leaving no group untouched, González Prada admonished the politicians and the military to live according to the standards of modern times or Peru would never recover its lost possessions. Finally,
with evident contempt for the generation in power, González
Prada issued the cry that would become a motif of his life: "Old
men to the tomb; young men to the task! "[10]
    In 1891 González Prada and other members of the Club Lite-
rario created their own political party, the Unión Nacional. Pro-
claiming their party to be one of principles and not *caudillos,*
the reformers presented the Unión Nacional as an alternative to
the petty personalist politics of the postwar years. The party
program called for a radical reform of Peruvian institutions, universal suffrage, decentralization of the government, and the end
of graft and corruption in politics. The party also announced
that it intended to emphasize social over political goals. Inspired by European radicalism, the Unión Nacional called for
the laicization of the state, religious tolerance, civil marriage and
burial, and the liberation of education from church control. Declaring that the Unión Nacional was not an "association of atheists
or communists," as some had charged, the reformers insisted that
they only proposed to do what the "liberal spirit of the age"
called for.[11]

For all their high-minded principles, or perhaps because of them, the reformers failed to attract any substantial following beyond the small group of cultured young men and women who surrounded González Prada. A spokesman for the party explained this lack of appeal in somewhat haughty terms: "A party which proclaims ideals so noble as the Unión Nacional would necessarily encounter resistance on account of the ignorance of the common people."[12] Several years later González Prada admitted that the goals of the Unión Nacional were utopian for Peru. At the same time he also revealed the somewhat individualistic and elitest notions of the reformers when he stated that he preferred a country of small but free property owners to a "huge republic of slaves and proletarians."[13] Furthermore, for all their emphasis on social goals, the reformers never made serious attempts to attract workers or other lower-class groups to the party.[14]

The same year as the founding of the party, González Prada set off to Europe to study and rethink many of his positions. His departure constituted a major setback for the new party, although he defended this action as a means of demonstrating that the party was one of principles, not *caudillos*.[15] He and his wife and son lived most of the six-year period in Europe in Paris, where he steeped himself in the ideas and atmosphere of the Enlightenment, the French Revolution, positivism, and anti-Christian historical criticism. Among the authors he studied were Victor Hugo, Louis Menard, Renan, Nietzsche, Bakunin, Spencer, and Darwin. He returned to Peru in 1898, a prophet thoroughly versed in every major nonconformist and advanced ideas of the day.

Shortly after returning from Europe, he left the Unión Nacional. He justified this separation later by claiming that the elitist youth who made up the party were incapable of bringing about what Peru really needed—a revolution.[16] After his European stay he accentuated his interest in social questions by turning toward anarchism and socialism. In 1905 he delivered a speech to the baker's union in Lima in which he called for an alliance of intellectuals and workers to pave the way for the coming revolution.[17] He also contributed regularly to anarchist newspapers, and until his death in 1918 he was the most articulate spokesman for anarchism and radical change in Peru.[18] In 1912 he succeeded Ricardo Palma as director of the National Library in Lima. In the nineteenth century Vigil had turned the National Library into an arsenal for his assault on the Roman curia. Now, in the early twentieth century, the National Library once again became a command post for a new battle: González Prada's campaign against all the repressive forces in Peruvian society.

INTERPRETING GONZALEZ PRADA

Both the man and his works defy simple classification. He was a retiring gentleman who evoked a passionate response from workers and anarchists. He was a positivist who mocked the dogmatism of sociologists. He was a fierce nationalist who inspired visions of a world brotherhood of anarchists and socialists. The Peruvian philosopher, Augusto Salazar Bondy, saw González Prada as primarily a man of letters who applied to Peruvian realities the two dominant thought currents in Europe in the nineteenth century—naturalism and positivism. Unlike the pessimistic positivists in the academic world, González Prada was a popularizer who sought to communicate his faith in science and progress to ordinary people.[19] Another author, Hugo García Salvatecci, compares González Prada to Nietzsche, Proudhon, and Vigil. All were essentially polemicists whose works and ideas became more intelligible when one understands the society against which they protested. Expanding somewhat on Salazar Bondy's analysis, García mentions these sources and influences that appear in González Prada's works: naturalism, romanticism, the paganism of Louis Menard, the positivism of Comte, the vitalism of Nietzsche, the historicism of Renan, the anarchism of Proudhon, Kropotkin, and Bakunin, the evolutionism of Darwin, and the oriental fatalism of Omar Khayyam.[20] It is somewhat more difficult to trace the lines of development in González Prada because there is little new at the end that was not there in the beginning. González Prada spent most of his life defining and refining the anticlericalism, the anti-Hispanism, and the anticonservatism of his youth.

In 1931 Jorge Basadre capitalized upon the theme of González Prada as a social protester. Basadre saw González Prada not so much as a spokesman to Peru of the radical new philosophies of Europe, but more as a symbol of the disillusioned Peruvian bourgeoisie faced with national defeat and disorder. Shocked by the defeat of their country in war and embittered by the alliance of the oligarchy with foreign capitalism in the postwar years, the Peruvian middle class found its voice in González Prada's nonconformist radicalism. Basadre described González Prada as an "apostate" because his message consisted in rejecting

the past, not in offering anything new for the future. To underline his view of González Prada as a spokesman for an alienated
bourgeois class, Basadre emphasizes the fact that in his later
years González Prada moved toward individualistic anarchism, not
not socialism.[21]

Three fundamental approaches to González Prada's religious
thought seem to emerge from this overview of his life and works.
First, González Prada may be studied from the point of view of
his personal reaction to the Spanish Catholic environment in
which he was raised and his lifelong public "debate" with himself
and others on the subjects of God, religion, life, and death. This
approach by itself, however, seems too narrow, for it excludes
the dynamic relationship between González Prada and Peruvian
society during the some thirty years or more in which he dominated the forces of social protest in Peru. A second approach is
to view González Prada as a prophet of the new and radical
ideas emanating from Europe. Under this aspect, he is seen as
an incarnation of the radical Enlightenment, rationalism, positivism, and evolutionism. Again, however, this viewpoint fails
to stress sufficiently the Latin American and Peruvian realities
to which González Prada applied these European philosophies.
Finally, to use Basadre's religiously charged word, González
Prada was an "apostate" whose supreme mission in life was to
bury the past. According to this view, González Prada was an
ardent nationalist who endeavored to expose the evils that in-
fested Peruvian society. He used radicalism and related advanced
positions as pedagogical devices to arrest the attention of fellow
Peruvians. The call to reform was the essence of González
Prada's message; the remedies he suggested were secondary.
These three approaches all concur in at least one observation:
González Prada was an eclectic thinker who did not achieve, or
never sought to achieve, a final, harmonious synthesis.

González Prada the Atheist

One of the clearest samples of the personal religious "world"
of González Prada is his essay, "La Muerte y la Vida," composed
in 1890. Like many of his later poems and essays, this composition is more of a searching dialogue than a dogmatic treatise.
The elements that pervade the essay are pagan sadness before a
blind and at times cruel universe, stoic determination to accept
life under these harsh circumstances, and a "pantheistic" human-

ism based on the common suffering of all things. In his opening
lines, González Prada announces the common fate of all men,
rich or poor: the tomb. To the question whether there is anything beyond the tomb, he replies that God and the soul are two
hypothetical entities invented by men to explain the origin of
things and how the mind functions. Men have invented God, said
González Prada, to compensate for the injustice of nature, which
rewards life with death.

But there is no escaping nature, which looks with indifference
on the plight of man. "We are born without being consulted,"
sighed the poet. "We die when we do not wish." González Prada
warned that it is ultimately useless to worry about what lies
beyond the grave. Yet he also displayed a marked resistance to
either fatalism or humble resignation. "It is undignified for a
man to die demanding the last place in the Heavenly Banquet
like a beggar," declared González Prada contemptuously. Rather,
he exhorted, like a pirate who sets sail without documents or
flag, a man should accept responsibility for his actions and "hurl
himself toward the Unknown."

Instead of gazing fixedly at the beyond, however, a man
should observe the condition of those who share life with him.
"There are times of generous solidarity," said González Prada,
"when we love not only humanity but the brutes and birds,
plants and lakes, clouds and stones as well." Who knows, questioned González Prada, but that all these things suffer with man,
too. Returning to the theme of Nature he observed that in all
this "infinite martyrdom" there is no bloodier irony than the im-
penetrable serenity of natural laws. What is the universe, demanded
González Prada: "Actor, accomplice, executioner, victim or instrument and stage for evil?" With stoic resignation, he responded that
there is no "superhuman light" to show the way in the night, nor
any friendly voice to encourage man in his failures. Ending on a
note of resignation, defiance, and generosity, González Prada exclaims:

> We did not ask for existence; but before the fact of life, let
> us accept life. Let us accept it, without monopolizing it or
> wanting to preserve it for our exclusive benefit. We laugh
> and love on the tombs of our parents; our children will
> laugh and love over ours.[22]

Even death must be accepted with stoic serenity. On one occasion González Prada envisioned death as one immense "Divine Unconsciousness" that swallows men like so many "conscious atoms."[23] On another occasion he announced that he intended to die "free and conscious, surrounded by fresh roses . . . facing the sun."[24] But suffering and cruelty were not to be born with the same equanimity. Anger, agonized skepticism, and even boastful paganism permeate González Prada's verses on these themes, While he was willing to share the sufferings of his fellow beings, he was not willing to resign himself to the suffering itself.

> Ante el inicuo drama de la vida
> Mi justiciero corazón protesta:
> Perdono mis dolores, no perdono
> La universal crucifixión eterna.[25]

In an anguished cry the poet demands to know who is responsible for this universal malaise:

> En la cosa y en el ser
> Hay una pena escondida,
> En la muerte y en la vida
> Hay oculto un padecer.
> ¿Qué puede un alma creer
> En este campo de horror?
> ¿Qué invisible sembrador
> Atraviesa el firmamento
> Derramando por el viento
> Sus semillas del dolor?[26]

In 1918, the year of his death, González Prada composed his last verses. He again evoked the image of an unjust God:

> No imaginemos un Padre
> Compasivo a los Clamores,
> Un buen Padre restañando
> Los heridos corazones.
> Si hay un Sér Omnipotente,
> Rey de hormigas y de soles
> Es acaso tan injusto
> Como nosotros los hombres.[27]

Finally, in another verse, imitating the style of Omar Khayyam, González Prada softened his anguished portrayal of God and nature by suggesting that perhaps some day God will come down to earth:

> Dicha en todo: ni un gemido
> Oyen tierra, mar y viento;
> Paz en todos: siempre juntos
> Andan lobos y corderos.
> ¿Quién obraba tal prodigio?
> Con el transcurso del tiempo,
> Dios se había humanizado,
> Era al fin clemente y bueno.[28]

These verses reveal a poet engaged in a passionate personal battle, the full meaning of which is only hinted at in language tinged with anger and bitterness. Although González Prada was capable of humor, there is an undertow of resentment and defiance in his works pointing to a struggle against an unredeemed past that weighed heavily on the present. González Prada the poet in stoic resistance against the unmerciful universe and an unknown God is a mysterious figure that eludes objective analysis. There are no clear or finished ideas that emerge from González Prada's religious essays and poems. More than anything else, the unresolved personal struggle enveloped in them is an atmosphere that pervades all of his other works.

González Prada the Positivist

González Prada the enlightened skeptic and prophet of positivism is a more well-known, if perhaps less original, figure. Although his faith in progress and science well antedated his European sojourn, his six years of study in the homeland of Voltaire, Renan, and Menard served to crystalize and broaden his ideas on these themes. Most of his prose and poetry exalting science or debunking Christian dogmas were composed either in Europe or shortly afterwards. The leitmotif of these writings is boldly proclaimed in this verse:

> Mas si hoy los Dioses de la fe Cristiana
> Decrépitos caminan a morir
> ¿Quién nuestro paso alumbrará mañana?
> La Ciencia, el solo Dios del porvenir.[29]

Although he mocked the new science of sociology as too dogmatic, González Prada accepted the general positivistic view of religion as an immature stage in the development of humanity.[30] The fully developed man destined to emerge from the superstitious grip of religion and metaphysics would be the enlightened man of reason and science. "To expect an intelligent mind to remain religious," said González Prada, "would be to attempt to prevent it from leaving adolescence."[31] Science and courageous good will were the arms that would liberate man from his myths. Furthermore, González Prada categorically rejected the idea that morality was a product of religion. On the contrary, he asserted, morality precedes religion and will supersede it. Religious "morality" hardly merits the name because it is based on ignorance and instinct. "Moral precepts," said González Prada, "like the laws of justice, do not proceed from religion; religions, in contact with philosophy, become more human."[32]

Atheism and skepticism are not mere negative stances before religion but rather positive weapons in the advance of morality. Giving an ironic twist to these words, González Prada announced that "there is no atheism when one worships justice from the depths of one's heart." Nor is there any room for skepticism when one places his faith in the "redemption of humanity by science."[33] Revealing his admiration for the iconoclasts who preached these doctrines, González Prada declared that there are men who have rejected religion and yet who are models of abnegation and virtue.[34]

With this general scheme, there are certain key people, events, and institutions that have advanced or retarded man in his forward march. González Prada grudgingly admitted that before it became vitiated and corrupted, primitive Christianity may have represented just such an advance by opposing "Roman Caesarism and the Jewish priesthood."[35] Relying heavily on certain French writers of the historicist school, he proposed the theory that Jesus was a basically good man in search of God, who was later deified by his followers. But it was not monotheistic Judaism but the politheistic Gentile world that deified Jesus. In its search for a new religion, the Gentile world paganized Christianity, making Jesus a symbol of protest against the empire and Mary a symbol of the poor woman. The imposition of the Trinity, a priesthood, the cult of the saints all formed part of the paganization of Christianity.[36] Thus, González Prada declared in verse: "What you enclose of paganism is what makes you survive, O Christianity."[37]

Whatever merits primitive Christianity may have had, it soon degenerated into Catholicism, which then became the great deviation retarding the growth of human liberty and reason. All religions follow a general law, declared González Prada: Every new religion is revolutionary and progressive, but every triumphant religion turns conservative and static.[38] Catholicism, which was an amalgam of paganism, Platonism, and the teachings of Jesus, soon became a priestly tyranny that sustained all the repressive states and governments from the time of the Roman Empire until the present. Catholicism, asserted González Prada, systematically and necessarily opposed every human advance in order to retain its dominant position in society. He went on to note that the best critical minds in modern times, including Lessing, Goethe, Sainte-Beuve, and Taine, have all been "freethinkers, Protestants or Jews." Catholicism, on the other hand, has only produced scholastics, philologists, and apologists—never original or critical minds. Darwin's theory, he added, could never have been conceived by a Catholic.[39]

Although its leaders and kings have been as fierce as the Catholics in implanting their ideas, Protestantism represented an advance for humanity because it opposed the power of Rome.[40] For a Catholic to become a Protestant, noted González Prada, although it may not represent a total emancipation, would at least signify an ascent up the "ethical ladder." With similar mixed approval, González Prada argued that until an essentially scientific education, "cured of all religious virus," were possible in Peru, Protestant schools represented a moral advance over Catholic education.[41] Of the two religions, Catholicism was the least equipped to survive the impact of science. Though it will die slowly because of the tenacity of superstition among uneducated people, Catholicism is already a "cemetery in the heart of a city."[42]

When González Prada returned to Peru in 1898, he turned with increasing attention and vigor to social questions, which was manifested by his conversion to anarchism. Anarchism was really the logical outcome of his vocation as a social protester and his broadened contacts with European rationalism and positivism. It was during this last period of his life that the third level of ideas predominated and González Prada the social apostate fully emerged. Writing in such freethinking publications as *El Libre Pensamiento*, *La Idea Libre*, the quasi-anarchist weekly *Germinal*, and especially in the openly anarchist organs, *La Protesta* and *Los Parias*, González Prada opened fire on nearly every institution in Peruvian society.

González Prada summed up his anarchist creed in two principal ideas: unlimited liberty for the individual and the abolition of the state and private property. The anarchist, said González Prada, enlarges upon the Christian ideal because he sees in his fellow man a brother to whom justice is owed and not a mere object of charity. The anarchist necessarily opposes Christianity, he declared, because Christianity seeks to resolve human problems in a world beyond the grave and tranquilize man's spirit of rebellion against injustice. If the members of different religions contented themselves with their dogmas and liturgies, there would be no need for antireligious campaigns. But as long as priests join forces with governments and soldiers to suppress the freedom of men, he warned, the anarchist must become an "aggressive anticlerical."

González Prada believed that anticlericalism by itself, however, was a sterile cause. The anarchist must also oppose the great ally of established religions, the state. In its own way, observed González Prada, politics is an "organized religion." Like a religion, politics has its own "providential fetish" in the state, its own liturgy in parliaments and its own priests in state functionaries. Given the general inclination of man to abuse power, he concluded, "All governments are bad and all authority is tyranny." To recognize the omnipotence of a parliament, he added, is more absurd than to recognize the infallibility of a council.[43]

The solution to human problems lies within man himself. The state with its penal laws and the church with its posthumous anathemas, González Prada pointed out, can neither correct nor moralize man. Morality arises not from the Bible or from civil codes, he affirmed, but from man himself. A man who loves himself and fears suffering, he declared, has the natural capacity to respect the similar desire to avoid suffering in others.[44]

González Prada's vision of the iniquitous alliance between religion and politics led him to inveigh against anticlericals and liberals who limited their efforts to only one of the two poles. With optimism, González Prada reported that the Freethinker's Congress in Geneva in 1902 had recognized the necessity of combating civil authorities and not just religious authorities.[45] With much less optimism, he noted that there were many anticlericals in Peru who imagined that in order to overthrow Catholicism it was only necessary to ferret out and expose to public view the priest's mistress and children. These same anticlericals, sighed

González Prada, have no interest in "social crimes nor political extortions." In order to liberate man, he warned, it is not sufficient to dethrone God "while the universe twists in agony, desperation and death."[46]

In González Prada's conception, however, the sacristy-obsessed anticlerical was only half-blind compared to the liberal who wishes to dethrone governments but not religion. Liberals who attempt this feat, González Prada believed, were doomed to failure because religion can no more be separated from social questions than politics from ethics. In his essay on Peruvian liberalism, González Prada set down his axiom on the inseparability of religion and politics: "Every political question can be reduced to an ethical question, and every ethical question envelops a religious one." The state, the church, and capital form an inseparable alliance. When one of the three is in danger, the other two rush to its defense because the vested interests of all are at stake. González Prada noted, however, that political changes may occur without a religious transformation, but every religious transformation necessarily precipitates a political transformation. The Protestant Reformation came first, he explained, then the French Revolution and the emancipation of Latin America. The religious revolt came first, then the German peasant's social war. In conclusion, he declared, there are not two kingdoms, that of God and that of man, but only one, the kingdom of justice. Professing the populist faith of anarchism, González Prada exclaimed: "According to divine justice, many are called, but few are chosen; according to human justice, all are called, and all are chosen."[47]

González Prada the Social Protester

González Prada found Peru far from being a "kingdom of justice" at the beginning of the twentieth century. While social misery grew worse, observed the new apostle of anarchism, Catholicism reigned unperturbed. Workers were being paid less even though they were paying more taxes, he noted, and women were prostituting themselves because of hunger or dying prematurely because of overwork. In the midst of all this the clergy lived "well-fed, contented and triumphant."[48] Everywhere that he looked, González Prada saw priests and religious living like vultures on a society sick with religious fanaticism. "Healthy and plump monks," he complained, "occupy the first place at the family table." These "black birds" symbolized exploitation in the name of mercy and religion.[49] The outstanding characteristic of Peruvian Catholicism, from González Prada's perspective, was hypocrisy. He excoriated the well-dressed women of high society who practiced their charity by visiting hospitals for the poor but who also deliberately ignored the hunger that wrecked the health of the patients.[50] He cited the case of a priest of an Indian parish who admitted that he believed in few of the church's teachings. "But if I let that be known," explained the priest, "I would lose my children's daily bread." Finally, González Prada pointed to the example of a canon who is alleged to have compared himself to a sleight-of-hand showman: if he were exposed, said the canon, he would lose his livelihood.[51]

Of all the churchmen in Peru, González Prada disliked the Spanish clergy the most. He found the Spanish to be rude, ignorant, and "fanatical," unlike the somewhat cultured French missionaries or the somewhat charitable Italian clergy.[52] This attitude reflected, of course, González Prada's opinion of Spain itself. While visiting Spain he described that nation as a "community of monks without tonsure."[53] He attributed the backwardness of Spain (and Ireland), moreover, to the dominance of Roman Catholicism.[54]

The area of church influence in Peru which González Prada feared the most was education. Lima, exclaimed the social critic, seems like a "Dead Sea" of churches and monasteries. Yet while churches and religious houses abounded, he lamented that there was not a "single municipal school worthy of a civilized people."[55] He blamed much of the religious fanaticism of the people on church-dominated education in Peru. Rejecting claims that Jesuit education was an exception to the mediocre level of religious education in Peru, he charged the Jesuits with forming "sectarians for Christ" and not "men for humanity." Furthermore, he accused the Jesuits of maintaining the aristocratic character of Catholicism by teaching only the sons of the wealthy in Lima.[56] By way of contrast, González Prada pointed to the Protestant schools in Puno, where the Indians learned to practice hygiene and to overcome alcoholism.[57]

Clerical domination of women was another recurrent theme of González Prada, who remembered the pious obsequiousness of his mother and sisters to priests. In a speech to the Italian Masons he termed such women "slaves of the Church." Rejecting the traditional notion that women are more religious than men, González Prada pointed to Catholicism's practice of holding women in tutelage as the real problem. He cited Louis Menard, moreover, to attack the belief that Christianity liberated the woman. Hellenistic monogamy and veneration of female deities, he claimed, did far more for women than the "masculine" Trinity of Christianity.[58] He went on to emphasize the greatly superior position of women in Protestant countries compared with the inferior status of women in Catholic cultures. The root of the problem, he explained, was the calculated state of ignorance in which both church and society conspired to maintain women. He contrasted the fidelity of women to the church with the poor treatment they received from the church. Furthermore, he charged the church with attempting to use women as weapons to achieve its objectives. This tactic, observed González Prada, is most evident in the homes of liberals and anticlericals whose wives occultly implant Catholic ideas in their children and send them to Catholic schools. He warned of the Catholic wife of a freethinker, who, like "a spy," will attempt to convert her spouse on his deathbed.[59] Finally, he called for the liberation of all women from the authority of God, pope, and autocratic husbands.[60]

One of González Prada's most important contributions in awakening the social conscience of Peru was his call to liberate the Indians from the social and economic exploitation to which they were subjected. It was in this area more than any other that he leveled his most sweeping indictment against liberalism and republicanism in Peru. "In Peru," he charged, "there are two great lies: the Republic and Christianity."[61] González Prada emphasized the fact that even though they made up the majority of the population, the Indians had made little or no progress since independence. Indeed, he believed that the Indians of republican Peru were far worse off than the Indians of colonial or pre-Columbian Peru. Republican institutions only changed the names of colonial institutions, while Indian servitude in the highlands remained unchanged. Republicanism in Peru, observed González Prada, consisted of rule by a tight clique of landed oligarchs and their political representatives in Lima who systematically exploited the Indians and bound them to the land in legal servitude.[62]

Furthermore, charged González Prada, all of the revolutions in Peru have been quarrels between factions of white men in which the Indians have shed much blood but received nothing in return. Reflecting on his own experience, he recalled that many Indians looked upon the War of the Pacific as a civil war between "General Chile and General Peru."[63] It is time for the Indian, he declared, to take rifle in hand and resist both the soldier who comes to recruit him for a white man's war and the revolutionary who summons him for a white man's cause.[64]

In the same vein, he attacked the liberal's panacea for all social problems—education. Public instruction alone, he warned, could turn out to be a new means of securing servitude on the part of the Indians. The Indian problem, he argued, is not primarily a pedagogical one but social and economic. Only when the Indian owns his own land will he overcome his hunger and feeling of servitude. When the Indian himself seizes the initiative and defends his own lands with violence, then he will be on the way to liberation. By the same token, concluded González Prada, the redemption of the Indians will not come through the good will of his oppressors.[65]

In González Prada's view, the church was one of the main oppressors of the Indians. In his Politeama speech he had decried the tacit alliance between the priest, the government officials and the landowners to hold the Indians in a state of servile obedience.[66] He claimed to perceive a direct relationship between the ignorance of the Indians and Negroes in Peru and the despotic power of the church over them. In fact, he declared, "The intensity of religious fervor increases in proportion to the darkness of the skin." To bear out this contention, he pointed to the enormous popularity of religious processions and feast days among the lower-class Indians, Negroes, and mestizos of Peru. Lest he be accused of racism, he added that a poor but educated Indian or Negro belongs to a "higher class" than a wealthy but superstitious white man. The white man who points with pride to his Catholicism as proof of his aristocratic background, he declared, in reality reveals his lower-class level of culture.[67]

González Prada's denunciation of Indian exploitation in Republican Peru underlines the major difference between himself and his liberal-reformist predecessors. The liberals had called for the reform of certain key institutions within what they believed to be a generally well-functioning society. Perceiving that the roots of Peru's problems went far deeper than the country's institutions, González Prada called for a radical transformation of all of society itself as a condition of reform. Although he displayed relatively little familiarity with Marxism, he anticipated many Marxist programs and slogans by subordinating education to land distribution as the key to ending injustice among the Indians. Furthermore, although he himself was not free from the obsession of many Latin American intellectuals to recast American realities in European terms, González Prada had the salutary effect of focusing reformist criticism on the real problems of Peru. There could hardly be a greater contrast, for example, between Vigil's notion of reform, which consisted in tediously resurrecting ancient church councils, and González

Prada's virulent condemnation of clerical exploitation of Indians in the highlands.

Moreover, although he arrived at a negative conclusion on the role of religion in society, González Prada forced other thinkers to see religion within the context of all of society, and not just as a church-state question. His distinction between church and religion is much clearer than among the liberals. According to his positivistic notions, religion represented a period of adolescence in the life of all men, while churches were but institutions that grew out of the ignorance and fears of that period. But religion was not an isolated symptom of man's backwardness. González Prada also demanded that reformers see religion as integrally related to the political structure of society. Unlike the liberals, who conceived of Catholicism as a stabilizing force potentially beneficient for any political order, monarchical or republican, González Prada believed that Catholicism was intrinsically allied to autocratic forms of government. He did share with the liberals, however, the belief that for all its defects, Protestantism might represent an advance over Roman Catholicism in Peru.

In judging the overall contribution of González Prada to social reform in Peru, however, a few fundamental reservations seem justified. In the first place, in spite of his passionate advocacy of Indians' and workers' rights, much of his knowledge of these groups was based upon personal observations but not on any critical or objective studies. He did not, for example, seem to appreciate the difference between popular Catholicism and the priest-dominated Catholicism in the highlands that he criticized so sharply. Although observers from colonial times on had noted the discrepancy between the popular devotions of the Indians and the official liturgy of the church, González Prada either did not think the distinction significant or else saw the latter as merely a more official form of "superstition." Indeed, on several occasions he identified Catholicism with the anti-intellectual pagansim of Roman times which survived among the uneducated masses simply because it was pagan, that is, "superstitious."

Furthermore, he was steeped in the a priori belief that Catholicism in itself contributed to the backwardness of the Indians. He saw the Protestant Reformation as the condition that paved the way for the political transformation of Europe and, hence, a possible good for the Peruvian Indians. In citing several of the many Indian rebellions in the nineteenth century, however he did not seem to be aware of the social and religious dynamics that accompanied them.[68] He did not ask the question, for example, why the Indians who revolted continued to maintain their traditional Roman Catholicism.

Finally, besides lacking empirical data on Indian life and customs, González Prada seemed at times to lack an insider's sympathy for the very groups he defended. On the one hand, he expressed a general sympathy for the misery and poverty of the Indians and workers, but, on the other hand, he satirized rather caustically their popular devotions and feast days.[69] From his perspective, of course, these manifestations of popular piety were but more symptoms of a general malaise. Nevertheless, in his satire there is an aloofness that casts him in the role of a reforming patrician before the ignorant plebs. It is true that he maintained close relationships with many workers who directed the new anarchist and socialist movements then appearing in Peru. But these workers were by and large the articulate leaders who shared González Prada's ideas, not the more representative members.

After his departure from the Unión Nacional in 1902, González Prada increasingly refrained from engaging in direct political action as a means of winning converts to his ideas. More and more he relied upon the power of the pen and private conversations in the National Library or his home to publicize his cause. A restrained and somewhat shy man who preferred to read his carefully composed speeches in public, González Prada felt more at home in the world of letters than in the turbulent and unrefined world of partisan politics. Although he was the most articulate voice of revolutionary ideas in Peru, he did not share the life of the lower classes who would benefit from the revolution. Certainly, in the area of popular religiosity, he remained an alien before the religious world of the ordinary worker and highland dweller.

His duties as director of the National Library did not, however, curtail all political activities or blunt his polemicist instincts. When Colonel Oscar Benavides overthrew the populist government of President Guillermo Billinghurst in 1914, he promptly offered his resignation in protest. Temporarily unemployed, he published a short-lived antigovernment newspaper, *La Lucha*.[70] In 1916 he was renamed director of the library by President

José Pardo. He continued to exert a great influence upon the new generation of writers, poets, and social thinkers who came to visit him in the library—José María Eguren, Percy Gibson, Abrahám Valdelomar, Alberto Hidalgo, José Carlos Mariátegui, Haya de la Torre, and many others.[71] On some occasions he conducted lengthy conversations with priests, who came to see the "Beast," as González Prada facetiously termed himself.[72]

A commanding figure at over six feet, he sat at his desk in the library like a lord in his castle. White-haired, with an aggressively upturned mustache, González Prada bore the hereditary marks of his Spanish-Irish-Galician ancestors: aquiline nose, blue eyes, and sharply chisled jaw. His proud exterior hid, however, a shy and sensitive man who was moved to engage in humorous repartee at times and, even more rarely, to make personal disclosures. One of the rare disclosures came in an interview which he granted two years before his death. Asked if he believed in God, González Prada paused for a while and then replied that in his youth he had been a convinced atheist, but after his European trip he had begun to doubt. Asked if he still doubted, he replied evasively, "The truth is there are days when I doubt, and there are days . . . but generally I don't believe."[73] Perhaps the knee had begun to bend.

González Prada's ideas on religion and reform may have influenced the reformist elite, but they did not necessarily reflect the attitudes of Peru's lower classes, especially the Indians. An examination of the many Indian rebellions that occurred in Peru during González Prada's own lifetime may serve to indicate how much more the reformers had to learn about their own countrymen before they could turn their ideas into popular movements.

3: HOLY WEEK IN HUARAZ, 1885: INDIAN REBELLIONS IN THE LATE NINETEENTH CENTURY

Throughout the nineteenth and early twentieth centuries, the Indian was frequently the subject of reformist debate but rarely a participant. More often than not, his was the last voice to be heard in any discussion of the "Indian problem" in the halls of the congress building in Lima or the drawing rooms of literary clubs in the provincial capitals of Peru. This was true not only for conservative landowners and their political representatives but for the liberal reformist elite as well. Rhetorical advocacy of Indian rights was, of course, a recurrent though hardly a passionate theme among Peruvian liberals. In his *Plan del Perú*, Vidaurre defended the Indians against the charge that they were by nature liars and thieves:

> Some believe that they are liars, revolutionaries, robbers, drunks and given over to concubinage and perjury. This is not true: they learned to steal, lie, drink and go back on their word at the cost of their lives and goods from the Spaniards.[1]

Rarely, however, did the church-obsessed liberals like Vigil or Mariátegui make references to the plight of the Indian.[2] Although a later generation of liberals represented by Pedro Gálvez argued in parliamentary debates in favor of Indian suffrage, it took the less doctrinaire and more pragmatic military *caudillo,* Ramón Castilla, to effect one of the first real reforms in favor of the Indians. In 1854 he abolished the *contribución personal,* or head tax, which all Indians had been obliged to pay since colonial times. His move was valiant, for the personal contribution accounted for roughly one-fourth of the national budget.[3] It was not until after the War of the Pacific that González Prada, Clorinda Matto de Turner, Joaquín Capelo, and others took a

45

more serious interest in the Indian and created the cult of *indigenismo,* which from the turn of the century on became a central theme of Peruvian liberalism.

RELATIONS BETWEEN INDIANS AND WHITES

For most members of Peru's educated elite, whether conservative or liberal, Indian Peru was a *terra incognita.* The general census of 1876 indicated that of Peru's 2,699,106 inhabitants, some 1,554,678, or 57.6 percent, were Indian. The mestizo population accounted for 24.8 percent of the total, while only 10.04 percent was listed as "white." Together Asiastics and Negroes made up 4 percent of the total.[4] Even if the mestizo population were added to the white population, the stark fact remained that Peru was a predominantly Indian country. This racial disparity was further accentuated by geographical factors. The white-mestizo population tended to be concentrated on the coast or in the provincial cities and towns, while the great bulk of the Indians lived in the central mountain valleys and the southern *altiplano* around Lake Titicaca. In 1876 the white-mestizo population of the department of Lima was approximately 71,000 while the combined total of Indians, Negroes, and Asiastics was 49,000. By way of contrast, in the department of Puno the white population was calculated at a mere 2,194, while the Indian population reached 51,124.[5] A similar enormous disproportion between the white-mestizo and Indian populations prevailed in all of the central mountain and *altiplano* departments of Peru: Puno, Cuzco, Apurímac, Ayacucho, Huancavelica, Junín, Pasco, Huánuco, and Ancash.

Within the Indian population of Peru there were numerous and profound differences, which a century of Inca domination and three centuries of Spanish rule had not been able to eradicate. The Aymara-speaking Indians around Lake Titicaca still held tenaciously to their ancestral customs and language. The Indian descendents of the Conchuco and Huaras Indians in Ancash spoke a Quechua dialect hardly recognizable by Quechua speakers from Cuzco. On the coast, where there had been a greater intermixture with whites, mestizos, Negroes, and in the nineteenth century with the Chinese, the Indians were at a far more advanced stage of acculturation into the white-mestizo world than the highland dwellers. Within this array of regional and cultural differences, however, there were two constant factors that produced a uniform pattern throughout all of Peru, excluding the jungle: the intense identification of the Indian with the land and the exploitation of the Indian by a small white-mestizo minority.

Despite the sudden splurge of prosperity on the coast brought about by the guano and nitrate industries before the War of the Pacific, Peru remained predominantly an agricultural country, and agriculture was predominantly an Indian occupation. On the coast, Negroes, Chinese, and Indians labored in huge sugar, cotton and rice plantations. The coastal economy was characterized by an incipient capitalism that tended to be urban based and oriented toward foreign exportation. In sharp contrast, the highland economy tended to be semifeudal in character and oriented toward internal consumption. In the mountains, where latifundia and minifundia existed side by side, the physical conditions for raising animals and crops were far less propitious than on the coast. The food crops raised—potatoes, camotes, yucca, and maize—had little earning value as exports and usually ended up in local markets. In the southern *altiplano* region, the Indians raised great herds of llama and alpaca, but no large-scale industry existed to affect living conditions significantly. In general, the main characteristics of agriculture in the highlands were subsistence farming, land scarcity, absentee landlords, and small local markets.[6]

Simplifying somewhat, the social structure in the highlands and the rural areas of the coast tended to correspond to one's land situation. At the apex was the white or mestizo *hacendado*, who ruled over vast tracts of land. Next came the small but independent property owners. Then came the *comuneros*, or Indians who had managed to retain their community lands since colonial times. In the practice, many of these *comuneros* owned individual plots of land (*chacras*) and worked part-time on a nearby hacienda or in a nearby town. Then there were the *colonos* or *yanaconas* who bound themselves in verbal contracts to turn over a certain portion of their crops and to offer services to the *hacendado* in return for the right to farm fringe areas of his hacienda. Finally, at the bottom of the scale were the contract workers who were recruited for work on the coast under a system known as the *enganche,* a type of collective contract. Most of the small, literate white-mestizo minority concentrated in the provincial towns consisted of landowners, merchants, craftsmen, lawyers, military, and government bureaucrats. The relationships within this social structure, as well as the nomenclature used to designate one's status, varied from region to region, but the overall pattern of *gamonalismo,* or paternalistic exploitation by a powerful elite, prevailed everywhere.[7]

Most of the most flagrant measures of exploitation of colonial times had been formally outlawed, but as the liberals frequently complained, these practices continued in republican times. The personal contribution, abolished in 1826 and again in 1854 by Castilla, continued to reappear late into the nineteenth century. The obligation of personal service (the *mita* or *pongaje*) had also been forbidden, but in practice continued to form part of the pattern of life in the highlands. As in most other areas of Latin America, the liberals themselves often created more problems for the Indians than they solved. In 1824 Bolívar ordered an end to communal lands among the Indians in the hopes of creating a country of productive private landowners. Unaccustomed to liberal doctrines of private property, thousands of Indians lost their lands to white and mestizo landowners and speculators.[8]

At times, articulate representatives of Peru's cultured elite underlined the psychological gulf between these two worlds in more expressive language than that of dry census statistics. One author who witnessed Peru's defeat in the War of the Pacific declared that as long as Peru was beset by great masses of Indians there could be no hope of liberty or political stability in Peru.[9] A faculty member who inaugurated the academic year of 1881 at the University of San Agustín in Arequipa called for a sweeping regeneration of Peru in light of its humiliating defeat and the subsequent occupation of its coast by Chile. According to the speaker, the principal reasons to account for Peru's debacle were the deleterious effects of three hundred years of Spanish rule and the presence of "impassive, timid and lazy" Indians in Peruvian society.[10] A similar call to regenerate Peru was made a few years later by the leading spokesman of positivism in Peru, Javier Prado y Ugarteche. In his inaugural address for the academic year at the University of San Marcos in 1894, he referred to the pernicious influence which the "inferior" races had exercised on Peru throughout its history. Prado called for the immigration of the "superior" races to Peru, particularly from northern Europe, as a remedy for the racial problem in Peru.[11]

It was in the interior provinces, however, that the polarity between the two classes was most evident. In his report to the prefect of Puno in 1898, the subprefect of Chucuito described the

Indians in his region. After noting that they outnumbered the whites 53,000 to 3,000, the author characterized the relations between the Indians, mestizos, and whites.

The Indians live in the fields and hills where they tend their farms and herds; they come to the populated areas on feast days, and only out of necessity on other occasions. They hate the white race from Spanish colonial times; they have a mortal hatred for the mestizo, who is their worst enemy, and for anyone who has served in the army, because these step on them without compassion, steal their animals and lands and force them to do whatever they want.[12]

The author also noted that the Indians resisted sending their children to school because they feared that they would learn the bad habits and lack of respect characteristic of the mestizos. The subprefect went on to describe the Indians as "lazy, boastful, liars, and thieves." Furthermore, he added, the Indian was "vindicative toward his enemies, even to the point of being fierce and savage." The Indian women were not much better than the men because they "get drunk, fight, sing, cry and make love drinking." The Indians all hate the army and would prefer to die rather than become soldiers. Yet, informed the author, once he has been in the army, the Indian considers himself superior to the other members of his race.

The author zealously argued that the practice of personal services should be retained because otherwise "there would be no one to carry official correspondence from one town to another or to aid the troops, travelers, justices of the peace, priests, or municipal officials." Besides, he added, the Indians themselves wanted the personal services so that their children could "learn to deal with the authorities" respectfully and obediently. Finally, the subprefect suggested as a remedy to the Indian's laziness and lack of entrepreneuring spirit that the government send up from the coast 3 percent of all the youth eighteen years of age and older to live among the Indians and set a good example for them.[13]

In this brief survey of the dismal relations between whites and Indians, it is somewhat difficult to uncover the Indian's own point of view, mainly because his illiteracy prevented him from writing his own history. The press in Lima and the provincial capitals generally ignored the Indian except when a major Indian uprising disrupted the peace and order of a particular region. Indeed, the Indian rebellions of the nineteenth century gave rise to practically the only substantial amount of literature and documents relating to Indian life and customs. It was primarily in these rebellions that the Indian found his voice and impressed upon the ruling minority his desires. Although the documentation on these uprisings is sparse, it is sufficient to provide an illuminating insight into the attitude of the Indians toward the church and religion. Of course, situations of social upheaval may tend to present a distorted view of normal patterns of living and thinking, but they may also reveal the Indians' true hostilities and sympathies, which might otherwise pass unrecorded in a study made under "normal" conditions.

Such a survey of Indian rebellions should also indicate, at least partially, to what extent González Prada's image of the church as an exploiting predator of the Indian was valid. The question is whether González Prada and other critics, for all their reforming zeal, possessed a greater insight into the reality of Indian Peru than most of the other members of the intellectual elite that ran Peru's universities and government. Furthermore, this overview may provide an interesting contrast with the far more well-studied and documented revolutions of the eighteenth century, particularly those of Juan Santos Atahualpa in 1742 and Tupac Amaru in 1780. A comparison between the uprisings of the eighteenth and nineteenth centuries might suggest to what extent the church had lost or gained influence among the Indians and to what extent the Indians continued to identify their interests with Christianity.

EIGHTEENTH-CENTURY INDIAN UPRISINGS

Little is known of the origins of Juan Santos Atahualpa, the Indian leader who for fourteen years dominated an enormous area of central eastern Peru. It appears certain that he was either a former servant or a student of the Jesuits and hence highly pro-Jesuit in his policies. He was also openly religious and even wore a cross. His movement may even be characterized as quasi-messianic, since he sought to rest his claim to sovereignty over Peru in a divine command.[14] Much more is known of the *Cuzqueño* landowner José Gabriel Condorcanqui, who assumed the title of Tupac Amaru II and initiated the greatest Indian rebellion in the New World. Though not nearly as overtly religious as Juan Santos Atahualpa, Tupac Amaru displayed a respectful attitude toward Christianity. He ordered his followers to remain Christian and prohibited the killing of priests or the destruction of churches. Yet the official church, as Boleslao Lewin observes in his work on the subject, opposed the revolution categorically, and few priests actually joined it although many had sympathized with it in the beginning. Lewin also noted that by 1780 most of the older strictly pagan practices had vanished and that what remained was a strange combination of pagan beliefs and Christian practices. Nevertheless, Lewin concluded that in spite of official church opposition and the survival of a pagan residue, the Indians continued to profess Christianity during and after the revolution.[15]

NINETEENTH-CENTURY INDIAN UPRISINGS

In general, there were three types of Indian rebellions in the nineteenth century: (1) those that were reverberations of a national political struggle between *caudillos,* as in the case of Miguel Iglesias and Andrés Cáceres in 1885 or Cáceres against Nicolás de Piérola in 1895; (2) those that reflected a more immediate social abuse at the local level, such as the personal contribution or the salt tax; and (3) those that reflected both local social dissatisfaction and a larger political struggle. Between 1850 and 1900 five Indian uprisings attracted national attention: Huancané, 1866–68; Huaraz, 1885; Huánuco, 1895; Huanta, 1896; Puno, 1895–97. In reality, the Puno movement consisted of a series of interrelated uprisings that flared up in different places at different times: at Chucuito in 1895; at Juli in 1896; and at Ilave in 1897. As in the case of Puno, many side rebellions barely mentioned in the official press were touched off by one of the major ones listed here. Furthermore, there were many civil uprisings before and after the War of the Pacific in which Indians participated, but these cannot be called "Indian" rebellions as the leaders were white or mestizo and the general orientation of these movements had little to do with Indian interests. During and after the War of the Pacific there were many cases of banditry.[16] Of all those which were clearly Indian rebellions, only that of Huaraz is relatively well documented.

Huancané, 1866–68

In November, 1866, a mass of Indians descended on the town of Huancané, just north of Lake Titicaca, to protest the attempts of the subprefect to exact the personal contribution, recently restored by President Mariano Ignacio Prado. After barricading himself in the local church with other officials, the subprefect was allowed to escape alive only through the intercession of other townsfolk. But the revolt quickly spread to many neighboring towns and villages around the lake region. The governor of the district was on the point of being shot when the bishop of Puno, Juan Ambrosio Huerta, arrived in time to save his life. Huerta had arrived only in April of that year as the first bishop of the new diocese of Puno. Before that he had been the rector of the seminary in Lima, and years later he was destined to become one of the most influential churchmen in Peru as the bishop of Arequipa, 1880–97. In the meantime, he was called upon to play a major role in the bloody events that disturbed the peace of the *altiplano* that year.

On November 11 Huerta arrived in Huancané and discovered that the townsfolk had wisely named a new subprefect, thus calming the situation considerably. Huerta spoke to the people and, according to a newspaper report, "with his words and by exercising some acts of his ministry, he reestablished order." Unfortunately, however, the prefect of the province in Puno had already equipped and armed a force of 200 men and sent them on their way to Huancané under a Colonel Lizares. Thoroughly alarmed, the townsfolk asked Huerta to intercede for them. When Lizares arrived, Huerta went out to meet him at the edge of the town and convinced him not to march on the town lest he provoke a new uprising among the Indians. Nevertheless, some time later Lizares chose to ignore the bishop's plea and took possession of the town. At the same time he forced Huerta to withdraw and then proceeded to unleash a bloody assault on the Indians in the area surrounding the town. After killing many Indians and plundering their herds, Lizares himself withdrew.[17]

On November 27, after the situation had calmed down again, the Indians of the district presented a memorial of complaints to Colonel Francisco Pimentel, the newly appointed prefect of Puno, a man held in favor by the Indians. In the preamble to the memorial, the Indians complained that the "barbaric customs" of Peru's conquerors had been reborn in their age "with even greater ferocity." The Indians complained of being compelled to perform unpaid personal services to private individuals (*pongaje*), being forced to labor on public roads and works without pay ("not even a little bit with which to buy coca") and receiving arbitrary whippings and jail sentences. On top of all these abuses, the Indians added, there was the new personal contribution of five pesos per head and an additional two reales for the church. Finally, the memorial went on to pay tribute to Huerta:

Fortunately, his Excellency the bishop of the diocese arrived among us. To him we humbly offer ourselves and express the most classic testimonies of our profound respect; and at the same time we offer this proof of our submission and obedience to the supreme authority of the department. In these circumstances a military force came from the province of Azángaro, organized by Colonel Lizares, who violently seized the plaza of Huancané and forced the bishop to depart immediately. When this happened we were left once again in a state of alarm.[18]

Slightly more than a year later, the barely healed wounds of Puno were violently reopened. This time the conflict was an extension of a revolt aimed at overthrowing President Prado. The pro-Prado faction was represented by Colonel Juan Bustamante, who was also a staunch advocate for the Indians. Supported by many Indians, Bustamante engaged in a series of pitched battles all over the department in the fall of 1867 with Colonel Andrés Luna y Recharte, the leader of the anti-Prado faction, who also had his own following of Indians. On October 12 Bustamante arrived in Huancané, but he was driven out by Recharte on November 12. On November 15 Bustamante counterattacked and took Huancané again. In December he left the town to confront Recharte in the open countryside. This proved to be a mistake because on January 2 he was defeated after a four-hour battle. In revenge, Recharte caused 70 Indians to die of asphyxiation in closed quarters in the small town of Pusi and ordered Bustamante shot.[19]

In an unsigned letter to *El Comercio* in Lima, an anti-Bustamante partisan expressed his point of view on the whole matter and at the same time shed a revealing light on the role that religion may have played in the conflict. The author of the letter accused Bustamante of having instigated the Indians to revolt by telling them that the movement against President Prado was antireligious and anti-Indian in nature. The author denounced Bustamante as the real enemy of religion and civilization because he had tried to convert the Indians into beasts.[20] Whether or not the accusation was true, Bustamante's detractor underlined the importance that he believed religion had for the Indians. Beyond that letter, the memorial of 1866 clearly emphasized the esteem in which the Indians held the religious leader of the area. If any important contrast stands out between this uprising and that of Tupac Amaru, it is between the decidedly pro-Indian stand of Huerta and the anti-Indian posture of the bishop of Cuzco, Juan Manual Moscoso, who had excommunicated Tupac Amaru a century earlier.[21]

Cáceres versus Piérola

Postwar Peru was subjected to a series of national and local struggles for power as different military and civilian *caudillos* vied with one another to impose their concept of order. Andrés Cáceres, the "Witch of the Andes" who stubbornly refused to surrender to the Chileans, marched on Lima and overthrew President Miguel Iglesias in 1885. At the same time, in the north Colonel José Mercedes Puga directed his own operations in Cajamarca against Iglesias. In the somewhat contrived elections of 1890, Cáceres turned the government over to Colonel Remigio Morales Bermúdez. Not content with his role of kingmaker, Cáceres again conspired to have himself elected president in 1895. This time, however, he was successfully opposed by another popular *caudillo,* Nicolás de Piérola, the former president who had somewhat ineptly commanded the Peruvian forces outside of Lima in 1881. Piérola waited for the public to forget his wartime conduct, and in the midst of strong anti-Cácerist feelings, marched on Lima in March, 1895, and drove Cáceres from the presidential palace after a three-day street battle. Though Cáceres left the country in exile, he was still revered as a hero in the mountain regions of central Peru. In almost every Indian uprising between 1895 and 1900, the Pierolists claimed to see a Cácerist lurking behind the scenes instigating the Indians to revolt. At times this was true, but at others it was an empty charge that masked the real social nature of the uprising.

Huánuco, 1895

In April, 1895, for reasons not entirely clear, the Indians of the north-central department of Huánuco rose up in arms and attacked the police force in the town of Chacabamba. The revolt spread and soon engulfed the two western provinces of Dos de

Mayo and Humalíes. One newspaper report placed the number
of Indians in arms in Huamalíes alone at 3,000. The citizens of
the departmental capital of Huánuco sent a petition to the government in Lima asking for immediate aid. In the letter they complained that the "civilized towns of the department are con-
stantly threatened by savage hordes." The letter emphasized the
danger by pointing out that all the roads to the capital were in
the hands of Indians.[22] By late May the prefect, Benjamín Novoa
set out with two companies of soldiers to pacify the regions in
arms.

During the pacification venture, the correspondent from *El
Comercio* reported that the soldiers had apprehended an Indian
bearing a secret missive signed by a priest of the region, Simeón
Zevallos. To their dismay, the soldiers discovered that the letter
contained a detailed description of the army's movements. The
correspondent expressed his own consternation that a "clergyman, bearer of the peace of Christ . . . should have been one of
the instigators of these mobs." He identified the priest as a one
time pastor of Yanaguara and a nephew of a local Cácerist
politician. Finally, the correspondent charged an ex-vicar of
the diocese of Huánuco with turning the seminarians in Huánuco
into pro-Cácerists, like Zevallos.[23] The fragmentary data on the
Huánuco uprising does not permit making a comparison between
the clergyman involved and Bishop Huerta of Puno, whose support
of the Indians was unmistakable. Nevertheless, it is revealing that
the local clergy was viewed by the government as potential allies
of the Indians.

Huanta, 1896

Another similarly ambiguous case occurred a year later in
Huanta, a northern town in the department of Ayacucho. Huanta
had frequently been either a nucleus or a crossroads of revolutionary movements. The Indians of Huanta had participated
in Juan Santos Atahualpa's insurrection a century earlier, and
in 1826, somewhat uncertain of which master to serve, they
fought under Spanish officials who remained after Ayacucho to
rally the Indians against the new Peruvian government. In 1882
a conflict flared up over the high-handed measures of the subprefect. The bishop of Ayacucho, who came to mediate in the
conflict, was killed in a case of mistaken identity.[24]

The immediate motive behind the 1896 uprising was to protest a new salt tax and to demand freer circulation of paper
money. But a more complex political factor was involved. Two
prominent families of the region, that of the pro-Cácerist Miguel
Lazón and that of the pro-Pierolist Feliciano Urbina, had been
engaged in a vendetta ever since Lazón murdered Urbina in 1890.
Both factions sought to use the Indians for their own ends.
Nevertheless, the uprising may be correctly considered an Indian
rebellion, since the vast majority of the participants were Indian
and the end for which they fought was social.

After the subprefect of Huanta refused to defer immediately
to their demands, several thousand Indians descended on the town
on September 27 and killed the subprefect and many local citizens. Similar outbursts against the salt tax erupted throughout
all the mountain departments, and the central government deemed
it necessary to make an example of Huanta by suppressing the
revolt there as hastily as possible. With 800 men under his command, Colonel Domingo Parra was dispatched from Lima to
carry out this task. By early November Parra reached Huanta,
only to find it deserted. Much to his discomfort, he learned
from his scouts that some 3,000 armed Indians had taken up positions in the hills surrounding the town. Forced to engage in
guerrilla tactics, Parra sent out numerous forays into the hills.
Finally, by mid-December he had managed to break the back of
the resistance, and in the process he incurred the lasting hatred
of the Indians for his brutal methods.[25]

The role played by the parish priest of Huanta, Pedro Betalleluz, is somewhat difficult to determine. In the violent clash
between the Lazón and Urbina families in 1890, he won the
esteem of both sides as a conciliator.[26] His attempts to serve as
a mediator between the Indians and the government in 1896,
however, made him an object of suspicion by the government
forces. The first reports from Huanta after the army had entered
charged the priest with sending Parra an ultimatum from the
Indians demanding the abolition of the salt tax within eight
days. Although the same report said that Betalleluz was probably
"pressured" into sending the ultimatum by the Indians, his con-
spicuous absence from town only served to draw more suspicion
toward himself.[27] A second report, however, stated that Betalleluz
presented himself before Parra two days later and apologized for
his actions, claiming that he had been forced to send the ultimatum
by Miguel Lazón, the pro-Cácerist instigator of the uprising. Ap-

parently the matter had given rise to contradictory speculation, because *El Comercio* found it necessary to deny a story in *La Opinión Nacional* to the effect that Parra had levied a fine *(cupo)* on Betalleluz of 8,000 soles and 200 rifles.[28]

Whether or not the pastor of Huanta supported the Indians remains unresolved. What is clear, however, is that once again the government did not take the loyalty of the local clergyman for granted, and indeed, viewed him with considerable suspicion. In other cases the role of the clergy was much less ambiguous. Parra himself reported with satisfaction that the Paris priest of Luricocha had aided greatly in pacifying the Indians.[29] Although the priest in question was obviously serving government intersts, Parra's reference was an indirect tribute to the priest's influence over the Indians.

Puno, 1895-97

That the clergy served government interests by pacifying the Indians is more evident in the series of uprising that broke out in the department of Puno between 1895 and 1897. The different reports from the troubled areas emphasized abuses by local government and church officials and the new salt tax as the immediate causes of the uprisings. The commanders of the expedition that marched on Chucuito in April, 1895, blamed the harsh strictures of the local politicians and ecclesiastical authorities.[30] In the Juli uprising of October, 1896, the subprefect singled out the repressive policies of the local governor as well as "certain priests" who exacted excessive stipends for marriages and burials.[31] At the same time, however, when a major uprising broke out in the Ilave, again in the province of Chucuito in March, 1897, the government officials counted on the same priests to aid the army in placating the Indians. The subprefect of Chucuito reported that when he departed from Juli with reinforcements to fight in Ilave, he ordered the pastor of Juli to accompany the expedition, "so that he could employ his religious influence to dissuade the Indians." The subprefect also noted that the priest spoke Aymara.[32] In May the prefect of the department reported that order had been reestablished in Chucuito. He went on to mention the two principal means he had employed to prevent future uprisings. The first was to leave behind a force of twenty-five policemen and twelve soldiers in the area. The second was to bring in a neighboring Franciscan mission:

Furthermore, I organized a mission of the Franciscan monks from Copacabana, which will be of decisive importance for reconciling the Indians with the residents of the area. It was the divorce between these two groups that was one of the determining factors in this last uprising.[33]

In all of these cases it seems manifest that the clergy still exercised an important influence over the Indian population of Peru. Judging by the reports emanating from the areas affected by rebellions, both the government officials and the local white and mestizo citizenry looked upon the priest as the key liaison man between themselves and the Indians. This recognition is even more important in light of the fact that the majority of the priests who worked in the Indian areas of Peru were themselves white or mestizo.[34] Furthermore, in some cases the army looked upon the priest as a potentially dangerous enemy of the government because of his influence over the Indians. In other cases, and these are probably more typical, the invading force saw the priest as a key instrument for placating the Indians. In a few cases, the clergy openly advocated the Indian side and sought to protect the Indians against armed attack. Such was the case of Bishop Huerta of Puno.

What is difficult to portray directly from these reports, however, is the religious attitude of the Indians themselves. It may be inferred, of course, from their acceptance of clerical influence that they maintained their respect for religion and traditional adherence to Christianity. Nevertheless, the charge of the anti-clericals that the Indians were "priest-dominated" and hence not expressing their true convictions still must be confronted by more direct evidence. Although far from being satisfactory, the documentation on the Huaraz uprising of 1885 is immeasurably more helpful for providing just such an insight into the religious attitude of the Indians while in a state of open rebellion.

Huaraz, 1885

The department of Ancash extends from the coast to the middle of the Peruvian Andes. In many ways it mirrors on a smaller scale the geographical disunity of all of Peru. It includes both

a coastal plantation culture and a highland Indian culture far
removed both physically and psychologically from the coastal
cities. It is somewhat indicative of this distance that the first
news dispatches of a major Indian rebellion in Huaraz did not
appear in the Lima dailies until about three weeks after the
event.

The actual focal point of the uprising was the Callejón de
Huaylas, a narrow corridor that stretches for approximately 150
miles between the *Cordillera Negra,* or "Black Range," and the
Cordillera Blanca, or "White Range," the latter so called because
its peaks, the highest in Peru, are snow-covered all year long.
The small cities in this mountain valley are arrayed like dots in
a straight file from south to north: Recuay, Huaraz, Carhuaz,
Yungay, Caraz. Numerous small Indian villages nestle in the foot-
hills of the two great mountain ranges. The cities are connected
by the river Santa, which flows downward from the bleak and
frozen heights of Lake Conococha at 13,780 feet past the semi-
tropical cities of Yungay and Caraz at 8,000 feet.

The Italian scientist, Antonio Raimondi, who thoroughly ex-
plored the Callejón de Huaylas before the War of the Pacific,
noted that the roads up to the Callejón were so narrow that
only mules could get by.[35] The main agricultural products of the
Callejón were wheat, rye, alfalfa, potatoes, yucca, and maize.
The principal animals raised were cows and sheep. Few indigenous
animals such as the llama were to be found. Raimondi also observed that the majority of the products were consumed in the
area. Although two large lead and copper mines were in operation in the *Cordillera Negra,* the main occupation of the valley
was agriculture.[36]

According to the 1876 census the total population of the department was 284,830, of whom 132,792 were listed as Indian.
Another 126,904 were described as mestizo, while the white
population was put at 18,706.[37] This general composition made
Ancash more typical of the central mountain departments and
less typical of the southern *antiplano* departments where there
had been far less *mestizaje,* or miscegenation, between whites
and Indians. Furthermore, there were more small property
owners and a better distribution of goods than in the Puno
region. Even with a higher mestizo population, however, only
33,194 persons claimed to be able to read or write in 1876.[38]

The immediate causes of the uprising were the abusive practices of the prefect, Francisco Noriega, and the reimposition of
the personal contribution. The more remote cause was the

devastated economy of Peru after the War of the Pacific. The Prefect Noriega was later accused of arbitrarily imposing the new head tax of two gold soles.[39] Nevertheless, it seems clear that he had the tacit approval of the central government of Iglesias to reinstitute the tax as a means of covering expenses that the bankrupt central government could ill afford. Onerous though the personal contribution was in itself, it also bore, as it always had in the past, an additional ominous significance for the Indians. The new tax almost necessarily meant placing themselves further in debt to the local *patrones*, who would be expected to advance the alloted sums for their hired hands.[40] Added to this fear were the high-handed methods of Noriega in collecting the tax.

In late February, 1885, some forty Indian mayors (*alcaldes pedáneos*) of the villages around Huaraz signed a memorial of complaints and sent it to Noriega. The principal complaints in the memorial were: forced labor on public works; state monopoly on salt; and the personal contribution. In the memorial the Indians requested that the contribution be either abolished or at least reduced to one sol per person.[41] The somewhat conciliatory tone of the memorial seemed to leave a door open for peaceful negotiations. Little prone to conciliate, especially with Indians, Noriega committed the first act of aggression in imprisoning one of the signers of the memorial, Pedro Pablo Atusparia, the mayor of Marián, on the pretext that Atusparia had refused to carry straw for repairing the roof of the military headquarters in Huaraz. Noriega exacerbated the situation by having Atusparia tortured to force him to reveal the name of the real "instigator" behind the memorial.[42]

When fourteen mayors presented themselves before Noriega to protest his treatment of Atusparia, the prefect compounded his ruthless tactics by arresting the mayors and turning them over to the local governor, José Collazos. While Noriega was away in the nearby town of Aija, Collazos committed the final act of tactlessness by ordering the long braids of the mayors, symbol of their authority, to be cut. Apparently the officials had no concept of the hostile feelings that had been engendered, for they released the mayors and Atusparia a short time later. A forewarning of impending trouble came on March 1 when a group of angry Indians descended on one of the districts of Huaraz and looted the stores of the resident Chinese. These Indians were driven out of the town by the local troops, but that night ominous campfires began appearing on the hills surrounding Huaraz.

The storm broke on the morning of March 2 when some 8,000 Indians armed with picks, hoes, machetes, sling shots, and rifles captured from the Chileans rushed upon the city. After a furious battle in the streets and main plaza of Huaraz, dozens of Indians and soldiers lay dead, while a few officials managed to flee the city. In a display of bravado, Noriega himself started for Huaraz dressed in full uniform. When he encountered a mass of Indians coming toward him on the road, he fled, and disguising himself as an Indian managed to escape down to the coast.[43]

The proclaimed leader of the revolution was Atusparia. Immediately after the capture of Huaylas he sent out emissaries throughout the entire Callejón de Huaylas to call for adhesion to his movement, and soon similar uprisings broke out in many parts of the valley. The Indian leader who emerged as second in command was a miner from Carhuaz, Pedro Cochachín, or "Uchcu Pedro," as he was popularly known.[44] On March 16 Uchcu Pedro took Carhuaz, and soon afterwards Atusparia and Uchcu Pedro together marched on Yungay and Caraz. At the same time a contingent of Indians swept down to the coast. News of the uprising in the Callejón de Huaylas touched off Indian uprisings in neighboring departments. By the end of March the greater part of the department of Ancash was under the sovereign power of Pedro Pablo Atusparia and his Indian followers.[45]

While Atusparia was in his ascendency, several white and mestizo pro-Indian supporters played minor but important roles. A lawyer from Huaraz, Manuel Mosquera, managed to ingratiate himself with Atusparia and was named prefect of the city. Mosquera attempted to turn the rebellion into a pro-Cácerist political movement, but by and large he was ignored by the Indians. Given over to drinking and quixotic pretensions, he left his post in Huaraz with an army of Indians and marched through the Callejón to rally the Indians around the banner of republicanism and Andrés Cáceres. Thoroughly incompetent as a soldier, he was killed by the government forces in Yungay in late April. A young journalist, Luis Felipe Montestruque, created a newspaper to become the voice of the revolution, *El Sol de Los Incas*, a potentially valuable source that has been lost. Finally, in Yungay, Simón Bambarén tried to stir up support for Atusparia among his fellow townsmen but was killed in reprisal.

Almost nothing is known about Atusparia himself from autotestimony. Even his baptismal record is missing. The first reports in Lima on Atusparia and his uprising were, of course, all negative and quite confused. *La Opinión Nacional* summed up this general ignorance and perjorative view with the statement that "the stupid phalanx recognizes as its principal chief the *alcalde pedáneo* of Huaraz, A. Atusparia."[46] *El Bien Público* claimed that the Indians called him "the Inca King."[47] *El Comercio* published the alarming "news" that Pedro Atusparia, known for his "audacious habits as a commander, dreams of bringing his numerous but unarmed hordes upon Lima."[48] But the testimony of eyewitness contemporaries of Atusparia produced a much clearer and far more sympathetic picture of the Indian leader. A young journalist, Ernesto Reyna, interviewed eyewitnesses of the uprising some forty years after the event and discovered the unanimous opinion of all, both Indians and whites, to be that Atusparia was one of the principal defenders of the white population against the vengeance of the Indians.[49]

Indeed, the press in Lima even admitted that the worst that could have happened in Huaraz did not happen. In its editorial of April 9, *El Comercio* reported that the Indians, after looting certain stores, "not only maintained order, but also offered all kinds of guarantees to government employees and soldiers" so that they could leave Huaraz. The editorial went on to observe that the Indians even designated local white residents as the new prefects of the different conquered cities.[50] When Colonel José Iraola, the new prefect appointed to replace Noriega, defeated the Indians in Huaraz, he went to visit the wounded Indian *caudillo*. In recognition of Atusparia's exemplary conduct while in command of the region, Iraola offered him guarantees and medical aid.[51] The most eloquent testimony of all, however, is provided by the diocesan priest of Huaraz, Fidel Olivas Escudero, who wrote two years after the uprising:

> The name of Atusparia will be remembered with gratitude always because he prevented with his energetic stance a new wave of looting that would have totally destroyed the goods and main buildings of Carhuaz, causing the ruin of the important families there.[52]

Carhuaz was the second city to fall after Huaraz. The commander of the attack on Carhuaz, Uchcu Pedro, represented the antiwhite faction among the Indians. Reyna reports in his somewhat dramaticized chronicle that Uchcu Pedro wanted to kill even the priests in Carhuaz when he entered, but was detained

by Atusparia personally.[53] Similar conflicts between Atusparia
and his second in command occurred repeatedly during the two
months that the uprising lasted. Atusparia always counseled pru-
dence, restraint, peace, and order, while Uchcu Pedro advocated
exterminating the whites and destroying their property.

Reyna also cast Uchcu Pedro in the role of an advocate for returning to the older, pre-Christian religion. There are important
reasons to doubt this portrayal of Uchcu Pedro. One is the great
popularity of the Catholic feast days among the Indians of the
region, a phenomenon to which Reyna himself attests in his chronicle. It is doubtful that Uchcu Pedro would have had a great following if he had advocated, at least publicly, anti-Catholic ideas.
Furthermore, in his last testament, composed right before being
executed by government forces, he declared himself to be an
"apostolic, Roman Catholic Christian, in which faith I have lived
and intend to die."[54] He also received the last rites of the church.
What is more probable is that Uchcu Pedro displayed hostility
toward the white priests in the area, which was the source of the
conflict between himself and Atusparia in Carhuaz.

Reyna seems to be closer to the truth, however, when he describes the religious behavior of Atusparia during Holy Week. According to Reyna, Holy Week, which began on March 29 and
ended the first week of April, marked the high point of Atusparia's "reign."

> Holy Week was celebrated with unusual pomp. There were
> many processions. Atusparia presided over all the ceremo-
> nies. In the ecclesiastical chapter he received the key of
> the tabernacle. . . . As the principal mayor he wore a
> black velvet cape (used only during Holy Week), a hom-
> burg hat with ribbons of three colors, and a great staff
> decorated with little silver bells.[55]

This description is in accord with the old Spanish custom by
which the mayor of the city wears the key to the tabernacle
around his neck during important feast days as a symbol of his
religious and political authority. Furthermore, the Indian mayors
always bring their staff (*vara*), symbol of their political authority,
to all major public functions.

A priest of the diocese of Huaraz, Alfonso Ponte, a contemporary of many of the participants in the uprising, confirms this
description of Atusparia's leadership during Holy Week. Ponte

records in a work on Huaraz, based upon the testimony of eye-witnesses, that Atusparia not only ordered all the Indians to attend the services but actually participated directly in them himself. Ponte describes Atusparia's participation during the Holy Thursday ceremonies:

> The priests offered him hyssop. He made the sign of the cross, then entered the church. The people arose and watched him, severe, calm, and in dominion of himself. At the appropriate moment the sign of peace was offered him with the ritual kiss. He arose and accepted it. In the afternoon he attended the Washing. He offered his contribution [*pesos de pina*] and kissed the feet of the "apostles." On Good Friday he made his act of adoration and offered his contribution [*óbolo*].[56]

Like Reyna, Ponte observes that religious fervor seemed to reach a high point that week. The entire "Indian aristocracy" showed up in their finest costumes, and unusually large numbers of Indians marched in the Holy Week processions. It was not only the first time since the Spanish conquest that the Indians had ruled in their own valley, but the first time that they had assumed official roles in the Catholic liturgy as well.[57]

The other major member of the dramatis personae of the uprising in Huaraz besides Atusparia and Uchcu Pedro was the priest Fidel Olivas Escudero. Born into a middle-class family in the district of Huari, not far from the Callejón de Huaylas, Olivas Escudero was sent to Lima to study in the *Colegio* of Our Lady of Guadalupe. In 1870 he entered Santo Toribio Seminary, but he was forced to withdraw because of bad health. He returned to Huari but was encouraged to try again by his uncle. Accordingly, he entered the seminary of Santiago, Chile, and was ordained a priest in 1874. After teaching briefly in the seminary in Santiago, he returned to the Callejón de Huaylas, where he began preaching missions. He joined the diocese of Huaraz in 1878 and remained there until 1900, when he was named bishop of Ayacucho. Two other priests of the diocese, Amadeo Figueroa and Pedro García Villón, also played influential roles in the religious life of Huaraz.

Olivas Escudero soon became one of the *notables* of the city. Along with Pedro García Villón, he founded a school for boys, San Agustín, as an alternative to the liberally oriented national school of La Libertad, where he also taught religion for a brief period. Shortly afterwards, he founded a similar school for girls, Santa Rosa de Viterbo. He also founded and directed three newspapers: the *Aurora de los Andes* (1877–78); *El Obrero de Ancash* 1880–81); and *La Justicia* (1892–1900). Many of the articles in these Catholic newspapers were written to combat atheism, Masonry, and liberal anticlericalism, although Olivas Escudero also took many advanced stands on women's rights. During the War of the Pacific he collaborated in raising funds to build a new warship after the loss of the Huascar. When the Chileans invaded Huaraz, he turned San Agustín into a hospital. A frequent target of the liberal press, he was assaulted once while traveling to Chiquián by anticlerical thugs from Huaraz.[58]

Tall, thin, and white-complexioned, Olivas Escudero impressed his contemporaries as being somewhat taciturn and even austere. Nevertheless, he was highly respected by both whites and Indians. After the fall of Huaraz, he organized a Red Cross mission for the wounded. He also went to Atusparia to plead for the lives of the inhabitants, a request readily granted by the Indian leader.[59]

In almost the same way in which Atusparia saved Carhuaz from destruction, Olivas Escudero appeared in time to save Yungay from the wrath of Uchcu Pedro. When Uchcu Pedro reached the outskirts of Yungay, he was greatly angered to hear that the prefect, Manuel Mosquera, whom Atusparia had left in charge of Huaraz, had followed him through the Callejón with the remaining Indian force, leaving Huaraz defenseless against a possible attack by government forces. The irate Indian chief announced his intention of destroying Yungay so that he could move back to Huaraz without fear of a rearguard attack. Olivas Escudero, who had accompanied Mosquera, petitioned the impatient warrior to detain his forces while he and a few of the leading citizens entered Yungay to ask for its peaceful submission. When the peace mission failed to return at the hour agreed upon Uchcu Pedro marched on the city and unleashed the full force of his anger. The several thousand Indians who flooded Yungay on Holy Saturday, April 4, massacred soldiers and civilians alike and looted most of the stores.[60] Olivas Escudero vividly recalled the tragic events of Uchcu Pedro's invasion of Yungay:

There are no words to express the panic and suffering of these families, who wandered about looking for a secure place to save themselves. . . . The intervention of the priests, which has always been the object of respect and veneration by the Indian race, was almost nil in those dark days. The very churches were profaned in the search for whites.[61]

In desperation, Olivas Escudero and the parish priest of Yungay took out the monstrance with the Blessed Sacrament and walked together through the streets of Yungay in the midst of the carnage. Olivas Escudero modestly stated later that this action as well as the "constant intercession of some priests" saved the city from total destruction.[62] At the same time Atusparia arrived from Huaraz to further stay the impulsive hand of Uchcu Pedro.

From Yungay Atusparia marched toward Caraz. This time the situation was quite different. Olivas Escudero and other priests of the area stood on the outskirts of the town in full liturgical regalia with the monstrance and the Blessed Sacrament held aloft. According to one eyewitness, Atusparia dismounted his horse, approached the monstrance, and knelt in adoration. Through the priests who acted as intermediaries, the city of Caraz surrendered peacefully, and Atusparia promised to respect the lives and property of its citizens.[63]

In the meantime, Colonel José Iraola, the newly appointed prefect, had arrived at Casma on the coast at the command of the pacification forces. He crossed the *Cordillera Negra* and took Yungay at the end of April. In a bloody battle outside of Yungay, Iraola's forces, under the direct command of Colonel Callirgos, clashed with an Indian army of approximately 10,000. Better armed, trained, and organized, Iraola's troops triumphed, leaving more than 1,000 Indians dead. From Yungay the government forces proceeded toward Huaraz, where Atusparia and Uchcu Pedro had concentrated their forces. Their arrival in Huaraz was set for May 3, the Feast of the Lord of Solitude.[64]

It seemed to be a fateful irony that while the high point of the uprising was Holy Week, the bloody denouement of the drama was acted out on the other great religious feast day of the Indians of Huaraz. The news of the advance of Colonel Callirgos threw the Indians into panic. Nevertheless, they chose to celebrate the feast day and proceeded to take out the statue of the Lord of Solitude for the annual procession.[65] Preceded by the *pallas*, the gaily decorated chorus of women cantors, the statue was borne through the streets, followed by thousands of respectful but apprehensive Indians, many of whom were inebriated. The procession had barely ended when Callirgos reached the outskirts of the city. At the head of some 6,000 Indians, Atusparia and Uchcu Pedro went out to battle together for the last time. In the violent clash that ensued, the Indians were defeated, Atusparia was wounded, and Uchcu Pedro fled into the mountains with many followers.

The flight of Uchcu Pedro made the mediating offices of Olivas Escudero necessary once again. Following his own proposal, Olivas Escudero led a delegation up to the *Cordillera Negra* to negotiate with the rebel chief, who had divided his forces, leaving the other half in the *Cordillera Blanca.* The Indians led the priest blindfolded to Uchcu Pedro so that he could not reveal their position. The content of the dialogue between the priest and the Indian *caudillo* is not known with certainty, but the outcome was failure for the peace mission.[66] Olivas Escudero returned to Huaraz, and on May 11 Uchcu Pedro attacked the city. This time the victory of the government forces was decisive, and Uchcu Pedro fled back into the mountains with a demoralized remnant. Hunted down, he was captured and shot in Casma in September, 1885.[67]

The fate of Atusparia was more fortunate, at least temporarily. His life was spared through the intercession of the women of Huaraz, and the new prefect, José Iraola, granted him full amnesty in recognition of his role of conciliator during the uprising. In December of that year, Andrés Cáceres overthrew the government of Miguel Iglesias and some time later he invited the Indian hero of Huaraz to visit him in the presidential palace in Lima. Atusparia brought his son for the interview with President Cáceres, who later granted the boy a scholarship. The death of Atusparia is shrouded in mystery. It appears that he was poisoned to death while attending a feast with other Indian chiefs in August, 1887, possibly because his dealings with the powerful men of the white world had placed him in suspicion.[68]

Olivas Escudero returned to his many activities in Huaraz. In 1886 he delivered a funeral oration for those who had died in the massacre of Yungay. He referred to "our unhappy Helots, who were hurled into the abyss of disorder by their ignorance, their undisciplined passions and most of all by the malice and weakness of their *caudillos.*"[69] A prolific writer and lecturer, he composed a great number of essays on diverse religious themes such as atheism, liberalism, the dignity of the woman, and the participation of the clergy in politics.[71] He was later elected deputy to congress from the district of Pomabamba during the tenure of

Nicolás de Piérola.[71] From that post he was named bishop of
Ayacucho, where he served until his death in 1935.

The exemplary behavior of Ambrosio Huerta in Puno and Fidel
Olivas Escudero in Huaraz must, of course, be complemented by
a study of other, less meritorious clergymen of the period. Scattered newspaper reports brought to light from time to time the
existence of clergymen who seemed to fit the most pejorative
descriptions of the anticlerical press. In 1866 a priest near Huancayo was accused of seducing an Indian girl.[72] That same year the
inhabitants of Pomabamba, Ancash, published a complaint against
the local priest, who refused absolution to an old man because he
had accused the priest of certain improprieties.[73] In 1888 in Bambamarca, la Libertad, a priest who was also the mayor of the town
presided over the condemnation of an Indian woman for witch-
craft, which resulted in her being burnt to death.[74]

On the other hand, there were indications that clergymen less
famous than Huerta and Olivas Escudero, but of the same quality,
also lived in this period. In October, 1896, the Indians of Huaylas
signed a petition asking for their return of a priest who had been
reassigned. In their petition, addressed to the archbishop, the Indians said that they wanted the priest back because he spoke
Quechua, because of his "gifts of piety and nobility," and because
he had been "charitable to the poor, and he was not a tyrant in
collecting your taxes."[75]

Important factor though it was, however, the conduct of the
clergy may not have been the most significant phenomenon in the
Indian uprisings of nineteenth-century Peru. What is most striking
was the allegiance of the Indians to traditional Catholicism during
periods of revolutionary stress. While it cannot be demonstrated
directly that religion itself was a motivating factor in the uprisings,
it does seem clear that religion did not inhibit the Indians from
fighting against social injustices. Indeed, as in the case of Huaraz,
religious fervor even seemed to increase in the midst of rebellion.
This may, of course, have reflected a momentary enthusiasm in
the wake of victory. But it may also have mirrored a new pride
among the Indians in being masters of their own land again.

There is something in the attitude of a solemn-faced Indian
caudillo presiding over Holy Week services in Huaraz that escapes
the mental schemes of Peru's intellectual elite. For a generation
of order-minded liberals, religion was perceived to be a force in

man that checked his passions and led him to be an obedient citizen of the republic. Atusparia, who ordered an end to looting and commanded his Indian followers to attend Mass, certainly viewed religion in this way too. But Atusparia had also done what the later anticlerical generation of González Prada conceived to be impossible. While remaining rigorously faithful to traditional Catholic practices, he and his followers revolted against the abuses of a liberal republican government. Unencumbered by enlightened philosophies the Indians had come to experience Catholic Christianity and social protest as compatible realities. Unfortunately, there is no evidence available to show that the Indians ever attempted to express this compatibility in formal terms. The lack of written testimony does not preclude the possibility that the Indians were aware of a new dynamic relationship between politics and religion; it merely means that they did not have the tools of communication with which to articulate their experience. Furthermore, it is important to note that the popular Catholicism of the Indians did not degenerate into a narrow racist sect. The conciliatory attitude manifested by Atusparia, Olivas Escudero, and others kept the universal, multiracial element alive in the Christianity professed by the Indians.

By and large the many Indian rebellions of the nineteenth and early twentieth centuries failed to have an immediate impact on national politics. For the most part, the uprisings were scattered regional outbursts with no substantial unity between groups. Furthermore, the Indians had no ideological program that committed them to pursue new goals after they achieved the redress of a particular abuse. More than anything else, the uprisings reflected a pattern of frustrated social aspirations as well as stubborn loyalty to traditional religious values. Nevertheless, Peru's intellectual elite was moved by the plight of the Indians, who increasingly became the object of the liberal's crusade for change and reform in Peru.[76] In this crusade, which became known as the *indigenista* ("Indianist") movement, many young reformers were challenged to go beyond González Prada's generalities about the Indians and reevaluate the role of religion among all of Peru's lower classes.

In the meantime, year after year thousands of Indians continued to pour out of the hills and mountains to celebrate Holy Week and the Feast of Our Lord of Solitude on May 3 in Huaraz. In the incense, singing, and festive tumult of the pilgrims, one can hear the clatter of hoofs and the roar of a distant battle swirling around the figure of an impassive Indian, Pedro Pablo Atusparia, the rebel *caudillo* who brought the hills and the city together for the first time in the history of the valley.

4: THE REDISCOVERY OF PERU: THE *INDIGENISTA* MOVEMENT, 1889-1930

At three decisive moments the Indian has been discovered and rediscovered in Peruvian history. The first moment was the first century after the conquest when soldiers, missionaries, and government officials composed numerous chronicles on Indian life and customs in their enthusiastic wonder at discovering a new world. For José de Acosta and other missionaries, the Indian was seen primarily as an object of evangelization, while the Viceroy Toledo and his officials saw the Indian as a prospective subject of a new empire, one who must be "civilized" and Hispanized.

Again in the late eighteenth century, in the wake of the scientific Enlightenment, creoles like Hipólito Unánue and José Baquíjano published tracts in the *Mercurio Peruano* on the psychology and characteristics of the Indians. For these enlightened precursors of independence, the Indian was viewed primarily as an object of scientific curiosity, although other creoles, moved by the revolution of Tupac Amaru, called for a curbing of injustices against the Indians.

The third moment of discovery began after the War of the Pacific and culminated in the *indigenista* movement of the early twentieth century. This time the Indian was viewed as an object of political and social reform. The writers, scholars, and political activists who created the *indigenista* school in Peru became the connecting link between the nineteenth-century liberals and the social reformers of the twentieth century. They also formed a bridge between the political radicalism of González Prada in Lima and the provinces where the Indian problem was the greatest. What began as a romantic literary movement in the nineteenth century became a militant political movement in the twentieth century. In their campaign to awaken their countrymen to the plight of the Indian, the *indigenistas* also uncovered for the intellectual elite a Peru which it had hitherto not known or ignored.[1]

A key theme of the *indigenista* movement was the cultural narcissism of Lima and the neglect of the provinces. Indeed, a significant number of the leaders of *indigenismo* were from provincial middle-class origins: Narciso Aréstegui, Clorinda Matto de Turner, José Uriel García, and José Frisancho were from Cuzco; Emilio Romero, Alejandro Peralta, and Juan Antonio Encinas came from Puno; Luis Valcárcel came from Moguegua; and Hildebrando Castro Pozo from Piura. Although González Prada, Dora Mayer, Pedro Zulen, Joaquín Capelo, and José Carlos Mariátegui were from Lima, they assumed the mission of directing the attention of their fellow *Limeños* to the reality of a country beyond the capital.

EL PADRE HORAN

The *indigenista* movement was born of a confluence of literary romanticism and political radicalism, two characteristics that lasted well into the decade of the thirties and forties of the twentieth century. An example of the first tendency was the first Peruvian novel, *El Padre Horán,* written by Narciso Aréstegui in 1848. Although the immediate influence of the novel was slight, *El Padre Horán* was important because it contained many themes that would appear in later *indigenista* works. Aréstegui was a lawyer and a military officer from Cuzco who also taught literature at the University of Cuzco and served as librarian of the College of Science. His novel, which first appeared in *El Comercio* of Lima, reflected many of his own political, religious, and social sentiments. He was opposed to the Peru-Bolivian confederation, which had only recently been dissolved when he composed the novel, and he manifested his pro-Indian sentiments by joining the Sociedad Amigos de los Indios, founded by the directors of *El Comercio* in 1867. In 1868 he was named prefect of Puno, but he died in a boating accident on Lake Titicaca a year later.

The novel fell within the literary genre known as *costumbrismo,* which aimed to uplift men morally by exposing the evil "customs" of some men in society and exalting the virtues of others.[2] The setting of the novel is Cuzco in 1836 at the height of Bolivian hegemony in southern Peru. The plot centers around the attempts of a priest, "El Padre Horán," to seduce an innocent young girl, Angélica, a story drawn from a real case.[3] The characters are all stereotyped figures drawn from nineteenth-century *Cuzqueña* society. Padre Horán is the "bad priest," a lecherous, scheming hypocrite, who goes to extravagant lengths to impress others, particularly susceptible, pious women, with his asceticism and "holiness." Once the women consent to become his "daughters of confession" (*hijas de confesión*), he envelops them in an evil web of conspiracy and carnal lust. As an instrument to trap new victims he uses a local *beata*, Brígida, an old crone whose life centers around the church but not around the poor or the needy. The mother of Angélica is an example of the pious women of the provincial city who are so bound by custom and respect for religion that they blindly follow the priest's advice. As a sort of an angelic alter ego to the evil Padre Horán, Aréstegui presents the good priest, Fray Lucas, who is everything that Horán is not—kindly, compassionate to the poor, and popular among the people for his abilities as a peacemaker. The final blow to Horán's pride, which drives him to murder Angélica, comes when he discovers that she has chosen Fray Lucas over himself as her confessor.

Although the main characters are all drawn from the middle class, in one brief but poignant section Aréstegui portrays an Indian couple, Dionicio and Leandra, discussing their fate in life as Indians. Aréstegui uses the couple to describe the entire gamut of abuses to which the Indians were subjected: tribute (not officially abolished until 1854); the *faenas*, or forced labor on pub- ·lic works; and the *reparto*, a system by which the agents from commercial houses forced the Indians to accept an advance on their woolen goods so that later the agents, accompanied by armed henchmen, could collect the goods far in excess of what was originally allotted. Aréstegui also depicts the couple as fundamentally religious and resigned to the will of God, although they both hope for a day when there will be real equality be- fore the law and not just before God.[4] A liberal, Aréstegui, of course, saw equality before the law as the key to Indian reform in Peru.

In another scene based upon an historical incident, Aréstegui describes a near riot that broke out in 1834 when the citizens learned that the image of the favorite cult of Cuzco, the Lord of Tremors, had been repainted. Provoked by the rumor that the re- touched version was really a fake and that the original had been carried off by Bolivian agents, the citizens take to the streets in angry consternation. They are calmed down only when Fray Lucas speaks to them and points out the contrast between their behavior and what Christianity teaches. Aréstegui's own sentiments are expressed in the words he has Fray Lucas proclaim to the people: "It is the people who lose in revolutions. We want only peace."[5]

Three basic elements in Aréstegui's novel reappear in *indigenista* literature well into the twentieth century: first of all, the emphasis upon clerical influence, for good or for evil; secondly, the stress on the strong religious feelings of the people as in the example of the outburst over the disappearance of the Lord of Tremors; and thirdly, a romantic portrayal of the Indians as good and innocent. Even given this tendency to romanticize, Aréstegui's novel represents a significant break from the liberal elitist tradition because he attempted to picture the Indians' life from their own point of view.[6]

ROMANTIC AND SOCIAL *INDIGENISMO*

Until the appearance of Clorinda Matto de Turner's *Aves sin Nido* in 1889, most works on Indians followed the romanticist pattern set by Ricardo Palma, whose witty vignettes on life in colonial Lima in his *Tradiciones Peruanas* focused the attention of Peruvians on their Spanish-creole past. An example of this genre is provided by Matto de Turner herself in a play that she composed and presented first in Arequipa in 1884 and in Lima in 1888. Entitled *Hima-Sumac,* it treats of an Indian princess in the time of Tupac Amaru II who falls in love with a Spanish youth. The princess, Hima-Sumac, knows the secret of the lost treasure of Atahaulpa, which is the real object of her suitor's designs. The princess is caught between her love for a son of her conquerors and her attraction to the movement of Tupac Amaru, which represents the cause of her people. In several scenes Hima-Sumac prays to "Pachacamac" and "Father Sun" to liberate her people.[7] While it is highly unlikely historically that the Indians of Tupac Amaru's time prayed to their ancestral gods, Matto de Turner's portrayal was the type of romanticized image of the descendents of the Incas that appealed to cultured audiences in Arequipa or Lima.

The social *indigenismo* of Aréstegui was reborn after the War of the Pacific in 1885 by José Itolararres in his novel, *La Trinidad del Indio.* Although Itolararres's novel never had the impact that Matto de Turner's works would have, it nevertheless serves as an example of the abrupt shift from prewar romanticism to postwar realism. The author dedicates his work to Mariátegui, Vigil, Gálvez, Grau, Bolognesi, and others as the "real patriots" of Peru. His predilection for anticlerical liberals suggests the influences on the author as he describes life in a small town somewhere in the Andes. According to the author, the town is a "nest of vultures" who feed upon the passive and long-suffering Indians. The three principal vultures who make up the "Trinity of the Indian" are the governor, the justice of the peace, and the local priest. The three spend most of their time conspiring to exploit the Indians or to rob one another. The priest is the "greatest vulture" of the three because he uses his priestly office of trust to relieve the Indians of their possessions. He is the first to arrive at the bedside of the dying to extract a person's worldly goods as insurance for the eternal rest of his soul.

The peace, or rather the iniquitous normal state of affairs, is momentarily interrupted when a young man from the coast appears in town. Angered by the lack of proper piety of the *costeño* at Mass, the priest leads a mob of Indians to imprison the offender, who symbolizes the rural priest's fear of outside influences which threaten his hold over the town. The story ends with the young man, thoroughly disillusioned about the possibility of finding justice on the local level, going to the level of the province prefecture, where the reader is led to believe that justice is unlikely to be procured either.[8]

CLORINDA MATTO DE TURNER

Indigenismo as a distinct literary form in Peru received its decisive impetus from Clorinda Matto de Turner. Like Aréstegui, she was born and raised in Cuzco, and after her marriage to an Englishman, John Turner, she moved to the nearby town of Tinta, where Tupac Amaru had begun his revolution a century earlier. She initiated her literary career under the influence of Ricardo Palma, whom she met frequently at the literary *veladas* held in the home of the Argentinian lady of letters, Juana Manuela Gorriti, in Lima around 1876–77. In imitation of Ricardo Palma, she wrote her *Tradiciones Cuzqueñas* in 1884–86. After a brief period in Arequipa, she returned to Lima in 1886 and this time fell sway to the influence of Manuel González Prada whom she met through the Club Literario and the Ateneo of Lima.[9] Her novel, *Aves sin Nido,* reflected to a great extent both the romanticism of Palma and the anti–status-quo revisionism of González Prada.

Matto de Turner situates her drama in a small town near Cuzco, which in reality is her own town of Tinta. As Itolararres had done earlier, she divides the world of "Kíllac" into the oppressors and the oppressed. The oppressors are the governor, the priest, and the justice of the peace, and his secretary, the ubiquitous *tinterillo* who exercises his ability to read and write to defraud the Indians of their rights and property. Unlike Itolararres, however, Matto de Turner gives life and substance to the oppressed. The Indian protagonists are Juan Yupanqui, a field hand, and his wife, Marcela. Weighed down by heavy debts owed the church, Juan Yupanqui and Marcela seek the intercession of Don Fernando and his wife, Lucía, a benign couple from Lima, who because they are white and educated, can speak to the priest and the governor as equals.

Lucía takes the initiative to ask the priest, Don Pascual Vargas, and his accomplice, the governor, to relieve Juan Yupanqui of his debts. Both the priest and the governor are taken aback by Lucía's boldness in advocating for an Indian. The governor informs Lucía that her request is against "custom" and that in Kíllac "custom is the law."[10] The story reaches a critical peak when the priest, the governor, and other town notables conspire to attack the home of the outsiders, Don Fernando and Lucía. The attempt is a failure, but Juan Yupanqui is killed defending the home of his protectors. Eventually, Marcela after being taken into the home of Don Fernando and Lucía, dies of poor health.

A secondary plot evolves around the figures of Manuel, an orphan raised by the governor, and Margarita, another orphan raised by Juan Yupanqui and Marcela. The two fall in love but discover to their dismay at the end of the novel that they are really brother and sister, the illegitimate children of the former pastor of Kíllac and now the bishop of the area. They thus find themselves to be "birds without a nest."

Like Aréstegui much earlier, Matto de Turner uses her pen to expose to public view the bad customs of life in an Andean town. As described by Matto de Turner, Don Pascual Vargas, the priest of Kíllac, is short, fat, and ill-kempt. He knows little theology and even less Latin. He mercilessly exacts payment of debts from the Indians and seduces Indian girls who are forced to serve the *mita* cleaning or cooking in the priest's house. Lucía expresses Matto de Turner's thoughts when she reflects to herself that Don Pascual is typical of the rural Andean priest and unlike the superior priests of the city who go about "wrapped in mystery" caring for the sick and dying.[11] But the Indians have no choice but to accept the tyranny of unscrupulous highland priests:

> The influence exercised by the priests in these parts is such that their word touches the limits of a sacred command; and the Indian is of such a docile character that even though he criticizes certain actions of the priests in the recesses of his hut with guarded words, the power of superstition levels all reasoning and turns the word of the priest into law for their parishioners.[12]

Matto de Turner interjects her own religious and humanitarian sentiments when she explains to the reader that attacking the bad customs of a town is useless if a foundation of belief in a Supreme Being is not first firmly laid. Above all else, the author observes, Kíllac needs good schools and good priests in order to instill this faith in God and to establish a "true civilization."[13] On another occasion, Matto de Turner places in the mouth of Manuel her own hopes for Christianity to regenerate mankind: "I have hope," says Manuel to his prospective father-in-law, Don Fernando, "that the civilization which will arise under the banner of a purified Christianity will not be long in appearing, because it will bring happiness for the family, and as a logical consequence, social happiness as well."[14]

The Indian couple, Juan and Marcela, symbolize the hope of the future because even though they are ignorant, they are free of the vile hypocrisy and avarice of the priest and other town leaders. For Matto de Turner, the Indians are the simple children of God whose prayers alone reach Heaven. On several occasions, she depicts Juan and Marcela praying the Magnificat and the Benedictus together in the midst of their suffering. Furthermore, Matto de Turner looked with forgiving sympathy even on the superstitions of the Indians. In her *Tradiciones Cuzqueñas* she describes an old Indian, Condorí, who tended her father's cattle near Cuzco. Condorí's beliefs, she noted, were a mixture of religious truths and "fantastic superstitions which were also poetic."[15]

REDISCOVERING THE INDIAN

Like Matto de Turner, many other Peruvians, moved by humanitarian and nationalistic concerns, set out to rediscover the Peruvian Indian and better the Indian's lot in life. In 1901, the government sent a commission under Alejandro Maguiña to report on the conditions of the Indians in the Puno area. In 1909 Pedro Zulen, a young student at San Marcos University, founded the Asociación Pro-Indígena, which counted among its members such leading *indigenistas* as Joaquín Capelo, Dora Mayer, Carlos Lissón, and Carlos Valdez de la Torre. The aims of the Association were to promote legislation in favor of the Indians, familiarize the public with the problems of the Indians in general, and change public attitudes toward them.[16] The main organ of the group was the *Deber Pro-Indígena*, which was published in Lima from 1912 until 1917. In 1915 Pedro Zulen founded a separate organ, *La Autonomía*, which came to replace the *Deber* as the main voice of the *indigenista* movement, until *La Sierra* and *Amauta* captured center stage in the late twenties.

In 1885 the Limanian novelist Mercedes Cabello de Carbonera, whose social criticism of city life complemented Matto de Turner's *indigenista* criticism, described a religious feast that she witnessed in an Indian town "near Lima." She arrived in January in time to observe the feast of the *Votapayas*, a celebration in which Indian women dancers bid farewell to the Baby Jesus. The author was shocked by the poverty of the Indians, who had lost many of their possessions during the War of the Pacific, and scandalized by what were for her the strange religious customs of the people. She found little that was pleasing in the celebrations: the dances were too long, the music was monotonous and cacophonous, the people were disorderly and inebriated, and the poetry recited was bereft of any religious sentiment. She was especially disconcerted by the lack of any apparent religious meaning in the dances and celebrations. So far removed was this Peruvian Indian feast from her idea of religion that she believed it could have taken place in pagan India.

When one beholds that huge multitude gathered there, the majority of whom are Indians, with their glazed eyes, stupified stares, creating an infernal din, drunk from aguardiente and sated from over-eating, without any religious idea in their minds or moral principle in their hearts, one would believe that he was witnessing, not a religious feast of a civilized people, but one of those feasts of Chelambrum in honor of the god Siva in the south of India. . . .[17]

The author went on to muse over how life must have been under the Incas. In those days, she wrote, the Inca represented the deity on earth. With "paternal Care" he provided for his "subject-children" and saw that justice was procured for all. There was neither poverty nor laziness under the Incas. In fact, she declared, the doctrines of Owen, Saint-Simon, and Fourier were fully realized in that great empire. Finally, she blamed much of the current religious degradation of the Indians on the Catholic church because it destroyed most of the good Inca customs that uplifted the people morally and socially.[18]

Moved by the frequent Indian uprisings between 1895 and 1900 and the rising indignation of pro-Indian advocates, the government sent Alejandro Maguiña to investigate abuses perpetrated against the Indians in Puno. In his report back to the central government, Maguiña described the poor economic conditions of the area, which he blamed partially on the church. In his opinion, Puno needed priests who would give an example of charity and morality and who would not use religion as a "means of speculation."[19] Many of the priests, he complained, used their priestly office to encourage the proliferation of religious feasts, a practice which brought lucrative returns to them but which also provoked much drunkenness and disorder in the towns and reduced the Indians to even greater poverty.[20] As an exception to the rule, Maguiña singled out the priest who accompanied him on his tour for his defense of the Indians.[21]

Even studies which claimed to be purely "scientific" in nature frequently turned polemical when the subject of the church was raised. In his bachelor's thesis on the Inca empire in 1909, Pedro Irigoyen, later a distinguished diplomat, concluded that the Spanish Catholic church was to blame in great part for the decline of the Indians since the fall of the Inca empire. According to Irigoyen, the monks and other "functionaries" who established their houses in Peru "impeded all mental and economic progress" during the colonial period.[22] A member of the Pro-Indian Association in Cuzco, Luis Aguilar, wrote a dissertation on "Indian Questions" in which he claimed that the Indians do not really worship the person of Jesus Christ but the image itself in the cult of the Lord of Tremors in the Cathedral of Cuzco. Furthermore, he charged the clergy with deliberately fomenting idolatry in order to fill their coffers.[23] Another author who composed a scholarly work on the ruins of Cuzco summed up his view of the religion of the Indians in one terse sentence: "In religious matters, they are fanatical and I can even say idolatrous."[24]

Other *indigenistas* resisted making such simplistic generalizations. The German-born advocate of Indian and women's rights, Dora Mayer, argued that the clergy did not exploit the Indian any more than the "other social classes" in Peru. She blamed the law for not providing some kind of assistance to the rural clergy so that it would not have to accept money from the Indians.[25]

The young director of the government section for Indian affairs, Hildebrando Castro Pozo, composed an exhaustive study of Indian life and customs in 1924, much of which was based on personal observation gathered from living in Indian communities. In his study, *Nuestra Comunidad Indígena*, he criticized the clergy for charging the Indians excessively for every procession, Mass, blessing, and religious act.[26] He also claimed that the church had failed to communicate to the Indians the "metaphysical" meaning of the Mass, which the Indians saw exclusively as a means of petitioning for their own needs.

Yet Castro Pozo had also witnessed the existence of an entire structure of popular beliefs and practices in the highlands that seemed to have little to do with the official church and its liturgy. He described extensively the cult of the dead, magical rites, incantations, and folk beliefs, the origins of which were lost in pre-Hispanic times. The young observer recorded that on every hill around an Indian village that had a pre-Columbian sacred significance the Christian missionaries had placed a cross to symbolize their "conquest" of the area. Yet, at certain times of the year the remains of food and other objects offered to the pre-Christian idols (*apachitas*) on those hills could be found scattered around the cross—silent testimony of the survival of preconquest religious beliefs.[27] In spite of all the efforts of the rural priests, concluded Castro Pozo, the Indians still firmly believed in Mamapacha, the goddess of the earth and fertility. Nevertheless, Castro Pozo warned the reader to view his conclusions as provisional because his study was one of the first of its kind in Peru and much more research would have to be carried out to fully understand the religious beliefs and practices of the Indians. He commented that the greatest difficulty that he experienced in collecting data was the "reserve" of the Indians themselves.[28]

POLITICAL *INDIGENISMO*

After World War I the success of the Russian and Mexican revolutions, the ideologies of socialism and nationalism, and the rise of Indian studies infused the *indigenista* movement with new enthusiasm and heightened its political consciousness. Young *indigenistas* began to view the Indian no longer as an object of scientific study but as a prospective agent of socialist-agrarian revolution. Others, influenced by their middle-class provincial background, saw the Indian as the catalyst of a new revolutionary nationalism that would transform Peru. An earlier generation of *indigenistas* had viewed Indian reform as one among many changes that would be necessary if Peru were to emerge from the lethargy of tradition and enter the modern world. The new post World War I generation, however, saw Indian reform as the essential *sine qua non* of the regeneration of all of Peru.

Above all else, the new *indigenistas* looked to the rugged Andes as the source of the coming revolution that would sweep aside traditions and revivify the country with the youthful energy of the Indian race. The mighty Inca empire, not the Spanish colonial experience, was to be the model for Peru's emergence into the modern world.

Two groups emerged in the decade of the twenties as the main spokesmen for the *indigenista* movement. In Cuzco, the Grupo Resurgimiento, which included Luis Valcárcel, José Uriel García, Dora Mayer de Zulen, Francisco Mostajo, José Guillermo Guevara, José Sabogal, and many others, put out *La Sierra* from 1927 to 1930. Claiming to be the organ of the "renovating youth of the

Andes," *La Sierra* pursued a nationalist line without identifying itself with any particular ideology, although its members were nearly all prosocialist. The other group centered around José Carlos Mariátegui's Marxist organ, *Amauta*, which appeared in Lima from 1926 to 1930. *Amauta*, which was more oriented toward worker's questions on the coast, openly identified socialism with *indigenismo*. Beyond these two principal organs, in all the provinces numerous pro-Indian publications appeared, most of them bearing Inca or regionalist titles, such as *Attusparia* in Huaraz, *Inti* in Huancayo, and *La Puna* in Ayaviri.[29]

Whatever their particular ideological differences, the *indigenistas* all concurred that Lima's traditional neglect of the provinces and the Indian had cost Peru the loss of a great potential source of spiritual and material energy. This was the belief of Luis Valcárcel, a student of Inca culture in Cuzco and later one of Peru's foremost ethnologists. "Andeanism," he declared, "is more than a political banner; above all else it is a doctrine of spiritual revivification."[30] Although the Spanish did their best to destroy the Indians and break their spirit, he stated, the Andes have infused new life and created a new race of Indians. This new race, he declared, "rejuvenated by contact with the earth, demands the right to act."[31] Modern culture may try to force the Indian to wear western dress and speak Spanish or English, said Valcárcel, but the vital touch of the Andes will keep the ancient race alive. In the meantime, he warned, a "storm" is brewing in the Andes as the Indians reassert the power of their race. Just as in Inca times, declared Valcárcel somewhat apocalyptically, culture will come down from the Andes once again. Another *indigenista* and early collaborator with Valcárcel, José Uriel García, predicted that the Andes, which he believed possessed a special creative power to regenerate men, would someday forge a "New Indian."[32]

In a similar way, *indigenistas* looked to Cuzco as the Mecca of the coming revolution. "All men turn their eyes toward you," exclaimed Valcárcel in a eulogy to the Inca capital, "because you are the body and soul of the people."[33] Cuzco symbolizes all that is authentically Peruvian, Valcárcel asserted, while Lima symbolizes the importation of European culture. A member of the court in Cuzco, José Frisancho, criticized the attempts of Limanian legislators to solve the problems of a part of Peru that few had actually seen. Peruvian legislation, he said, has rarely taken into consideration the condition or geographical situation of the Indian. Lima, he complained, is always looking to foreign models

to solve the problems of the Indians when it should be looking
to the Indians themselves. Finally, the author deplored the pernicious attraction that Lima held for the provinces: "What Europe
is for the *Limeño,* Lima has become for the mountain people: a
paradise for those predestined to acquire fortunes."[34]

CATHOLIC LITURGY AND INCA PAGEANTRY

Emilio Romero, a young student of the new science of economic geography and later a senator from Puno, believed that Cuzco
hid hitherto unexplored facets of the rich culture of the highlands.
He was especially fascinated by the way Spanish Catholicism had
superimposed itself on Inca culture. He greatly influenced other
indigenistas with his belief that Inca paganism not only did not
die with the conquest but may even have been strengthened by
the Catholicism of the conquerors. Though his work synthesizing
these ideas, *3 Ciudades del Perú,* did not appear until 1929, as
early as 1927 he had expressed his insights in *Amauta* and *La
Sierra.*[35]

Calling his work an "essay on human geography," Romero
blended historical studies with personal insights into the cultural
life of his native highlands. He was especially impressed by the
widespread depth of religious sentiment among the Indians. "More
than by the sword," he observed, "Peru was conquered by the
cross."[36] He also noted that the sixteenth-century Spanish monks
chose as their centers of operations precisely those sites that had
been foci of Inca religiosity: Cuzco, the capital of the empire,
and Copacabana, the island of the sun in Lake Titicaca. From
these sites the Dominicans, and later the Jesuits, radiated out-
wards in their evangelization of the region. It was also in these
sites that the Virgin of the Spanish made her appearances to the
Indians, giving rise to the cults of Our Lady of Copacabana and
Our Lady of Pomata. So great was the religious impact of the first
missionaries on the Indians that "the formulas of Catholic ritual
penetrated into all the *ayllus"* and even reached isolated Indians
in distant mountain plateaus who had never heard of the conquest.[37]

In colonial Cuzco it was the church that governed the pace of
life and gave coherence to the culture. "The Church," said Romero, "was undoubtedly the social center, the club of the colonial period."[38] The slow, monotonous rhythm of colonial life

was interrupted only by the arrival of the mail and the great religious feasts and processions of the church. In fact, continued Romero, Cuzco outdid all other Peruvian cities, possibly even Lima itself, in the splendor, extravagance, and sheer outpouring of energy in its religious feasts and processions. Romero found the explanation for this effusion of religious fervor in Cuzco precisely in the way in which the Spanish Catholic liturgy recalled Inca pageantry. In Cuzco, he argued, the Indians were accustomed to witness the great solemn religious festivals of the Incas. They were naturally attracted to the equally magnificent displays put on by the Catholic church in its liturgy and processions. Indeed, suggested Romero, in the Catholic liturgy the Indians relived the grandeur of the Inca empire.

> The Indians vibrated with emotion before the solemnity of Catholic ritual. In the flowing, golden-embroidered chasubles and pluvial capes they saw the image of the sun; and in the fine violet silk of the surplices they beheld the colors of the rainbow. In the purple tassles of the priests or the cintures of the discalced they saw perhaps the symbol of the *quipus*.[39]

This affinity between Inca and Christian symbols explains the "pagan furor" with which the Indians of Cuzco shook with fear before the image of the Lord of Tremors in which they saw the tangible incarnation of their memories. They offered to the Catholic saints the same libations that they had offered before to the sun god. *Cuzqueña* religiosity, said Romero, is sensual, proud, and voluptuous; it is full of the ancient sentiments which the Indians felt when they danced in mystic trance on the feast of Inti Raymi. Nevertheless, even though they changed fetiches, said Romero, it was always God whom they adored.[40]

The Indians in colonial and even republican times clung tenaciously to their religious traditions, fortifying even more the hold of the past on them. Nevertheless, pointed out Romero, this strength of religious custom has had a double positive effect. First of all, it served to counter the impact of Spanish culture on the Indians, thus helping to preserve their Indian identity. Secondly, religion checked the excesses of materialism in the colony. On the negative side, Romero believed that Catholicism turned the sun-worshipping Incas away from the open spaces to which they were accustomed and to the narrow confines of medieval churches. "The prayer to the Sun . . . was replaced by the smoking candle and the dank interior of air-starved temples."[41]

Yet these very temples were at the same time original creations of the newly evangelized Indians. If the Inca dance and other artistic manifestations of the people suffered on account of Christianity, architecture flourished as a result of the imposition of the new faith. Indeed, declared Romero, the churches and great cathedrals in southern Peru are the most beautiful architectural monuments of Spanish-Indian art. So great was the impact of the church in the southern highlands, he noted, that the Indians do not consider a populated area a "town" (*pueblo*) if there is no church there. Yet, even in the architecture of the colonial church Romero discerned the powerful imprint of the Inca past. In his description of the Cathedral of Cuzco, he underlined the symbolic fusion of the Inca past with the Christian present.

The walls are Spanish, but the earth, the black stone, is Indian. Strange, twisted spirits which provoke the imagination climb the columns along the walls. But through the skylights the sun which shone on Tamputtoko defiantly breaks through. A proud and majestic temple . . . its stone crypts and pillars and gargoyles turn into indigenous symbols before the *Cuzqueño* countryside.[42]

Uncertain which tradition influenced the spirit of Cuzco the most, Spanish Catholicism or Inca paganism, Romero gazed nostalgically at the past and concluded that in either case religion had been the dominant force in the history of the city.

THE NEW INDIAN

Another member of the Grupo Resurgimiento, the writer, historian, and later senator from Cuzco, José Uriel García, also emphasized the importance of the religious factor for understanding the history of the highlands. Like Valcárcel, he accepted the theory of the juxtaposition of Catholic forms on Inca realities. Unlike Valcárcel, however, he believed that the real religious force of both the Inca and the Spanish past had become incarnated in the mestizo, not the Indian. He held that the history of Cuzco must be understood by reference to the Christianized mestizos, who assimilated many of the exterior forms and doctrines of the Spanish, but who also created at the same time a "neo-Indian religious sentiment" that profoundly influenced the piety, the art, and even the politics of the city. In his search for God in nature, the mestizo resisted abstract medieval dogmas and infused

Catholicism with a vital realism. Even as an artist the mestizo was a rebel against the imposition of Spanish culture. The image of the Virgin in the church of Belén, pointed out Uriel García, is definitely that of a mestizo girl, while that of the Lord of Tremors is an Indian field-laborer.[43]

It was this same "neo-Indian religious sentiment" that lived on in republican times and reinforced the conservative political feelings of the lower classes of Cuzco. In reality, said the author, politics and religion were but a continuum of the same instinct to cling to the past. The same mass of people who rioted in protest because the image of the Lord of Tremors had been retouched in 1834 made up the mobs that poured out into the streets to support popular military *caudillos*. Idolatry and demagoguery are two sides of the same mask. According to Uriel García, García Moreno's "Republic of the Sacred Heart" could very well have been transplanted to Cuzco.[44]

But Cuzco merely represented on a larger scale what was true of the multitude of mestizo villages and towns that formed the "heart of the Andean countryside." For Uriel García, the Andean village church symbolized the triumph of mestizo Catholicism. The Indian of the *ayllu* who looks to the mountain peaks in pantheistic contemplation, sees the church as an enigma that he accepts without questioning or understanding. He enters the church in awe and dread; his prayer is the "cry of a child lost in the desert." But if the church crushes the spirit of the Indian, it uplifts and fills with pride the mestizo for whom it is a refuge and an extension of his being. He fills the local church with his realistic and at times grotesque art objects and decorates the interior with vivid colors and symbols drawn from his daily life. He comes to the church to visit his "saints," to organize his processions and fiestas, and to share life with his fellow villagers. For the mestizo the church is both an "incentive to fight" and a heavy weight pinning him to tradition. Beneath the church are the tombs of his ancestors and in the cross on the tower he beholds the symbol of his conquerors. For him, the church is both the "axis of rural emotion" and a "giant millstone that holds him in bondage."[45]

Sunday morning Mass in the Andes is the great event of the week that brings the village to life. Most of all, the Mass and the inevitable *fiesta* that follows are a mestizo celebration. The gold of the altar, brightened by the morning sun's rays, the organist's music, and the Latin incantations all awaken the sensual and poetic sense of the gaily attired villagers. The mestizo priest's sermon, a mixture of pious moralisms, local anecdotes, and theological dogmas, is badly translated into Quechua and dissolved into pagan ideas and sentiments. After the Mass, the people gather in front of the church and to the tune of their musical instruments they sing and dance, nostalgically calling to mind their pagan ancestors.[46]

But the mestizo village does not belong to the past. It is the crucible of energy and passion where the future of Peru is being forged. In spite of all his defects, concluded Uriel García, the mestizo is the "heart of our people," who nourishes us with "our feeling of being Americans." It will be the mestizo with his violent passions, not the apathetic Indian, who will regenerate Peru.[47]

THE CHALLENGE OF POPULAR RELIGIOSITY

For many *indigenistas,* the obvious widespread tenacity of religious sentiment among the Indians and lower-class mestizos posed a challenge to their renovating program. Some, like Uriel García, viewed the paganized Catholicism of the Indians as another force from the past that oppressed them and destroyed their spirit of rebellion.[48] One author in *Amauta* asked what three centuries of evangelization had gained for the Indians. He responded by pointing to a cumbersome church-state that lorded it over the Indians and exploited them mercilessly. For this author, the religious problem was an economic one: Give the land back to the Indians, and the church will have no more power over them.[49] Others, however, believed that their mission was to exalt and incorporate the best of Indian culture and tradition into Peruvian national life. An element so basic as popular religiosity could not be so easily dismissed as "superstitious" or "conservative." In their quest to discover positive values in the religious traditions of the lower classes, the *indigenistas* ran the entire gamut of possibilities.

A few authors looked nostalgically to the Inca religion, unsullied by Spanish Catholicism. In 1925 Luis Valcárcel wrote that the essential difference between the European man and the man of Tawantinsuyu was the idea of conquering a spiritual world beyond the grave. In the Inca world, he explained, there was no room for a heaven or a hell. The Incas were a contented, this-worldly people who possessed a supreme sense of confidence in life.[50] On another occasion he described the Incas as a "happy and believing people who never lost faith in the superhuman power of their king."[51] Other authors saw in the Indian's pantheism a mystical communion with the earth that inspired him to construct great temples and works of art. One author in *La Sierra* concluded that the Indian is neither Catholic nor Protestant but a "pantheist" whose real divinities are Achachila and Pachamama, the male and female earth gods.[52]

The work of the Adventists in the Puno region impressed many *indigenistas* as a promising, though partial, solution to the Indian's backwardness. The spokesman for liberalism in Arequipa, Francisco Mostajo, compared the work of the Adventist missionaries with that of the Catholic priests in Puno. While the Catholic clergy was busy fomenting prodigious feast days among the Indians, he pointed out, the Protestant missionaries offered medical assistance and established schools for the Indians.[53] Valcárcel too praised the Adventists on numerous occasions for their cultural contributions to the Indians, although he mentioned that he did not understand their dogmas.[54] Dora Mayer de Zulen, however, was skeptical of the missionaries, whom she believed were the advance guard of Yankee imperialism. She claimed that their success was due to the "corruption" of the rural clergy. Nevertheless, she believed that it would be typical of religious "fanaticism" to recall the missionaries. The answer, she said, would be to build schools to replace those of the Adventists and replace the diocesan clergy with "monastic congregations" that were better prepared to raise the educational and social level of the people.[55] While not precisely identifying the religion of the future with Protestantism, Emilio Romero believed that the quaint rural clergy of the highlands would be replaced some day by "Priests of the Vanguard, with a new mysticism, a new religion." These "lay priests" will preach the true gospel of justice, truth, and love.[56]

In 1921, César Falcón, collaborator with Mariátegui in *La Razón* and later a militant loyalist in Spain, wrote a short story, "Los Buenos Hijos de Dios," in which he suggested that the popular Catholicism of the people, as opposed to the official Catholicism of the priest and local provincial upper class, could be a possible source of revolutionary action. In his story, Tadea, an orphan girl in a small Andean town, is taken with fever. The townsfolk come to believe in her sanctity and interpret her delirious utterances as divine reproaches against the excessive drinking in the town. Out of fear of Saint Michael, whom they believe to be Tadea's protector, the Indians cease drinking. The new sobriety

in town rapidly depletes the coffers of the priest and town officials
who draw much of their revenue from the frequent religious processions and drinking that accompanies them. The story ends tragically
when the child is kidnapped and the priest tells the people to return to their old ways.[57]

Like Falcón, almost all social thinkers sensed the importance
of understanding the popular Catholicism of the lower classes,
whether they were sympathetic to it or not. Indeed, there was an
accelerated rise after World War I in the number of articles and
studies on the "people's" religion. For example, nearly every important *indigenista* or social thinker described one or another of
the great religious processions in Peru. In 1917 José Carlos Mariátegui described with great sympathy the Lord of Miracles procession in Lima.[58] In 1926 José Frisancho depicted poetically the
Holy Week processions of Cuzco.[59] José Uriel García recreated
the Corpus Christi procession of colonial Cuzco,[60] and in his *3
Ciudades del Perú,* Emilio Romero contrasted the religious processions of Cuzco with those of Arequipa and Puno.[61] Although
all of these authors censured clerical exploitation of the processions and the consumption of alcohol associated with them, they
also expressed wonder at the size and the pageantry of these popular manifestations.

Romero summarized the thinking of other *indigenistas* when he
stated that the "religious formulas" of the sixteenth century "have
remained profoundly imprinted on the spirit of the Indians." He
concluded, rather negatively, that even after eighty years of republican life, the "new spirit" still had not arrived in southern
Peru.[62] But the anarchist newspaper of Ayaviri, *La Puna,* in the
department of Puno, viewed the popular Catholicism of that
region in a more positive light. The editors saw no incongruity
in dedicating a special edition of the newspaper, normally full
of articles on socialism and anarchism, to the great annual Virgin
of High Grace (*La Virgen de Alta Gracia*) feast on September 8,
1927. The editors deplored the commercialization of the feast,
pointing out that the Indians had come from all around for "religious reasons." After underlining that this was undoubtedly the
most important event in the year for Ayaviri, they went on to
describe with great sympathy the great mass of brightly decorated
Quechua and Aymara Indians who had come to participate in the
feast.[63]

In 1925 the young socialist, Ernesto Reyna, participated in a
protest sympathizing with an Indian uprising that year in Huaraz

against the compulsory road-work law of President Augusto B.
Leguía. Moved by the plight of the Indians, Reyna composed his
chronicle on the uprising of 1885 in order to publicize the cause of
the Indians and glorify the figure of Atusparia. In the course of
gathering data for his chronicle and interviewing the Indians, he
became aware of the strength of popular Catholicism among the
Indians not only in Atusparia's time but in his own time as well.
According to Reyna's somewhat fictionalized account of the uprising,
Atusparia issued a proclamation in which he ordered all the Indians
of the area to attend a Mass of thanksgiving for the success of
their rebellion. In his proclamation Atusparia stated that the Mass
would be offered "so that the Lord of Solitude would forgive all
sins committed and so that He would even send Saint James and the
Archangel Gabriel to fight for his devout Indian sons and daughters."[64]
While the exact historical veracity of his chronicle is questionable
because of Reyna's imaginative addition of colorful details, the
chronicle is valuable for what it reveals of the author's own attitudes.
Though an anticlerical and later a militant Aprista, Reyna clearly
sympathized with the popular religious traditions of the Indians
he defended. Furthermore, he astutely observed that the religious
traditions of the Indians could be exploited for revolutionary action
in the future.

In their quest to rediscover the Indian, the *indigenistas* found it
necessary to question their own a priori concepts about the values,
beliefs, and capacities of Peru's lower classes. Most *indigenistas* in
the 1920s retained the same image of the rural priest as a greedy
predator of the Indians that appeared in *Aves sin Nido* in 1889. Nor
did most pro-Indian writers entirely free themselves of the romanticized image of the "good Indians" heralded by Aréstegui and
exalted by Matto de Turner. Nevertheless, there was a significant
difference in the way Indian reformers perceived the Indians' customs and beliefs from the disdainful contempt that González
Prada had expressed for popular processions and the repugnance
that the citified Merecedes Cabello de Carbonera had felt toward
the Indian religious feast that she described in 1885. The new
indigenistas had come to take both the Indian and his culture
seriously, even if they did not entirely understand or sympathize
with all aspects of that culture.

Although the Andes were the focal point of the *indigenista* movement, most social thinkers transferred many of the *indigenistas'*

conclusions to include all of Peru's lower classes—coastal workers as well as highland Indians. Both *indigenistas* and socialists shared much of González Prada's hostility toward the church, but they could not reject such an integral and important element of the culture of the lower classes as popular Catholicism and remain consistent with their principal objective, which was to exalt native values over the aristocratic Spanish Catholic culture of the upper class. Furthermore, while the lower classes had also been formed in the same general Spanish Catholic culture as that of the upper-class elite, it became apparent to many *indigenistas* that they had evolved in addition their own separate "popular" religiosity that allowed them to be both Catholic and "Peruvian" at the same time. Finally, a few observers had even reached the conclusion that the popular Catholicism of the lower classes could even become an integral factor in the coming revolution.

The greatest contribution of the *indigenistas* to social thought was to give form and substance to the image of Peru's Indians and lower-class mestizos. It was this knowledge of their own people that enabled social revolutionaries of the next several decades to make their plans and summon the people to rise up. What the *indigenistas* did not do, however, was to construct a theory relating popular religiosity to revolution. The task of doing that was undertaken by *indigenismo's* leading spokesman in Lima, José Carlos Mariátegui.

5: EULOGY TO AN ASCETIC CELL: JOSE CARLOS MARIATEGUI AND THE MYTH OF THE REVOLUTION

It was particularly auspicious for the course of social reform in Peru that its first great Marxist thinker was also its first great revisionist. José Carlos Mariátegui's eclectic fusion of spiritual and Marxist elements in his essays and articles on religion, art, and politics has posed a fundamental dilemma for many of his interpreters: Was Mariátegui a Christian in search of a new faith, Marxism, or was he really a convinced Marxist returning to the Christianity of his youth? This discrepancy over which is the real Mariátegui has led to the interesting phenomenon whereby both Marxists and Christians look to Mariátegui as a source of inspiration for social reform in Peru.

Perhaps the greatest contribution of Mariátegui to the advance of political and religious thought in Peru was to create just such a dilemma. By refusing to deny the traditional Roman Catholicism of his youth as well as the spiritual culture of Latin America, he left the door open for Christians to look with sympathy on his Marxism; by preaching a humanistic Marxism that integrated the best of Peru's past with the new socialist future, he won the sympathy of leftist humanists who looked with distrust on a tradition-bound Catholic church. Most importantly, where the *indigenistas* had treated the Indians' religion as an object of esthetical appreciation but without identifying it with their own interests, Mariátegui created the first intellectual bridge in Peruvian history between popular Catholicism and the reformist elite.

A SPIRITUAL MARXIST

When Mariátegui returned from Europe in 1923, he declared himself to be a professed and convinced Marxist. He envisioned as his mission in life to give birth to a socialist party that in turn would create the conditions for a sweeping revolution in Peru. During the next seven years, until his death in 1930, he dedicated himself fervently to that task. He wrote extensively in journals and newspapers, organized workers' groups, and lectured on Marxism. His own journal, *Amauta,* attracted the attention of intellectuals in Peru, the rest of Latin America, and Europe, and his work, *Siete Ensayos de Interpretación de la Realidad Peruana,* gave wider circulation to his ideas. When he died, the first socialist parties were firmly established in Peru. Most of all, from Mariátegui's time on, Marxism became a powerful intellectual force among Peruvian reformers.[1]

Ironically, however, for all his espousal of historical materialism, contemporaries found Mariátegui to be one of Peru's most "spiritual" men. María Wiesse, wife of the *indigenista* artist José Sabogal and member of the original *Amauta* group, stated in her biography of Mariátegui that he never left the God of his youth. Rather, she claimed, he reorientated his religious faith away from the otherworldly Catholicism of his day toward the world and the concerns of men.[2] Shortly after Mariátegui's death, Luis Alberto Sánchez commented that Mariátegui distinguished himself for his "religious sense and political intuition."[3] Perhaps even more telling was the interesting claim in the conservative organ of the archdiocese of Lima, *El Amigo del Clero,* that after having defended communism and "flirted" with Protestantism, Mariátegui was on his way to a "full return" to Catholicism.[4]

Although these testimonies merely reflect a general impression of Mariátegui the man without referring to any particular event in his later life, Mariátegui himself confirmed at times this "spiritual" image of himself. He once described himself as a mixture of Spanish and Indian blood. But more than an "Indian" of Latin America, he declared that he was an "oriental." "I am," he said, "at times sensual and at times mystical."[5] Even more significant was an interview for *Mundial* in 1926 in which he was asked to characterize his conversion to Marxism. He replied, somewhat enigmatically, that as a youth his "attitude was more literary and esthetic than religious or political." He went on to explain that he had not really changed, only matured. Referring to his Marxism, he stated that "in my search I found a faith. That is all. But I found it because my soul went out very early in search of God." He described himself as a "soul in agony" like that portrayed by Unamuno. As a soul in agony, he felt he had a mission, a destiny to fulfill in life.[6]

It seems clear that there was a continuity between Mariátegui's openly religious feelings as a youth and his later vocation as the founder of Marxism in Peru. The question is precisely what elements or insights of his early experiences influenced and molded his later, more universal vision of history and society.

THE SEARCH FOR GOD

Born into a lower-class family in Moquegua in 1894, Mariátegui was raised in the traditional Catholicism of his parents. At an early age he underwent an operation on his knee, which caused him to limp thereafter, the first of many health problems that eventually led to his premature death at the age of 36. When his father left the family in 1907 for reasons unknown, his mother was forced to support the family of four children as a seamstress. Financially unable to continue studies beyond primary school, Mariátegui sought employment as a copy boy in *La Prensa* of Lima in 1909. He soon advanced to become a linotypist's assistant, and by 1913 he made the editorial staff. In 1914 he began publishing his own articles, frequently using the pseudonym "Juan Croniqueur."

That same year he wrote two articles on Lima's religious life. The first one, on "Holy Week in Lima," was basically an objective narration of events.[7] But the second one on the Lord of Miracles procession in October was an interpretative essay that reveals remarkable historical intuition for a self-educated youth not yet twenty years old. He characterized the procession as a legacy from colonial Lima. What had once been a favorite devotion among Negroes and lower-class mestizos had now also become a cult among "aristocrats and gentiles." In spite of the snobbish attitudes engendered by modern progress, he said, the enthusiasm of Limanians for the procession had not diminished over the years. Nevertheless, the young journalist doubted that it was really "religious fervor" that attracted the people. Rather, he believed, it was a nostalgic clinging to the only popular celebration which reminded them of their colonial traditions. The procession reveals, he said, "an instinctive and affectionate respect for a past that rapidly fades."[8]

In 1916 Mariátegui joined the staff of the more avant-garde newspaper, *El Tiempo*, founded that year. He reported regularly on parliamentary debates and the political gossip of the day. That year also seemed to mark a decisive deepening of his religious spirit. In February he made a retreat at the monastery of the Discalced

Friars in Rimac, and he published a sonnet a few months later evoking memories of the occasion, affectionately entitled "Eulogy to an Ascetic Cell." The last two stanzas suggest the feelings of Mariátegui during his retreat:

> Christ Crucified cries at our ungrateful wanderings.
> The skull stares with empty eyes
> which seem to glow at night with a disturbing light.
>
> And in the rumor of the country and the prayers
> the sweet solitude of John of the Cross
> speaks to the melancholic peace of hearts.[9]

Besides writing for *El Tiempo*, Mariátegui collaborated with César Falcón and Felix del Valle in a new literary review, *Colónida*, founded by the novelist Abraham Valdelomar. *Colónida* represented an important phase in Mariátegui's career because the review was created as a protest against the conventional literary molds of the day. Among other compositions Mariátegui wrote a series of verses entitled "Psalms of Sorrow." In one line he likened himself to a "Child who is a bit mystic and a bit sensual." He also announced at the same time his intention of writing a book, *Tristeza*, which never appeared.[10]

One of the clearest statements of his religious convictions appeared in *El Tiempo*, January 1917, in an open letter addressed to the poet Alberto Hidalgo. In a short book of verse published in 1916, Hidalgo had praised the military might of Germany and glorified Kaiser Wilhelm, terming him a "New Jesus." He dedicated the book to his younger brother who had died tragically and unexpectedly at the age of fifteen. In bitterness Hidalgo blamed the death of his brother on "the injustice of God, that impotent, stupid, foolish and petty God."[11] In his letter, Mariátegui replied that while he believed in the sincerity of Hidalgo's praise of the Kaiser, he did not believe in the sincerity of the poet's attack on God. In reality, said Mariátegui, Hidalgo loves God but in his grief he is defying God with the gesture of a fallen angel. Then, in a particularly uninhibited revelation for a secular newspaper, Mariátegui made a public profession of his own faith:

> I believe in God above all things and I do all things devoutly and zealously in his holy name. Like the Emperor Constantine, I carry out my tasks with the sign of the holy cross. I am a humble and weak Christian, and I cannot find it within me to become a

Lucifer. I believe that God helps me and consoles me when I call on him.[12]

Mariátegui ended his article imploring his friend to return to the same Catholic faith in which Mariátegui found himself at home. Finally, he admonished Hidalgo to overcome the romantic attitude of blaming God because he is not born in better times.

The death of another poet-friend, Leónidas Yerovi, who was shot by a jealous rival a few weeks later, inspired Mariátegui to compose a poetical eulogy, "Prayer to the Immortal Spirit of Leónidas Yerovi." Referring to himself as a "brother in laughter, sorrow, faith and doubt" with Yerovi, Mariátegui compared his friend to Christ: "And now I behold your bloodless and cold body, wounded in the chest like that of our Lord Jesus Christ."[13]

THE LORD OF MIRACLES, 1917

Undoubtedly the most artistically well-written religious composition of Mariátegui was his description of the Lord of Miracles procession in 1917, which won a prize from the journalists' circle of Lima. His earlier narrations of the same procession and Holy Week were formative exercises preparing him for this final effort. Also, his accentuated religious experiences from 1916 on undoubtedly influenced his attitude toward the procession. His general point of view is that of a sympathetic bystander who moves from an objective description of events to an impressionistic description of the procession's effect on him. In the first lines he captures the mood of Lima during the time of the procession:

> In the spring in Lima, that bland, cloudy, grey, undefined and cowardly spring, there are two days which suddenly resurrect the tradition and the faith of the city. During them the procession of the Lord of Miracles signifies the renovation and flowering of the city's religiosity, while it sends forth through its hybrid viceregal and modern streets a strong, melancholic and picturesque wave of emotion.[14]

During these days, continued Mariátegui, there is an "intense resurrection of mysticism"—a favorite word of the author—in which skeptical and indifferent Limanians turn pious and fervent. With his usual sharp insight, he observed that "Lima is a Catholic city, but not a fervent one." *Limeños,* he said, are more sentimental than religious, more fearful of the end of the world than conscious of the need to love. Nevertheless, the poet-chronicler admitted that such demonstrations of faith as the Lord of Miracles procession were indeed impressive: "The contemplation of a multitude which invokes God always moves one with irresistible force and deep tenderness." It seemed as though the entire city were caught up in an "innocent, seductive and religious sentiment." The sound of the bells, the "Christian smell of incense," and the melancholic march of the procession moves even the curious bystander who may be in anything but a devout mood.

I felt and I saw the procession. I understood what it means and what it represents in the life of the city. I loved the instant in which this magnificent spectacle of a tumultuous and sonorous mass seized hold of and softened my heart.

Mariátegui admired the robust *zambos*, Negroes, and mestizos who carried on their shoulders for long hours the heavy stand bearing the image of the Lord of Miracles. These pious members of the confraternity of the Lord of Miracles believe that each year the Lord of Miracles will call one of them to Heaven. Hence, explained Mariátegui, they willingly endure such a burden for hours on end. The procession slowly and majestically winds its way through the streets of Lima, stopping at different churches along the way so that the Lord of Miracles can "rest."

During these two days, concluded Mariátegui, colonial Lima lives again in the long litanies, the music, the flowered balconies, the monks and children singing, the Negroes and mestizos selling their wares in the streets, and the beggars asking for a few coins. Most of all, the city fulfills its obligation to do penance.

For a brief moment the city of sinners asks pardon for all that it has committed in thought, word and deed, and for its failure to be good; and above all else, the Lordship of Our Lord Jesus Christ, who died on a cross to redeem us from original sin, triumphs again. Amen.[15]

RELIGION AND LATER LIFE

After he returned from Europe, Mariátegui made few references to his formative literary period.[16] He repudiated the esthetic dilettantism of *Colónida* and its nearly total neglect of political and social questions. Nor did he ever express again his personal religious convictions at any length. Nevertheless, an overview of his prolific writings during and after his conversion to Marxism suggests that at least two elements of those early years molded and inspired his later insights. Firstly, his view of religion as a universal component of human culture seemed to stem from his own experience of religion as an integral part of his being. For Mariátegui, politics was not a substitute for, but an extension of, his religious experience.[17] Unlike militant atheistic Communists, Mariátegui never considered a rejection of religion a necessary prerequisite for engaging in the social struggle. Secondly, his conviction that religious belief, or any belief in an absolute, was a source of strength to man and society seemed to be influenced by his experience of the popular religiosity of the lower classes. The contrast he drew between the religious fervor of the ordinary people and the skepticism of the onlookers foreshadows his later contrast between the proletariat, which is empowered by the myth of the revolution, and the bourgeoisie, which is dying for want of a myth in which to believe.

Undoubtedly Mariátegui's own humble background predisposed him to view with critical but forgiving sympathy the religious displays of the lower classes. At no time in later life did he criticize the religious beliefs of others, and he was always respectful of the Catholicity of his mother and wife.[18] He looked with disdain on the anticlerical attitudes of many middle-class university-educated reformers. On one occasion he rebuked a close collaborator, Luis Bustamante, for his anticlerical remarks, admonishing him to learn what real religion is from Theresa of Avila and Francis of Assisi.[19] He did, of course, criticize the church on a few occasions, but in general he avoided identifying criticism of the church with criticism of religion.[20]

EUROPE, 1919-23

Like most other young intellectuals in Latin America, Mariátegui was stirred by the great social cataclysms that disrupted the old order in Mexico, Russia, and central Europe during those years. In 1918 he, César Falcón, and Felix del Valle created a new review, *Nuestra Epoca,* which was modeled on Luis Arasquitain's avant-garde journal, *España,* to which Miguel de Unamuno regularly contributed. The majority of Mariátegui's articles during this period took on a more political tone and revealed a marked sympathy for socialism. When the war ended, he wrote an article in his column in *La Prensa,* calling for all socialists, like himself, to come out into the streets to celebrate.[21] When President José Pardo forbade *Nuestra Epoca* to continue publication, Mariátegui and Falcón founded a new newspaper, *La Razón,* in 1919, which suffered the same fate at the hands of President Augusto B. Leguía in August of that year. Because of his criticism of the government and the military, as well as his support of the strike for the eight-hour day and the university reform, the government pressured Mariátegui to accept a scholarship abroad lest he suffer possible imprisonment at home.

From October 1919 until March 1923, Mariátegui lived and studied in Europe. He once quipped that in Europe he acquired a wife and "a few ideas." In reality, this autobiographical understatement glossed over the enormous humanistic formation that he acquired in Europe. He assiduously put himself in contact with every important literary, cultural, and political movement of postwar Europe. In France he conversed with Henri Barbusse and avidly read the novels of Romain Rolland, Anatole France, and many others. He steeped himself in the ideas of the leaders of French socialism, especially Jean Jaures and Georges Sorel. In Italy, where he spent most of his time, he witnessed the rise of fascism to power as well as the internal disputes between Marxists and socialists. He was especially impressed by the works of Benedetto Croce, Adriano Tilgher, Giovanni Papini, Antonio Labriola, and the socialists Piero Gobetti and Antonio Gramsci.[22]

From Italy, where he married and attended the baptism of his first son, he went to Germany and eastern Europe and then back to France. Before returning to Peru he completed his education by studying the works of Miguel de Unamuno, who later contributed to *Amauta,* George Bernard Shaw, James Joyce, Henri Bergson, Nietzsche, and, of course, Marx and Engels. He later commented in an essay on Waldo Frank, his favorite North American author, that, like Frank, he discovered America through his European experience.[23] He acquired a firmer and richer sense of identity as an American by discovering at once both the depths and the limitations of the Old World.

There are two fundamental common denominators of most of the authors that Mariátegui studied in Europe and later in Peru.

They were all prophets who heralded the decline and collapse of
Western capitalism and the rise of a new social order, and they
were all rebels against the deterministic and rationalist philosophical systems of the nineteenth century. Nietzsche's pagan voluntarism, Henri Bergson's *élan vital,* and Georges Sorel's myth of
the general strike reflected the emergence of a new, dynamic concept of man, culture, and history. Even Mariátegui's Marxism was
learned through thinkers like Sorel, Croce, and Labriola, who emphasized the dynamic vision of the early Marx over the more rigid
and deterministic elements of the later Marx. Most of all, the
authors whom Mariátegui studied and sought out complemented,
expanded, and deepened in a more sophisticated, intellectual way
the religious instincts of his youth. In a similar way, Mariátegui
returned to Peru with an organic vision of history and culture
that creatively affirmed the positive values and directions of
Peruvian culture. González Prada's way of anarchical denial belonged to the past.

THE MYTH OF THE REVOLUTION

When he returned to Peru in 1923 he joined the Popular Universities founded by Víctor Raúl Haya de la Torre and companion
students from San Marcos. When Haya and his collaborators were
exiled later that same year by Leguía, Mariátegui took over the
direction of the organ of the Popular Universities, *Claridad.* In
1925 he published his first book, *La Escena Contemporánea,* and
in 1929 his master work, *Siete Ensayos de Interpretación de la
Realidad Peruana,* appeared. Most of the essays of the latter work
had appeared previously in the organ of the new socialist movement, *Amauta,* founded by Mariátegui in 1926, and in the
Limanian review *Mundial.* Many of his other articles appeared in
El Tiempo, the cultural review *Variedades,* and in a proworker's
newspaper *Labor,* which he founded in 1928.[24] Only in one essay,
"The Religious Factor" in *Siete Ensayos,* does Mariátegui formally
study the role of religion in Peruvian history. But his study can
best be appreciated by analyzing first his concept of "religion,"
which appears in most of his other articles and essays under Sorel's
notion of "myth."
    Mariátegui viewed religion as a dynamic and intuitive element
in man that inspires him to act and sustains him in his actions.
Given this definition, religion need not be identified with a particular religion or church. Rather, it is an innate impulse in all men

that permeates all human culture and society. During periods of equilibrium religion serves to undergird and give coherence to a culture. But in periods of stress, religion may stand in opposition to the dominant culture by signaling a new order struggling to emerge from the old. Because men tend to understand religion in too narrow a sense, Mariátegui preferred to subsume religion under the concept of "myth."

In a posthumous work, *El Alma Matinal,* Mariátegui develops his notion of "myth" more extensively. Man, he said, is a "metaphysical animal" who needs a "metaphysical conception of life" by which to live. This metaphysical conception is a myth that provides a coherent explanation of the world and sustains a man in his commitment to that world.[25] Observing the signs of decay in the Western world, Mariátegui attributed the cynicism and skepticism of Western man to the fact that he had lost a myth in which to believe. The rationalistic and positivistic philosophies of the nineteenth century, which extolled reason and progress, had failed to usher in either a reasonable or a progressive world. In the face of this failure, men have elected three courses of action: to suspend belief and fall into skepticism; to grope for a myth in the past in which to believe; or to reach out for an entirely new myth.

Fascism was the example of the second response. Mussolini's fascist state was essentially an attempt to resurrect the medieval myth of hierarchical order rooted in nationhood and functional roles. Mariátegui astutely observed two phenomena about Italian fascism that escaped the attention of other observers. The first was that Mussolini triumphed not because of the appeal of his political or economic programs but because he offered the people a new faith. Mussolini challenged his followers to "live dangerously" and to risk all for the new order. A weak and dispassionate liberal bourgeoisie had no comparable arresting message to compete with Mussolini's challenge.[26] Secondly, Mussolini's diplomatic overtures to the Vatican represented in reality his attempts to strengthen the fascist myth by linking it with the one great symbol of the Middle Ages that survived in republican Italy, the Catholic church.[27]

But a return to the past cannot long satisfy the needs of most men. The third course was to embrace a new myth that looked to the future. To commit oneself to this myth one must also "live dangerously" and in open defiance of the dominant culture, which may even qualify the myth as totally irrational. This myth, which is a "religious, mystical and spiritual force" destined to supersede the dying myths of bourgeois progress and democracy is, of course, that of the coming social revolution.[28]

Henri Bergson

It is important to trace the sources of Mariátegui's concept of "myth" in order to understand how distant he was from not only mechanistic positivism but orthodox Marxism as well. Indeed the fundamental analogue of Mariátegui's vision of the coming revolution, via Georges Sorel and Henri Bergson, was Christianity itself. In a lengthy passage in *El Alma Matinal* he acknowledges his indebtedness to both Bergson and Sorel:

> For some time the religious, mystical and metaphysical character of socialism has been pointed out. Georges Sorel, one of the greatest representatives of French thought in the twentieth century, said in his *Reflections on Violence:* "An analogy between religion and revolutionary socialism, which aims to prepare and reconstruct the individual for a giant task, has been discovered. But Bergson has taught us that not only religion can occupy the deepest region of the self: revolutionary myths can also occupy that region in the same way."[29]

Henri Bergson's vitalistic and evolutionary philosophy made a major impact on intellectuals in Europe and Latin America who were searching for a way out of the impasse created by the mechanistic world view of positivism and rationalism. Especially in Latin America many thinkers believed that these philosophies smothered the spiritual values inherent in their cultural tradition. In Peru Bergsonism deeply influenced Mariano Iberico, who became its main spokesman, Francisco García Calderón, Alejandro Deústua, Pedro Zulen, and Víctor Andrés Belaúnde, who attributed his conversion from positivism in part to Bergson.[30] Somewhat paralleling the debate between the Hegelian Right and Left, Belaúnde's debate with Mariátegui over his Marxist interpretation of Peruvian history was in reality a match between Bergson on the Right and Bergson on the Left.[31]

The two fundamental ideas of Bergson that most influenced Sorel and later Mariátegui were his concepts of the vital impulse and intuition. Bergson sympathized with thinkers of the different spiritualistic schools who wanted to safeguard the concepts of human liberty, the dignity of the person, and even life after death from the assaults of empiricists and rationalists enthralled by the triumphs of science. But Bergson took these same thinkers to task for attempting to construct their philosophical systems in isolation from the major currents of science and history and especially from the new concept of evolution, which to many appeared to be nothing else but a blind, mechanistic process.

According to Bergson, the key to resurrecting spiritual man lay in the very movement of evolution itself. The French philosopher perceived in the heart of the evolutionary process a dynamic "vital impulse" (*l'élan vital*) that infused inert matter with life.[32] This same primitive "spiritual" current, indivisibly linked to matter but not produced by matter, is the basis of consciousness in animals and men. Bergson reacted against the popular idea that man's greatest "achievement" was to subordinate "animal" instinct to intelligence. On the contrary, instinct and intelligence, both products of the vital impulse, exist side by side and even complement each other in man.

Bergson's distinction between instinct, or intuition, and intelligence constituted his devastating blow against scientism. For Bergson intelligence is man's capacity to grasp relationships and perceive overall forms and unities. But instinct is the power of consciousness that allows him to know individual things and their unique essence. Intelligence produces scientific concepts and physical laws, but instinct alone knows what life is. Intelligence, in its quest for the universal, can only understand an immobile world; instinct grasps the meaning of a world in flux.[33]

In his essay on metaphysics, Bergson distinguished between the parallel concepts of intuition and analysis.

> We call intuition the *sympathy* by which we are transported to the interior of an object so that we coincide with what is unique and therefore inexpressible about it. On the other hand, analysis is the operation which dissolves the object into elements already known, that is to say, common to that object and to others.[34]

Intuition was not a mysterious deus ex machina, which Bergson superimposed on homo sapiens, but the very spirit of man himself, which empowers him to know himself as a free person. In the midst of transient psychological states man intuitively experiences a deeper self, which in turn grasps reality intuitively and not by an elaborate study of disparate parts. Intuition, said Bergson, is the light in the darkness of mechanistic determinism that illuminates the way to spiritual and transcendent man.[35]

Georges Sorel

The French socialist Georges Sorel (1847-1922) found in Bergsonism a philosophy that liberated Marxism from both determinism and reformist socialism. He believed that the way of parliamentary elections and patient waiting for the hour of socialism to arrive had enervated the socialists' will to fight. He was profoundly impressed by Bergson's notion that intuition allowed man to grasp the essence of reality in contrast to intelligence or analysis, which contented itself with the exterior data of reality.[36] Under the notion of "myth," Sorel took Bergson's idea of intuition and raised it to the level of a collective insight that men have into the process of history. Inspired by such an intuitive vision, or myth, men are emboldened to anticipate the future by contructing their dream world in the present. Sorel believed that without myths it was useless to urge people to revolutionary action. Reformist socialism, with its rational program, unnecessarily delayed the advent of socialism.

As an antidote to reformism, Sorel urged his fellow socialists to adopt the myth of the general strike. By the general strike he meant not a particular strike but rather an act of faith in the need for many continuous battles against the bourgeoisie. The strike is both an outlet for enthusiasm and a stimulus to new action. Victory is in faith and action, not rational planning and parliamentary debates. It hardly matters, said Sorel, if revolutionaries err completely in instigating a particular strike. The important issue is to strengthen the sentiment and longing for the final great battle that will bring down bourgeois civilization.[37]

Sorel's prime analogue for revolutionary socialism was Christianity. He saw a parallel between socialism's struggle against capitalism in the twentieth century and Christianity's struggle against paganism in the first centuries after Christ. The early Christians saw themselves as participants in a great cosmic battle between Christ and Satan in which the ultimate triumph of Christ was inevitable. Inspired by this vision, the Christians never grew discouraged in spite of the apparent solidity and strength of the pagan world. For them, each new battle constituted an episode in the cosmic war and, hence, a new step forward toward victory. They saw martyrdom as part of this great battle against the antichrist. Martyrs were needed, said Sorel, so that Christians could demonstrate to themselves the absolute truth of their religion. Above all else, the Christians had a sense of impending catastrophe for the pagan world and of certain victory for their cause.[38]

It was this apocalyptic vision of catastrophe and triumph, which constituted the essence of the Christian myth, that Sorel wished to transfer to socialism. Because both the Christian and the revolutionary live by a myth, they have in common the same detractors—the cynic and the rationalist. As an example of the latter, Sorel singled out Renan, who understood neither religion nor revolution. In his myopic rationalism Renan failed to account for the heroic virtues of men who fight for glory or for conquest. Renan once expressed surprise that socialists never seemed to grow discouraged, but, as Sorel pointed out, this is because Renan judged socialism as a rational program, not as a faith.[39] Similarly, the rationalist is mystified by the survival and even the renewed vigor of the Catholic church in the nineteenth century in the wake of the anticlerical and rationalist campaigns launched against it. The church remains strong, said Sorel, because it has the myth of the Church Militant engaged in battle against the antichrist. When it loses that myth, then it will die.[40]

RELIGION AND REVOLUTION

Sorel also inveighed against intellectualizing socialists who scoffed at manifestations of popular piety. For him, as for Bergson, the mystical vision and the miraculous appearance constitute the intuitive element in religion. The mystical insight and the miracle come first, then the theological or scientific explanation. People go to Lourdes, he observed, because they are looking for happiness, something which science cannot offer them.[41] Like these ordinary people, Sorel concluded, the revolutionary should search for the intuitive insight that cuts across rationalistic argumentation. Referring to Bergson, Sorel added that those who oppose socialism to religion display an ignorance of the latest advances of psychology.[42]

Mariátegui absorbed these ideas of Bergson and Sorel and applied them to Latin America and Peru throughout all of his writings. He stated on different occasions that though the hour of formal religions is passing, the religious emotion lives on in the myth of the revolution. He refuted the charge that, compared with Mahatma Gandhi's movement in India, revolution in the

West was materialistic and prosaic. On the contrary, he replied, "Is not the emotion of revolution a religious emotion? " The difference, he observed, is that in the West religion has come down from heaven to earth.[43] On another occasion he criticized Miguel de Unamuno's characterization of Marx as a "Jewish Sadducee, a materialist." Rather, said Mariátegui, he was a "soul in agony" who was closer to Christ than Thomas Aquinas.[44]

Mariátegui directed his main attacks not against religion or the church but against positivists or liberal anticlericals who attempted to uproot religion without offering men a new ideal in its place. Referring to Sorel's criticism of French laicism, Mariátegui declared that "lay morality" lacks the necessary "spiritual elements" to create heroic and superior characters. The lay school in particular utterly fails to satisfy the real necessity in men for an absolute in life. The product of a purely lay education is destined to be a mediocre conformist, devoid of enthusiasm for an ideal that might inspire him to heroic action.[45] In particular, he hoped that the Mexican revolution would overcome its anticlerical phase and that the Mexican state would cease to call itself "neutral and lay, but socialist."

> Then it will not be possible to consider it antireligious, because socialism is also a religion, a mystique. And that great word, religion, which will continue to influence human history with the same force as always, should not be confused with the word Church.[46]

In like manner, Mariátegui acclaimed González Prada for his spirit of protest but said that the apostle of positivism suffered from an illusion when he preached irreligiosity. "We know now," said Mariátegui, "that a revolution is always religious." Without quite realizing it, he pointed out, González Prada had a type of religious commitment in his atheism. Similarly, in spite of the Soviets' belligerent slogan, "Religion is the opium of the people," communism is essentially religious.[47] Those who are offended by the word *materialism,* said Mariátegui, fail to realize that just as Christian metaphysics did not impede great material conquests, so neither will materialistic Marxism impede the flowering of moral and spiritual values. The creative spirit of the former has reasserted itself in the latter.[48]

Mariátegui's sense of the inner unity of spirit and matter, religion and politics, is the source of the controversy over whether or not he was really a Marxist at all, at least in the strict sense of the word. The Peruvian educator, Antonio San Cristóbal-Sebastián, C.F.M., claims that Mariátegui departed from orthodox Marxism by making spirit a determining factor of history.[49] Although Mariátegui's preference for voluntaristic language seems to confirm this opinion, he never formally clarified his concept of the relationship between the economic base of society and the cultural superstructure. Nevertheless, given the philosophical currents that he adopted approvingly, as well as his predilection for voluntarism it is difficult to avoid the conclusion that for Mariátegui myth moves history just as faith moves the individual.

The East German professor Adalbert Dessau interprets Mariátegui's use of the word "myth" in a more orthodox Marxist-Leninist fashion. By "myth," says Dessau, Mariátegui meant a model of the future that inspires the proletariat to look for something beyond a mere satisfaction of material aspirations. Religion in Mariátegui is nothing other than man's innate drive to contribute creatively to the good of his fellow beings. In this sense, "religion" refers to the revolutionary role of the workers.[50]

Without denying this interpretation, however, one senses in Mariátegui's frequent identification of myth with "faith" something deeper than an exciting sociological model for the future. For him, myth was an archetypical constitutive element of man himself, without which he cannot live or create. On one occasion Mariátegui spoke of the need of the artist to have a faith in order to create:

> The literature of decadence is a literature without an absolute. As such, it can only take a few steps forward. Man cannot proceed without a faith, because to not have a faith is to not have a goal. To go forward without a faith is *patiner sûr place*. The artist who most exasperatingly professes his skepticism and nihilism is, generally, the one who most desperately needs a myth.[51]

Mariátegui's own faith in the revolutionary intuition of the masses reinforced his disdain for doctrinaire Marxists and his admiration for socialists who emphasized action over pedantic repetition of Marx or Engels.[52] He looked with admiration on Lenin, who according to Unamuno is supposed to have declared when informed that his ideas went contrary to reality, "Too bad for reality!"[53] For Mariátegui, Marxism was less a finished metaphysical explanation of reality than a tool for interpreting and changing that reality. More than anything else, Marxism for him was a discipline that guided the revolutionary toward his goal. The essential ingredient of the struggle was not the means but the myth, not fixed rules but faith and action.[54]

It is man's search for a myth that constitutes the basis of the revolutionary populism in Mariátegui. In Bergsonian language, Mariátegui pointed to the "vital impulse" in man that provides him with the answers to the questions posed by life long before philosophical speculation offers its interpretation. The ordinary, semieducated man does not concern himself with the relativity of the myth in which he believes. He finds his road in life better than the philosopher: "Because he must act, he acts. Because he must believe, he believes. Because he must fight, he fights."[55] In his introduction to Luis Valcárcel's *Tempestad en los Andes,* Mariátegui praised the author's faith in the Indians and called for *indigenistas* in general to apply Sorel's concept of myth to the Indians' struggle for justice: "We should not neglect or underestimate the perennial value of the myth in the formation of the great popular movements."[56] On another occasion he noted the profound strength of religion among the Indians and declared that only the myth of the revolution could substitute for the "artificial myths" imposed by their conquerors who identified religion with servile obedience to authority.[57]

THE RELIGIOUS FACTOR IN PERU

It was this humanistic vision of the underlying unity of religion and politics in man and history, inspired by Bergson, Sorel, and others, that profoundly influenced Mariátegui's interpretation of the role of religion in Peruvian history. Unlike the *indigenistas,* who tended to see religion as competing cultural expressions—Inca paganism versus Spanish Catholicism—Mariátegui viewed religion as a universal mode of expression of all of humanity and, hence, an essential factor of Peruvian history without which that history would be unintelligible. Most of all, Mariátegui believed that an element so deeply rooted in Peru's traditions as religion should not be ignored. He wanted the coming social revolution to incorporate and bring to fruition the best of Peru's traditions, and that included the religious impulse that had up until then so decisively influenced the course of events. In one significant section Mariátegui, wishing to balance the overenthusiasm of some *indigenistas* for the Inca past, declared that the Christian Gospel too must be counted as a valuable contribution to Peru's nationhood.

National tradition has been broadened by the reincorporation of Indian culture, but this reincorporation does not annul other factors and values which have definitively entered into our existence and our personality as a nation. With the conquest, Spain, its language and its religion entered forever into Peruvian history, communicating to it and articulating it in terms of western civilization. The Gospel, either as truth or as a religious conception, was certainly more valuable than Indian mythology.[58]

Mariátegui prefaced his remarks to his essay on "The Religious Factor" by stating that the period of a priori anticlericalism is over. It is time now, he declared, to recognize that the notion of religion is deeper and wider than any particular church or rite and to acknowledge the services offered by religion to the progress of humanity.[59] Mariátegui studied first the interrelation of religion and society in the Inca empire and secondly the impact of Catholicism on the course of Peruvian history after the conquest.

Andean Religiosity

The two fundamental characteristics of the Inca religion were its "theocratic collectivism" and its "materialism." Mariátegui did not entirely agree with Luis Valcárcel's belief that the man of Tawantinsuyu did not have a concept of life after death. Nevertheless, Mariátegui agreed that "metaphysics" was a marginal reality in the life of the Incas. More than a metaphysical concept, the Inca religion was a moral code that specified the conduct of the ordinary inhabitant in his service to the community.[60]

Mariátegui cited Sir James Georges Frazer's *The Golden Bough*, which considerably influenced his views on the role of religion in the Inca empire, to show that the Inca religion was more like the state religions of Greece or Rome than the different oriental religions. In Greece and Rome the citizen identified religion with service to the community or to the state, whereas the oriental religions posited communion of the soul with God as the end of religion, thus distracting the individual from public service, and for that matter, from this present life. So closely identified was the Inca religion with the Inca state that the former could not survive the destruction of the latter.[61]

Yet part of the work of the *indigenista* movement had been to uncover the myriad agrarian rites, magic practices, and, most of all, the widespread pantheistic sentiment of most highland dwellers that made up Andean religiosity. One must speak of two religious systems operating simultaneously even in Inca times, observed Mariátegui: the official state religion and the "Quechua religion" of the vast majority of the subjects. Somewhat like the assimilationist Romans, the Incas did not proselytize conquered subjects. Rather, they added the conquered people's gods to the national pantheon. The Incas merely superimposed in a rather loose way the cult of the sun on local myths and rites. The Incas believed not so much in the divinity of a religion or a dogma as in the divinity of the Inca himself.

Hence, the most significant religious factor among the Indians of preconquest Peru was what Mariátegui termed, following the schemes of Frazer, the "primary elements": magic, mythical beliefs, local gods, animism. These primary elements were what the people felt and understood more than the official Inca cult and later on offered the greatest resistance to Christian evangelization.

The Evangelization of Latin America

Mariátegui viewed the evangelization of Latin America as the last crusade of Spanish Catholicism. He developed the theme of the evangelization of Spanish America by contrasting it with the colonization of North America as portrayed in Waldo Frank's *Our America*. Mariátegui envisioned a double dynamics at work in these twin processes that caused them to be so different. The Spanish missionary represented Spain of the Golden Age, which, though it was in its ascendancy religiously and culturally, was beginning its decline economically and politically. By way of contrast, the Puritan in North America represented a new bourgeois-capitalist culture that was in its decline religiously, but on the rise economically and politically.

According to Frank, the individualistic Puritan and the materialistic Jew created the pragmatic and utilitarian culture that so distinguishes North America from Spanish America. Unlike the triumphant Spanish conqueror, the Puritan came to the New World as a nonconformist who had broken with his past. He had intentionally renounced pleasure in order to accept the discipline of colonization. The Puritan turned his piety toward the task of conquering an alien hostile world and acquiring wealth. His successor was the pioneer, an exteriorly free but interiorly closed man, who subordinated religion to his utilitarian ethics. Like the Puritan, the Jew saw himself as part of a New Israel in the middle of the North American wilderness. Like the Puritan, he directed his religious instincts toward domination and material satisfaction. The end product of both types is the aggressive self-made man of American business and politics.[62]

Paralleling this New World process, while northern Europe spent its religious energies in constructing the bases of capitalism, Spain spent its spiritual energies in the Counter-Reformation. Spanish mysticism reached its flowering in the great figures of Saint Theresa of Avila and Saint Ignatius of Loyola, but the curve had reached its crest and the Counter-Reformation soon degenerated into the Inquisition. Similarly, in Latin America the first wave of missionaries were cast in the heroic mold of a Bartolomé de las Casas, whom Mariátegui admired enormously. But the evangelizer and advocate of the Indians was soon followed by a wave of mediocre ecclesiastics, and the crusade devolved into a bureaucratic church.

The Impact of Catholicism

To a great degree Mariátegui accepted the sociological theses of Emilio Romero and those of the positivistic Javier Prado on the impact of Catholicism on the Indians and on the Negro slaves. Unlike the individualistic Puritan who was poorly prepared psychologically and materially to catechize the Indians of North America, the Spanish missionary came with an elaborate army of catechists and the official support of his counterpart, the military conqueror. Given this militant crusading nature of evangelization, noted Mariátegui, the church did not win the Indians over to a new metaphysical-religious world view. Rather, the missionaries imposed an exterior cult and a liturgy on the Indians, while the old paganism subsisted under the forms of Catholicism.[63]

Mariátegui underlined two reasons for this "successful" syncretism of Catholicism and paganism in the Andean highlands. The first is the Catholic church's centuries-long experience in adapting to foreign cultures, beginning with its absorption of pagan feasts in Roman times. But this ability to adapt is also, as Frazer observed, the church's weakness.[64] Mariátegui referred to Unamuno's *L'Agonie du Christianisme* to illustrate his belief that unlike Saint Paul who struggled in ardent agony with Christianity before he accepted it, the Indians accepted the Gospel without resistance. The second reason for syncretism in the highlands, therefore, is that there had been no real evangelization because there had been no agony. The Indians contented themselves with the exterior forms of Catholicism while continuing to nourish themselves spiritually on their pagan past.

One consequence of this passive acceptance of Christianity was a general weakening of Catholicism in the early colonial period. The spiritual energy of Catholicism was further dissipated by the grafting of Catholicism onto the "sensual fetishism" of the Negro slaves, who turned Christianity into a superstitious and immoral cult.[65] For their own part, the religious in the monasteries and convents spent most of their energy in internal disputes and in looking for heretics.

Although Mariátegui accepted the view of a general religious decline throughout the colonial period, he did not embrace all aspects of the positivists' and other Marxists' criticism of the church. He did not believe, for example, that Catholicism in itself retarded the economic growth of Latin America. The feudal system which Spain implanted in the New World was to blame for that. In another section of *Siete Ensayos*, he states: "The religious spirit in itself, in my judgment, was not an obstacle for the economic organization of the colonies."[66] He expressed admiration for the Jesuits and other religious orders for their enterprising spirit in organizing and defending the Indians. Indeed, he believed that they were the only groups in Latin America that created wealth for the Indians instead of exploiting them.[67] Finally, Mariátegui praised the many Indian and creole priests at the time of independence in whom the mysticism and passion of true religion had survived.[68]

Anticlericalism and Protestantism

While Latin Americans echoed the slogans of the French Revolution, they preserved intact the feudal-agrarian economy of the colony during and after independence. Because of this there was no basis for the rabid anticlericalism of the French Revolution, much less for a cult to reason. Even when anticlerical liberalism appeared in Peru it was but a pale reflection of the anticlericalism in Mexico where the church owned vast properties. Mariátegui found that even the attitude of Vigil, "which was the impassioned attitude of a freethinker who had left the ranks of the Church," hardly belonged to modern liberalism because he sought neither to liberate the state from the feudal oligarchy nor to laicize it.[69]

Social reform in the late nineteenth century took two basic forms: the conservative positivism of the middle and upper classes and the radical anticlericalism of González Prada. But anticlericalism was, as Mariátegui had observed on a number of occasions, but a stage of bourgeois liberalism because it never seriously addressed itself to the social and economic structures of the country. Nor was Protestantism a viable alternative. Mariátegui believed that for all its worthwhile contributions by way of its schools and clinics, Protestantism was too late in Latin America because it was overly identified with capitalism, which had already ceased to be a revolutionary force in the world.

In his concluding remarks on "The Religious Factor," Mariátegui declared that only an analysis inspired by "historical materialism," which he carefully distinguished from "philosophical materialism," could accurately point the way to reform in Peru. Socialism, he said, believes that ecclesiastical forms and religious doctrines are peculiar to and inherent in the socio-economic structure that produces and sustains them. The aim of socialism is to change the latter, not the former. Finally, Mariátegui returned to the theme of the myth of the revolution. Nineteenth-century rationalism had attempted futilely to dissolve religion into philosophy. But pragmatic experience had shown that religion is a far deeper sentiment in men than rational concepts. Only the myth of the revolution, declared Mariátegui, can exist in man's consciousness with the same intensity and fullness as the ancient religious myths.[70]

Mariátegui's death two years after writing *Siete Ensayos* left many questions unanswered. In his enthusiastic call to fellow socialists to embrace a wider and deeper notion of religion, he never defined more precisely what he meant by such key terms in his lexicon as *religion, politics,* or *myth.* It seems clear that religion for him referred to man's fundamental quest for an absolute, but Mariátegui never identified that absolute with a personal God, which is the traditional notion of religion. Nor did he discuss the origin of man's "vital impulse" to create myths. Furthermore, he did not deal at length nor attempt to resolve the dilemma over which decisively influences history in the long run—the material infrastructure or the spiritual suprastructure.

Mariátegui should not, of course, be approached as an historian or even as a philosopher whose task it was to tie neatly together loose strands from the past. Rather, he was a visionary groping for a new synthesis of elements in his experience and in Peruvian history that many other contemporary thinkers considered antagonistic.[71] To repudiate traditional Spanish Catholicism in favor of an agnostic socialism would have made him a direct successor of González Prada. But to discover an underlying unity between the two pointing to a new synthesis called for an intuitive insight that defied many popular concepts on the nature of religion and reform. Mariátegui saw that just as the Inca religion had not absorbed all the religious potential of the Indians, so neither did Roman Catholicism in its time. Like a powerful underground current in man and society, the religious instinct now sought to rechannel itself into the realm of the secular and the political. What many *indigenistas* had hinted at, Mariátegui formally asserted: the instinct that inspired the Indians to worship Pachamama or the Christian God was the same instinct that would now lead them to embrace the myth of the revolution.

Among the fundamental contributions of Mariátegui to the history of ideas in Peru was to give a wider and a richer meaning to the words "religion" and "politics." In so doing he cast a positive light on both Andean religiosity and the popular Catholicism of lower-class mestizos, which hitherto most reformers had considered to be stumbling blocks to reform. Progressive Christians too were able to find in Mariátegui a sympathetic humanist whose ideas encouraged rather than discouraged them in their desire to support major national reform. In a land with deep religious traditions, such amplitude of thought would be necessary if social reform were to be carried out without rending the country asunder as in the case of Mexico or other Latin Catholic countries.

Mariátegui's own vision of the unity of politics and religion did not arise, however, from such pragmatic political considerations. Rather, the general tenor of his life and ideas suggests that it was born in the agony and solitude of an ascetic cell and in the press of a crowd at a religious procession some time ago in a past that he never seemed to leave behind.

6: A PROTEST AGAINST THE SACRED HEART:
THE ORIGINS OF APRA, 1919-31

José Carlos Mariátegui once warned fellow socialists against a rising wave of "messianic sentiment," which he detected in many young intellectuals of the postwar generation. In particular, he accused Víctor Raúl Haya de la Torre, with whom he had recently parted company, of stirring up "racial and nationalistic" sentiments among the people with his "messianic and confusionist preaching."[1] Yet it was not the more sober and restrained Mariátegui who was destined to speak for leftist reform in the chaotic and turbulent thirties and forties in Peru but the messianic Haya de la Torre and his Aprista movement.

The Aprista movement traced its inspiration remotely to the liberalism of Vigil but more immediately to the vitriolic social criticism of González Prada, many of the ideas of José Carlos Mariátegui and the *indigenistas*, and of course, Haya de la Torre. The general idea of the Aprista movement arose out of the confluence of the university reform movement in Peru, led by Haya de la Torre and like-minded fellow San Marcos University students, and the new anarcho-syndicalist movement among factory workers in Lima and the textile town of Vitarte. In 1919 the students and the workers collaborated in the workers' successful strike for the eight-hour day, and in 1921 the two groups joined together to create the González Prada Popular Universities under the leadership of Haya de la Torre. In 1923 President Augusto B. Leguía suppressed these centers of culture for workers and deported most of the leaders.

In Mexico in 1924 Haya de la Torre proclaimed the creation of Apra (Alianza Popular Revolucionaria Americana, or Popular Revolutionary Alliance of America, from which the Spanish adjective, *Aprista*, is derived). Although intended to be an alliance of all Latin American countries against foreign imperialism, Apra really made a major impact only in Peru, although an Aprista

115

party in Cuba and similar parties did make significant headway in other Latin American countries. During the next several years in exile, principally in Europe, Haya de la Torre and companions forged the essential points of Aprista ideology.

When Colonel Luis Sánchez Cerro overthrew President Leguía in 1930, Aprista leaders returned from exile and established the Partido Aprista Peruano (Peruvian Aprista party) in preparation for the presidential elections set for October 1931. The all-embracing Aprista party program of 1931 called for the redistribution of lands to the Indians, the nationalization of many industries, a sweeping renovation of national education, full women's rights, the separation of church from state, and a whole host of other progressive proposals. Haya de la Torre was, of course, the party's candidate for the presidency.

By the very fact of being the first great mass movement in Peruvian history, Apra would have attracted much attention. But in addition, it appeared at a critical moment in Peruvian history when the working class on the coast and many disenchanted sectors of the new middle class were ready for a full-scale social reform in the wake of the economic depression and the downfall of President Leguía. During the presidential elections of 1931, which Apra apparently lost, and especially during the subsequent persecution of the party under the repressive regimes of Colonel Sánchez Cerro (1931–33), General Oscar Benavides (1933–39) and Manuel Prado (1939–45), Apra captured the sympathies of reformers throughout the world.[2]

A CONTROVERSIAL MOVEMENT

Yet no other organization or institution in Peruvian society, not the church or the military, has provoked such feelings of hostility and given rise to such widely divergent interpretations as the Peruvian Aprista movement. As soon as Apra was constituted as a political party in Peru in 1930, it was heatedly accused of being a "communist" movement in disguise by conservatives, who feared that Haya de la Torre would become, as the poet Alberto Hidalgo ecstatically prophesied on the eve of the Aprista leader's return from exile, "our Lenin."[3] But other leftists and some frightened moderate groups saw Haya de la Torre as the new "Mussolini" of a rising fascist movement in Peru.[4]

Mindful of Apra's official advocacy of democratic methods,

other Peruvians viewed that movement's frequent association with political assassinations and uprisings throughout the thirties as clear proof of the hypocrisy of its leaders. But youthful revolutionaries within the party were continually disillusioned by the party's failure to organize and support openly and enthusiastically the great national revolution that they believed Apra alone was capable of bringing about.

Most critics and Aprista sympathizers agree on only two points. The first is that the Aprista party was undoubtedly the first real political party in the history of the country. Although the dominant role of Haya de la Torre in the party and his decisive influence on the party's ideology may make Apra appear to be a one-man caudillistic party, Apra also commands respect because of its comprehensive ideology and programs and because of the fervent discipline that welds rank-and-file members to the party hierarchy into one cohesive organization. Indeed, it was the public demonstrations of its massed, disciplined followers that attracted the admiration of observers and instilled fear in Apra's enemies. The second area of agreement is that even given its great regional concentration among sugar-plantation laborers in the northern coast, Apra came the closest to being the only truly national party in Peru until the late fifties. Beyond these points there is little agreement. Conservatives at one time viewed Apra as the most dangerous threat to the stability and order of Peru in modern times. But three decades later, hostile leftists singled out Apra as the most important obstacle to real change in Peru.[5]

APRISTA POPULISM

A frequent, nonsympathetic explanation for the Apra's ideological maneuvering from revolutionary to reformist tactics and vice versa is that the party leaders are basically pragmatic opportunists in pursuit of power. A more sympathetic explanation is that under the impact of bloody repression and extended periods of legal proscription (1932–33; 1934–45), the pristine revolutionary fervor of weary party members simply faded.[6] While these explanations must be given due consideration, another, perhaps more important, factor is the very populist nature of the party. Especially after the decisive ideological split with Mariátegui in 1928 in which the Apristas rejected Mariátegui's call for the establishment of a single-class socialist party, Apra openly welcomed all exploited classes, both middle and lower into the movement.

In the presidential campaign of 1931, representatives from nearly every dissident and alienated sector of Peruvian society poured into the Aprista movement: urban factory workers, blue-collar workers, northern sugar-plantation laborers, shopkeepers, middle-class professionals, university students, and some Indians. The greatest strength of Apra was in the northern coastal departments where organized sugar-hacienda workers felt deep resentment against the great foreign concerns that ran most of the haciendas. Apra was strong too among factory workers in Lima and the lower middle class that felt the impact of the world depression.

But Apra did considerably poorer among the more Indian sections of Peru in the *sierra* and southern *altiplano* departments. One reason for this was simply that the majority of the Indians were excluded from voting because they were illiterate. Another is that the Aprista anti-imperialist program had little meaning for people in the interior provinces who had never directly felt the impact of foreign imperialism as coastal workers had. A more fundamental reason was that the vast majority of Indians in Peru in 1931 still had not gone through a politicization process and looked with suspicion on the new Aprista party with its Marxist slogans and complex economic and social programs.[7]

In general, Apra was the party of the newly self-conscious mestizo class, which resented the all-pervasive influence of the Spanish culture of Peru's wealthy ruling elite. Furthermore, in many ways Apra represented a revolt of the provinces against the dominant role of Lima in setting the cultural and political pace of the nation. In this respect, the Apristas were deeply influenced by the *indigenistas*, many of whom became Apristas not so much in their pro-Indian stance as in their anti-Limanian bias. Indeed, at least half of Aprista leaders and other noted Aprista figures came from the northern departments of La Libertad, Lambayeque, and Cajamarca: Haya de la Torre, Antenor Orrego, Alcides Spelucín, Carlos Manuel Cox, Luis Heysen, and Ciro Alegría, while Ramiro Prialé came from the central *sierra* province of Junín. Most of the other eminent Apristas came from Lima: Luis Alberto Sánchez, Pedro Muñiz, Manuel Seoane, Magda Portal, and others.

Looking askance at the apparent hodgepodge composition of

Apra, Mariátegui's former secretary Ricardo Martínez de la Torre concluded that Apra was condemned to perpetual ideological instability as a result of the wide diversity among its component elements. Declared Martínez de la Torre in 1934:

> If the Right is under the control of a defined class, the ranks of Aprismo are made up of the most diverse elements: Civilists, bourgeoisie, professionals, petty bourgeoisie, working class aristocracy, extremely poor field hands. Apra is obliged to follow a policy of incessant switches, accommodations, sell-outs, in order to maintain more or less unified the heterogeneity of its components.[8]

But for Apristas the diversity within the party was a cause for pride. The artist and biographer, Felipe Cossío del Pomar, described with affectionate approval the great geographical and social heterogeneity of the Aprista National Convention of 1945, held secretly on the outskirts of Lima:

> The three hundred and eight delegates settled down in the great hall. [There were] delegates from all the syndicates: lawyers, engineers, teachers, farmers, doctors, students, miners, leaders of the Old Guard and youth of the JAP. [There were] pale-faced *Loretanos* and sun-burnt mountain dwellers; slow-talking northerners and closed-mouthed southerners. There were representatives from Tumbes in the extreme North and from Tacna in the extreme South. The hot airs of the Amazon mixed with the winter fog which the suffering *Limeños* breathe: the collective experience of persecuted men.[9]

The presence of these disparate groups within its ranks necessarily limited Apra's possible range of action. The collective hopes, fears, and resentments of such a variegated constituency dictated revolutionary stances on some occasions but patient endurance on others. After the electoral defeat of 1931 and the imprisonment of Haya de la Torre by Sánchez Cerro, in anger and frustration the Apristas of Trujillo rose up in 1932 in the bloodiest confrontation between civilians and the military in modern Peruvian history. Yet these same Apristas were willing to wait through long years of political voicelessness while their leaders parleyed with the conservative elite in the hope of seeing a better day.

POPULISM AND RELIGION

Professor Emanuel de Kadt offers this characterization of a populist movement:

"Populism" is used . . . to refer to a social movement led by elements of the intelligentsia whose main preoccupation is the life situation of the downtrodden groups in society, "the people," caught in the mill of social change. The wisdom and purity of the people are set against the evil and corruption of the elites.[10]

This definition stresses the fact that within a populist movement there are two different levels, the intelligentsia and the "people". This distinction can be further extended to suggest that there are also two levels of expression within a movement: the ideological level in which the goals of the movement are stated in more rational and abstract terms, and the "popular" level that includes the inarticulate feelings and emotions of the movement's followers. This level includes the fears, hostilities, dreams, and basic religious and human values of rank-and-file members. Obviously, the two levels must intersect, or the movement would suffer from a total schizophrenia. Nevertheless, it is quite possible that the real values and feelings of ordinary party members, to which sensitive party leaders are continually attuned, may only be vaguely hinted at in the cold language of ideological pronouncements. A study of the Aprista movement, therefore, must include more than a review of the formal ideology or policy statements of its leaders; it must also include an examination of the underlying "feelings" and motivating values of party members, to whatever extent that is possible.

An example of the Aprista leaders' willingness to shift tactics and develop new psychological techniques in response to the sentiments of their vast constituency was religion. Although the party officially eschewed the anticlericalism of González Prada in the elections of 1931, it suffered from a popular stigma of being anticlerical and even antireligious. Part of this impression was fomented by the conservative Catholic press, which saw in the Aprista movement a local incarnation of the Mexican revolution with its accompanying official persecution of the church. But some Apristas themselves contributed to this image of the party by espousing a few of the anticlerical sentiments of González Prada. What Aprista leaders began to appreciate only after the party had already be-come a mass movement was that the newly politicized lower classes, which eventually formed the main base of support within the party, had come to the party not by the path of philosophi-cal speculation but rather by that of the simple pragmatic desire for political and economic change. These rank-and-file party mem-bers, raised in the environment of traditional popular Catholicism and largely unfamiliar with either Marxism or radicalism, were the same "ignorant" common people whom González Prada had failed to attract to his Unión Nacional a generation earlier.

Thus, two different cultural groups with two different back-grounds converged in the Aprista movement. On the one hand, there were the Aprista leaders, most of whom were middle-class, university-educated intellectuals, who had been born into the white Spanish culture of Trujillo or Lima, and who were inspired by the liberalism of Vigil, the radicalism of González Prada, the Marxism of Mariátegui, and the revolutionary populism of Haya de la Torre. On the other hand, there were the Aprista "masses"—ordinary workers, field hands, lower-class secretaries and shop-keepers—most of whom belonged to the coastal mestizo culture, which was a racial, religious, and psychological fusion of the Spanish and Indian cultures but quite distinct from both.

There were, of course, many workers in Lima and in the north-ern coast who had also become radicalized through contact with González Prada and the anarcho-syndicalist movement before the student-worker alliance of 1919. In this sense a rigid line cannot be drawn between the workers and the students who eventually formed the Aprista movement. Nevertheless, it was largely in recog-nition of the great disparity between the cultural worlds of these two groups that Haya de la Torre and companion students founded the Popular Universities to close the gap between them.

The intermingling of these two cultural groups in the Aprista movement was of special significance because it was the first time in Peruvian history that the cultural elite and the lower classes of the country came together in a single permanent move-ment. It was also the first time that the reformist and enlightened theories of Vigil, González Prada, and Mariátegui came into di-rect and sustained contact with the traditional popular Catholi-cism of Peru's lower classes. The mixing and blending of these two currents produced results that only Mariátegui and a few Apristas could have envisioned. Certainly, neither Vigil nor Gon-zález Prada could have foreseen or understood the strange inscription that appears on one of the walls of the great assembly hall of the Aprista party headquarters in Lima: "God alone will save my soul; Aprismo alone will save Peru! "

This transformation within Apra, from an official neutrality toward religion with undertones of an unofficial anticlericalism among some Aprista leaders to an open and deliberate mixing of political and religious sentiments, corresponds approximately to two stages in Apra's history. The first stage, in which the anticlerical attitudes prevailed, included the formative years of Apra from the student-worker alliance of 1919, the period of the Popular Universities, and ended sometime after the elections of 1931. The second stage, in which Aprista leaders openly appealed to the religious sentiments of their followers and largely left behind the anticlericalism of their youth, began during the persecutions following the 1931 elections and continued well beyond World War II.

It was during the second stage especially that Aprista leaders displayed their awareness that the popular Catholicism of the lower classes far from being a stumbling block to reform as González Prada had presumed, could actually be a key resource for galvanizing the people to revolt against and to resist the dictatorial regimes of Sánchez Cerro and his successors. What Mariátegui had proposed as a theory on the relationship between political and religious sentiments in the twenties, the Apristas put into practice in the thirties. The compatibility between traditional religion and political protest which Atusparia and other Indians had experienced but not articulated in the last century the Apristas not only articulated but enthusiastically exalted in songs, speeches, and slogans. An overview of the major events in these two periods of Apra's history will help to clarify this transformation in the Apristas' approach to religion.

VICTOR RAUL HAYA DE LA TORRE

Víctor Raúl Haya de la Torre's background and formation was fairly representative of that of most of the other founders of Aprismo. Born in the northern coastal city of Trujillo on February 22, 1895, he was raised in a middle-class family of practicing Catholics with strong political interests. His father, Raúl Edmundo Haya, was a pro-Cácerist deputy from Trujillo from 1904 to 1908 and was the founder of a local newspaper, *La Industria*. For a brief period he considered becoming a priest, when he was nearly thwarted in his plans to marry the girl of his choice.[11] Years later, in the midst of the turbulent campaign of 1931 Haya once responded to the charge of being anti-Catholic by pointing to the devout Catholicity of his parents.[12] An uncle on his father's side, Samuel Octavio Haya de Cárdenas, became a priest and was always held in esteem by Haya.

At an early age he was sent to San Carlos Seminary in Trujillo, run by the French-based Lazarist fathers, where his father and grandfather had also studied. Haya entered the University of La Libertad to study law and soon became an active participant in a literary circle that included some of the brightest minds among young intellectuals and artists in the north: César Vallejo, Antenor Orrego, Alcides Spelucín, Carlos Manuel Cox, and many others.

In 1917, after a short visit to Lima in which he continued his law studies at San Marcos, Haya accepted the invitation of friends of the family to study at the University of Cuzco. There in the old Inca capital he developed a new appreciation of Peru's Indian culture as well as a heightened sense of indignation at the social injustices to which the Indians were subjected. During his eight-month tour of the southern *altiplano* region, Haya witnessed a far more manifest and cruder exploitation of human beings than he had seen in his native Trujillo, where the Indian "problem" hardly seemed real.[13] Along with this new sense of social indignation Haya also felt his first anticlerical sentiments when he beheld the low cultural level of many rural priests who worked among the Indians. On one occasion he was scandalized by the sight of an intoxicated priest.[14]

Back in Lima in 1918, Haya sought to deepen his new social and political awareness. His reading during his university days included Renan, Sarmiento, Marx, and, of course, González Prada, whom Haya had visited on a number of occasions. Like many young *provincianos,* he shared González Prada's hostility toward the gracious and elegant capital city that ignored the human misery in the rest of the country. For a while too he shared González Prada's contempt for religion. "Every time I try to pronounce the word 'God'," he declared in his early Lima days, "it nauseates in my mouth."[15]

But his disdain for religion was soon modified by the benevolent influence of a newly found friend, Dr. John A. MacKay, a Scottish Presbyterian minister and founder and director of the Anglo-Peruvian Colegio in Lima, where Haya taught part-time in order to support himself while studying at San Marcos and directing

the Popular Universities. Dr. MacKay had studied Spanish Literature in Madrid, with a special interest in the great Spanish mystics, before coming to Peru in 1917. In Peru he entered San Marcos in order to obtain a degree in letters and wrote his doctoral
thesis on the religious thought of Miguel de Unamuno. His study
of Unamuno and the Spanish mystics convinced him of the profound spiritual values inherent in Spanish culture. In his work de-
veloping this theme, *The Other Spanish Christ*, Dr. MacKay comments on Haya's discovery of the message of social justice in the
prophets and in Jesus:

> He later made the discovery that in the writings of the Old
> Testament prophets and in the teachings of Jesus were more
> incandescent denunciations of oppression and wrong than he
> or his companions had ever made. It dawned upon him not
> only that there could be a union between religion and ethics,
> but that there should be, and that in the religion of the Bible
> there was. The Book began to take on a new meaning.[16]

By a coincidence, many other young rising intellectuals also
taught in the Anglo-Peruvian Colegio along with Haya: Luis Alberto Sánchez, Raúl Porras Barrenechea, and, at a later date,
Jorge Guillermo Leguía.[17] For a while Haya also regularly attended a literary circle held in Raúl Porras Barrenechea's home
in Lima. But Haya's increased involvement in university politics
left him little time for participation in sedate, scholarly discussion
groups. In 1918 he volunteered to serve as one of the university
delegates to the textile workers of Lima and Vitarte during their
strike for the eight-hour day. Later, Haya worked on a committee
headed by Jorge Guillermo Leguía to spearhead the university reform movement in Peru, which was inspired by that of Córdoba
of 1918. In October, 1919, Haya was elected president of the
newly founded Federation of Students and one of his first acts
was to convoke a national student congress, the first of its kind
in Peru, to implement the aims of the university reform in Peru.
The congress, which included representatives from the four
universities of Peru, took place in Cuzco in 1920. At the urging
of Haya, who presided over the congress, the students resolved
to create popular universities to bridge the gap between the elitist
universities and the workers and Indians who made up the majority
of the population of the country. In January, 1921, Haya and
companion students from San Marcos presided over the inaugur-
ation of the first Popular University centers in Lima and the nearby
textile town of Vitarte.

THE POPULAR UNIVERSITIES

Although Haya was the founder and director of the Popular Universities, a great many other young enthusiastic and idealistic students who would win fame in their own right also collaborated in them: the historians Raúl Porras Barrenechea and Jorge Basadre; Luis Heysen, a top Aprista leader; Oscar Herrera, also an Aprista and later rector of Federico Villareal University; Eudocio Ravines, cofounder of the Communist party in Peru and later a director of *La Prensa*; Luciano Castillo, founder of a small socialist party; and in 1923, José Carlos Mariátegui, who was one of the few non-students among the leaders of the Popular University.[18]

The young student-teachers offered free nocturnal classes in history, mathematics, Spanish grammar, hygiene, first aid, and even music appreciation. The Popular University also sponsored a whole host of cultural events and campaigns to awaken the civic consciousness of the workers. At times the Popular University held literary-musical *veladas* to glorify Peru's Inca heritage. At other times it conducted temperance campaigns and even put on morality plays to demonstrate the evils of alcoholism. Finally, the teachers and students went on picnics together near Vitarte to foster an appreciation of Peru's natural beauty and to deepen the ties of friendship between themselves.[19]

The Popular University was an enormous success, far beyond the original expectations of its creators. At the height of its influence as many as one thousand workers, men and women, would gather in the Palacio de la Exposición, where the Lima Popular University was housed, to hear Haya de la Torre expound on social justice or José Carlos Mariátegui lecture on the new Russia. By 1923, besides new centers in Lima, popular universities had been established in Arequipa, Trujillo, Ica, Cuzco, Jauja, Chiclayo, Piura, Huaraz, Puno, and in the jungle department of Madre de Dios.

In Lima the majority of the "students" were lower-class factory workers who were racially and culturally mestizos. But in Vitarte some ten miles inland there were many Quechua-speaking hacienda laborers who rode in on horseback to listen to the lectures in the local cinema where the Popular University functioned.[20] Like many coastal towns, Vitarte was a community in transition from the Andean Indian culture to the westernized urban culture of the coast. Most of the workers in the textile plant in Vitarte were Spanish-speaking mestizos, but most of the workers on the haciendas around the town either spoke Quechua or had been raised in a Quechua-speaking environment.

Photographs taken of the workers and students during their picnics (*pachamancas*) in Vitarte reveal much about the social composition of the Popular University. In the center of the workers, seated on the grass in a woods, attired in formal white shirts and ties are Haya de la Torre and several other San Marcos University students. Surrounding them are workers, darker-complected and dressed in the coarse, plain white shirt and pants typical of hacienda laborers. Finally, accompanying the workers are their quite unwesternized wives, arrayed in the long braids, straw hats and *polleras* (skirts) typical of the highlands. Some of the women listening attentively to the young students are carrying their young ones wrapped up in *mantas* (blankets) on their backs.[21]

CHRIST AND THE ANARCHISTS

This wide diversity of cultural background and degree of political awareness gave rise to a curious mixture of González Prada radicalism and simple biblical social Christianity within the Popular University, anticipating a similar phenomenon a few years later in the Aprista party. The directors of the Popular University waited until a year after its founding to baptize their cultural center with the name "González Prada," in order not to prematurely arouse the fears of the oligarchy and the government.[22] The memory of González Prada was enshrined in one of his quotations on the walls of the Popular University: "In Peru there are four million illiterates, thanks to the clergy and the politicians!"[23] A teacher in the Popular University expressed the feelings of many of his colleagues when he wrote in his literary review *Bohemia Azul*: "Let us throw the monks out of Peru and thus perform a mission of social purification."[24]

The most important link between the university students and the anarchist movement was a young worker, Arturo Sabroso, who first met Haya during the strike of 1918–19 and who later became the head of the powerful pro-Aprista syndicate, the Confederation of Peruvian Workers. In 1919 Sabroso cofounded with José Sandóval *El Obrero Textil*, which was the official organ of the textile workers in Peru. In 1921 it also became the unofficial voice of the Popular Universities which included many textile workers, especially in Vitarte. Many of the articles in *El Obrero Textil* revived the antireligious and anticlerical positivism and anarchism of González Prada. One article, dedicated to Lenin,

attacked the notion of an other-worldly God who fails to hear
the cries of a suffering humanity:

> Twenty centuries have passed since the sacrifice of Golgotha to
> better humanity and [humanity] has not been able to practice
> that injunction to "Love one another . . .", and that is because
> justice does not look to other worlds nor is it the patrimony
> of an imaginary being, of a being which places itself at a dis-
> tance from us, which hides and does not hear the cries of those
> who invoke it.[25]

Nevertheless, the anarchist press did esteem the figure of Jesus
as a social protester. *El Obrero Textil* published an essay entitled
"Jesus was an Anarchist," in which the author expressed his belief that "Jesus of Nazareth was a perfect revolutionary," although
he may have been "too sentimental and mystical." The author
went on to accuse "exploiters from the priestly caste" of disfigur-
ing the personality of the real Jesus, whose sayings and actions
clearly reveal him to have been a "perfect anarchist." Anyone
who studies the life of Jesus, declared the writer, can only arrive
at one conclusion:

> The Martyr of Golgotha was, in his age, a Gorki, only more
> altruistic and courageous, a Tolstoy, only more intransigent
> and committed, a Bakunin, only more self-sacrificing and at-
> tractive! Jesus, in our century, would have produced better
> results. His great suggestive power would impress upon the
> Social Revolution a uniform direction.[26]

In May, 1923, Haya de la Torre founded his own separate organ
for the Popular Universities, *Claridad,* modeled on Henri Barbusse's
Clarté. Like *El Obrero Textil, Claridad* mixed anticlerical broadsides with biblical allusions. In a series of articles addressed "To
Catholics," *Claridad* urged "bourgeois Catholics and their national
clerical servants" to heed the call to social justice found in the
Bible and in the Fathers of the church. Naturally, the biblical
passages reproduced were those containing the most caustic condemnations of abuses and injustices by the wealthy and the powerful: Matthew 4, 10; Mark 10:23-25; James 5:1-6; Amos 5:21-24,
and others.[27] Frequent quotations from Vigil and González Prada
interspersed in the pages of *Claridad* revealed what some of the
other sources of inspiration were for the new publication.

This same exaltation of the figure of Jesus was also characteristic

of Haya de la Torre's classes in the Popular University, a reflection
of his recent contact with John MacKay. A former student of the
Popular University of Vitarte recalls fondly a lecture on religion
that Haya delivered to the workers. In it, Haya described the
apostolic labor of Jesus and the apostles and praised the "legitimate Christian religion," which consists in practicing "justice,
truth, love and forgiveness." At the end of the lecture, Haya exhorted the workers not to reduce their Catholicism to popular
devotions, but to practice it in acts of charity: "The Apostolic
Roman Catholic Religion," said Haya, "is not just candles and
flowers. What aroma is more pure than that of a generous action? What flame is more ardent than the fire of love which is
practiced?"[28]

MAY 23, 1923

Officially, the Popular University was intended to be a purely
cultural institution with no direct political orientation. In practice, however, it was impossible to separate culture from politics
precisely because a great number of both students and teachers
envisioned the Popular University as a cultural complement to
their awakened political consciousness. Even the motto of the
Popular University, "The Popular University has no dogma but
that of Social Justice," had obvious political overtones. Some
young students, especially Eudocio Ravines, Jacobo Hurwitz,
Nicolás Terreros, and Luis Bustamante, who all became Communists later, used the Popular University as a forum in which to
teach Marxism and lecture on the social advances of Soviet
Russia. When José Carlos Mariátegui returned from Europe, he
too envisioned the Popular University as a platform for creating
his socialist party. By coincidence, the announcement of Mariátegui's first lecture in the Popular University appeared on May 23,
1923, the date on which the Popular University launched its
most serious venture into politics: the protest movement against
the consecration of Peru to the Sacred Heart.[29]

In a pastoral letter of April 25, 1923, Archbishop Emilio
Lisson announced his intention of consecrating Peru to the Sacred Heart in a ceremony in the Plaza de Armas in Lima. This
somewhat innocent proposal might not have provoked such a
storm as it did were it not for the fact that the archbishop had

also invited President Leguía to preside over the ceremony as
"Patron of the Church." Undoubtedly the statement that the consecration represented the "will of the faithful" throughout Peru
was irritating to some.[30]

Soon protests began to appear in different Limanian reviews
and dailies. The mildly anticlerical Clemente Palma announced
sarcastically in *Variedades* that Peru was about to do "what
García Moreno did fifty years ago in Eucador." "What satisfaction," he added, "our southern neighbors [Chile] will have to
see us make an alliance with the Heart of Jesus."[31] A writer in
La Crónica, seconding Palma's denunciation asked, "Why add
the religious question to political divisions?" Declaring that such
an official ceremony infringed on liberty of conscience, the
author suggested that the archbishop confine the ceremony to
consecrating Catholic homes to the Sacred Heart, not consecrating the entire Republic.[32] Besides attacking a ceremony which
symbolized the union of church and state as anachronistic,
others accused Leguía of using the ceremony to court the Catholic vote in his move to defy the constitution by seeking another
term. A few devout Catholics found it somewhat incongruous
that Leguía, a high-ranking Mason, should assume such an hono-
rific role. Finally, critics on the Left viewed the public act as a
symbolic alliance of the oligarchy with the conservative upper
clergy.[33]

Although many voices were raised in protest, the key leader
of the protest movement turned out to be Haya de la Torre.
Weeks before the announced date of the event, Haya set about
to pull together into a unified movement a number of disparate
groups that objected to the ceremony. He agitated through the
student federation to win support among university students and
he attracted Protestant friends from the YMCA, of which he
was a member, as well as many Masons, Catholics, and anarchists.
But the bulk of support came from the workers of the Popular
Universities and students from San Marcos.[34]

An Anticlerical Protest?

Years later, Aprista apologists offered a considerably revised
interpretation of the general tone of the protest movement. In
their desire to disassociate themselves from the charge of being

antireligious, some Aprista leaders greatly deemphasized the strong
anticlerical thrust of the protest. In 1931 Luis Heysen claimed
that it was really President Leguía who wanted to consecrate
Peru to the Sacred Heart and therefore it was against Leguía that
the students protested.[35] In an interview in 1961, Manuel Seoane
claimed that the students objected to the political character of
the ceremony, not its religious orientation. "It was not a movement against the crowning of the Sacred Heart for religious
motives," the Aprista leader stressed, "because those of us who
took part in that protest were Catholics."[36] Cossío del Pomar,
however, is closer to the truth when he states that the movement
was directed against both Leguía and the upper clergy who supported the dictator's regime.[37]

An examination of the documents and speeches of the students
during the events of May 23, however, reveals that they did not
limit their protest to the consecration ceremony or the upper
clergy. On the contrary, inspired by the liberalism of Vigil and
the radicalism of González Prada, they also demanded the separation of church from state, a sweeping reform of the church, and
the enactment of many other measures left unfinished by the
anticlerical liberals of the previous century.

On May 19, the Popular University issued the first of several
polemical manifestos that filled the editorial sections of the
major dailies. The manifestos invited all "free men of Peru" to
form a united front to block the projected consecration ceremony:

> Students, workers, intellectuals, employees, journalists, free
> men of Peru: let us form a United Front against the projected
> consecration of the Peruvian nation to the image of the Heart
> of Jesus.
> The student body of the González Prada Popular Universi-
> ties of Lima and Vitarte . . . invokes the adhesion of all free
> men of the country, and agrees:
> To create a "United Front," without distinction of religious,
> political or social creeds, to see that the imposition of clerical-
> ism with the projected consecration does not offend against
> the privilege of liberty of conscience which the Nation should
> guarantee to the fullest.
> To make a special appeal to the working classes, intellectuals,
> students and journalists so that they, in support of the propa-
> ganda of the United Front, will seek the adhesion of all free
> citizens of Peru to favor the separation of the Church and the
> State and the laicization of public education.[38]

Three days later, on the afternoon of May 22, the students of
the departments of philosophy, history, and letters and the workers
of the Popular University assembled in the courtyard of San Marcos
and affiliated themselves with the League of the Free Youth in
Peru (La Liga de la Juventud Libre del Perú), an organism created
especially for the occasion. That same afternoon Haya organized
a United Front Committee (Comité de Frente Unico) to organize
a protest march for the next day.

The following fateful afternoon of Wednesday, May 23, 1923,
the students and workers assembled again in the Great Hall of
San Marcos. During the assembly a lengthy "Declaration of Prin-
ciples" was passed around and signed by most of the student
leaders, including Augusto Rodríguez Larraín (the principal author),
Manuel Seoane, Haya de la Torre, Carlos González Posada, Luis
Bustamante, Jacobo Hurwitz, Enrique Cornejo Costa, Edgardo
Seoane, Edwin Elmore, and many others.

In the general prologue to the Declaration, the students announced
that they aimed to defend freedom of religion and "to reject the
advances of fanaticism and fight for the adoption of radical principles
which would integrate the Republic into the ideological currents
affecting humanity today." They went on to term the consecration
"absurd and anarchronistic" because it threatened the liberty of
conscience of the majority of Peruvians.

The eight resolutions in the body of the document called upon
the students to (1) protest against the consecration; (2) demand the
absolute separation of the church from the state; (3) seek a reform
of article 5 of the constitution, which still restricted full liberty
of religion in Peru; (4) work for a reform of the current "dogmatic
education" by suppressing obligatory religion courses and practices
and by replacing them with the teaching of moral principles that
would "orient the spirit toward reason, tolerance and the ideal";
(5) ask for the inclusion of civil marriage and the right of divorce
in the new civil code, as well as the suppression of ecclesiastical
tribunals; (6) advocate special laws to control the behavior of
priests so that a "priesthood capable of understanding and living
religion on the margin of the civil and political life of the country"
can be formed; (7) solicit the complete suppression of "parish
rights" as well as the nationalization of all clergy; and (8) work
for the abrogation of the section of the penal code on "acts
against the Catholic religion."

In the peroration of the document the students were exhorted
to diffuse scientific and moral ideas that might dissipate "infantile

superstitions and absurd dogmatic positions" that imprison the human spirit. One student in the assembly proposed that another resolution calling for the secularization of religious houses and the turning over of their goods for the benefit of public education also be included among the resolutions. This motion and the entire Declaration were unanimously approved by the assembly.[39]

After the preliminary speeches were delivered, Haya de la Torre assumed direction of the meeting. Making full use of his considerable oratorical talents, he launched into a fiery attack against the idea of the consecration and then delivered an encomium to the memory of the great men of Peruvian liberalism—Luna Pizarro, González Vigil, and González Prada. Finally, he contrasted the figure of Christ, whom he praised as a model of idealism and justice, with the "prejudices and absurd methods" employed by Catholicism.[40]

The Protest Marches

Led by Haya de la Torre and the students of the Popular University, several thousand demonstrators marched from San Marcos through downtown Lima toward the principal plaza. Unexpectedly, however, mounted police advanced on the students and workers from the rear, and in the ensuing melee two protesters and three policemen were killed and many wounded. This bloody encounter served to exacerbate tempers more and corrode further whatever moderating instincts there may have been. In an angry public letter the next day Haya blamed the government and the clergy for the bloody clash.[41] In another protest letter, the deputy from Puno, who was not associated with the Popular Universities, declared bitterly that "Don Emilio Lisson can be satisfied with his work. Now he has something with which to bless the image of the Sacred Heart. He has innocent blood instead of Holy Water."

The day after the confrontation, after calling for a general strike, several thousand students and workers once again took to the streets, this time to protest the attack by the police on the preceding day. As they moved through the streets toward the Plaza de Armas they cried such slogans as "down with the clergy!" and "down with the Archbishop!" and "away with clericalism!" Once in the plaza, Haya addressed the marchers from the front door of the cathedral. After hurling another broadside against clericalism, which he accused of trying to smother liberty of conscience, he compared the church's methods of acting to the Inquisition, "which assassinated innocent men in the name of Jesus Christ."[42]

The third great protest march, which took place on May 25, was the funeral procession for the two demonstrators who had been killed. At the cementery Haya climbed aloft the crypt of heroes and delivered the funeral oration before the silent crowds that surrounded him. Although weary from the pressure of the past few days, he fulfilled beyond expectation his role as interpreter and spokesman for the repressed anger of his audience. After praising the virtues of those who were to be buried, he delivered a panegyric on the fifth commandment. In an angry and hoarse voice he cried repeatedly: "The Fifth, Thou shalt not kill! The Fifth, Thou shalt not kill! The Fifth, Thou shalt not kill!"[43]

The brief drama of the consecration of Peru to the Sacred Heart ended that same day when Archbishop Lisson issued a decree suspending the ceremony. In the first article of the decree he observed, quite accurately, "that the projected consecration of the nation to the Sacred Heart of Jesus has been turned into an arm against the legitimately established government and social institutions."[44] Later, somewhat less accurately, he blamed the protest movement on Protestant propaganda and the political machinations of certain persons who manipulated the students and workers.[45] While many anti-Leguía forces stood to gain by discrediting the dictator, however, there seems to be little evidence that anyone besides Haya de la Torre and his fellow students and the workers of the Popular Universities originated and led the protest movement.[46]

Haya and Lisson

Years later the conservative Catholic press would resurrect the specter of Haya de la Torre haranguing angry crowds to protest against a religious ceremony. With the distortion that comes with time and the heated passions of an election campaign, one newspaper in 1931 announced that it could not support Haya de la Torre because he was an "enemy of the Heart of Jesus, and therefore of Christ and God."[47]

Yet there are a number of reasons for arriving at a considerably different view of the future Aprista leader's role in the events of

May, 1923. An irony known only to a few was that Archbishop
Lisson had once been a teacher of Haya (English and natural
science) at San Carlos Seminary in Trujillo. On at least two other
occasions Lisson and his former pupil met again. When Lisson,
who had been bishop of Chachapoyas, was installed as the new
archbishop of Lima in 1918, young Haya went to greet him and
his priest-uncle, Samuel Octavio Haya, who by coincidence was
Lisson's secretary. Later, again by coincidence, both Lisson and
Haya were included in the same program to inaugurate a new
school for workers' children in Lima on May 3, 1923, the former
to bless the new school and the latter as representative of the
Popular Universities.

The archbishop, who remembered his former pupil well, stayed
on to engage in a friendly debate with Haya after the formal program had ended. After reminiscing briefly on the days when he
taught Haya, Lisson declared that he could not agree with Haya's
statement that revolutions are not destructive. The archbishop
concluded his remarks by stating that he preferred Saint Vincent
de Paul to Haya de la Torre's "civil saint," González Prada. In
the same spirit, Haya praised the archbishop for his openness in
discussing social issues with himself and the workers. Haya then
returned to the theme of revolution, and after reviewing the impact of the Reformation and the French and Russian revolutions
on history, he reaffirmed his original thesis that a revolution is
not necessarily destructive but could be creative as well. Finally,
Haya stressed the revolutionary character of Christ and early
Christianity, but noted that the church had lost this early revolutionary spirit. The reporter who recorded the exchange between
the archbishop and the new spokesman for radical reform observed
that the audience experienced "a strong feeling of sympathy for
both speakers."[48]

From this encounter and later comments of Haya, it appears
certain that neither Haya nor most of the students bore any ill
will toward the archbishop personally. In Haya's opinion, Lisson
was "irreproachable" in his personal moral conduct, although he
may have been somewhat "rigid" in his religious ideas.[49]

Other incidents and considerations suggest that the anticlericalism of the students was not so threatening as later critics came
to believe. According to Haya de la Torre, the protest had the
tacit approval of the apostolic nuncio, Bishop José Petrelli, who
had assured the young student leader through his secretary that
he believed that the archbishop's ceremony was politically ill-

advised. In symbolic recognition of this support, on the day of the burial of Alarcón and Ponce, Haya led the funeral procession away from the normal route past the papal nunciature.[50]

One slightly humorous incident occurred as a result of the virulent anticlerical propaganda of the Popular University. On the day of the clash between students and police, a group of clergymen encountered workers from the Popular University coming down the street toward them from the opposite direction. In panic, the clergymen attempted to enter a strange house but found the door locked. The workers calmed the clergymen down by assuring them that they were not "assassins."[51]

Finally, the anticlericalism of Haya and companions of the Popular University was no greater than that of most of the other San Marcos University students of the period. Apristas later defended their participation in the protest by pointing out that a great number of other students who never became Apristas or Communists had also participated in the movement. Indeed, the most anticlerical document of the movement, the "Declaration of Principles" was composed largely by Augusto Rodríguez Larraín, who was not affiliated with the Popular University or involved in politics later on.[52] Even *El Comercio,* which became the principal anti-Aprista organ after 1930, supported the Popular University in the protest.[53]

Religious and Political Messianism

But the most significant phenomenon of the events of late May, 1923, was not the anticlerical language used by Haya de la Torre, which was quite common among the other students, but rather his strong appeal to the religious sentiments and emotions of his followers. Here, indeed, was a total reversal from González Prada's approach to social reform only five years after the great anticlerical's death. Both his reading of the Bible and his sustained close contact with simple lower-class workers in the Popular University had taught Haya not only that religion and social change could be compatible realities but that religious sentiment was a powerful motivating force among lower-class Peruvians steeped in traditional Roman Catholicism. In particular, the figure of Christ had a strong attraction among these classes, a reality that the anarchist press clearly recognized and exploited.

The greatest irony of the May 23 protest was that it was the allegedly anticlerical leader of the movement, Haya de la Torre, who made the most persuasive appeals to the religious sentiments of his followers, not the Catholic hierarchy or press. Nor was it the cold rationalism of liberal anticlericalism that stirred the thousands of workers and middle-class students to march in defiance of a dictator and an archbishop but the mixed passions of religious righteousness and political indignation. This was the wave of of rising messianic sentiment that Mariátegui beheld when he returned from Europe and that he associated with the personality of Haya de la Torre.

The immediate effect of the protest marches was to win fame for Haya de la Torre among leftist sympathizers throughout Peru and Latin America and to incur the wrath of President Leguía, who sensed danger for his regime from this new force in Peruvian political life. After returning briefly to normal life, and rejecting a government bribe to leave Peru, Haya found himself pursued by the police and his Popular University under attack. Finally, after hiding for a period in Dr. MacKay's house in Miraflores, Lima, he was apprehended and deported in October, 1923. In 1924 most of the other leaders of the Popular University were also deported, leaving José Carlos Mariátegui in charge of both the Popular University and its organ, *Claridad*.

THE FORMATION OF APRA

In Mexico in May, 1924, Haya brought Apra into existence. During the next eight years of exile he schooled himself through extensive reading and traveling while he and his fellow exiles further refined Aprista ideology and planned their return to Peru. From Mexico Haya went to Russia, where he admired the achievements of the new workers' state but was less enthusiastic about the possibility of applying Russian communism to Latin America.[54] After a trip through Switzerland and Italy he reached England in 1926. In London he studied at the University of London and wrote his first article in English, "What is Apra?" in the *Labour Monthly*.[55]

From London Haya went to Paris, where he established the first Aprista cell, composed of Peruvian students and writers living in Paris. In January, 1926, the Aprista cell of Paris staged the first anti-imperialist congress of the movement, and in 1927 Haya attended the World Anti-imperialist Congress in Brussels. It was here that he definitively rejected the Communist solution to the problem of imperialism. He systematically developed his own thinking on the subject of imperialism in his first book, *Por la Emancipación de América Latina,* which he published in 1927 shortly after a visit to the United States.[56] After a trip to Mexico and Central America, he was apprehended in the Canal Zone by the police and deported to Germany where he remained until 1931.

Haya's decision to convert the Popular Revolutionary Alliance into a political party designed to win power in Peru motivated Mariátegui to break with Haya and form his own socialist party in 1929. For the first three or four years after his return to Peru, Mariátegui had collaborated quite harmoniously with the future founders of Aprismo in the Popular University and other related projects such as Haya's review, *Claridad.* The Apristas too had viewed Mariátegui's ideas with great sympathy and collaborated regularly in his review, *Amauta.*[57] Although Mariátegui at first condemned the protest movement of May 23 as anarchistic, he later praised it as the "historic baptism" of the Popular University as a center of political protest.[58] But the two issues that ultimately divided Mariátegui from the Apristas were the populist nature of the new movement and its gradualist approach to foreign economic imperialism. The Apristas believed that a party of reform in Peru, to be truly effective, should be a multiclass movement, including both the middle, lower-middle, and the very poorest classes. Furthermore, the Apristas called for a middle course in the fight against foreign economic imperialism. In recognition of the need to attract foreign capital to Peru, the Aprista program called for the progressive nationalization of foreign companies, not an abrupt break with foreign capitalism.[59]

In 1929 John MacKay visited Haya in Berlin and noted with satisfaction that the exiled leader had matured and retained his enthusiasm for the Bible. Haya confided to his mentor that he was writing a new book on Latin America that would be "full of quotations from the Bible." This work never appeared. Haya also indicated to MacKay his belief that the next government in Peru should separate church from state. Furthermore, reiterating an idea of Vidaurre and Vigil a century earlier, Haya went on to suggest the advisability of severing the church from Rome in order to create a "free and independent Catholic Church" that would then make a decisive contribution to national life.[60]

After the fall of Leguía the Apristas set about feverishly creating an effective party apparatus within Peru that would carry them to victory in the promised presidential elections. Mariátegui's death in April, 1930, deprived leftist Marxism of its most articulate voice and cleared the way for Apra to dominate the Left in Peru. On September 21, 1930, the Partido Aprista Peruano was officially established and legalized. Luis Heysen and Manuel Seoane returned from exile immediately to help organize the campiagn. Seoane, who was to assume a role second only to that of Haya until his death in 1963, founded the new party organ, *La Tribuna*. In March, 1931, Sánchez Cerro left for Europe in self-imposed exile after a dispute with the other military leaders in his interim government, but he returned in four months to oppose Haya de la Torre in the presidential contest. In May and June regional Aprista congresses were held to prepare for the national party congress in August.

Haya himself did not return to Peru until July, a scant three months before the elections. In the meantime, a wave of "messianic sentiment" was stirring up the passions of Peruvians as they prepared to welcome home the hero who thwarted an archbishop's plans to consecrate Peru to the Sacred Heart.

7: APRISMO ALONE WILL SAVE PERU!

THE APRISTA MARTYRDOM, 1931-45

THE RELIGIOUS ISSUE, 1931

The vertiginous growth of the Aprista party, especially after Haya de la Torre's triumphant tour of the northern departments and his tumultuous welcome in Lima in mid-August, 1931, can be fairly accurately measured by the rising note of alarm in the Catholic press from an initial cool indifference to nearly dooms-day panic. In early August the conservative voice of the Catholic workers of Arequipa, *La Colmena*, dismissed Haya de la Torre as a serious candidate because he was supported by only a "few social-climbing youths."[1] But by mid-September, the Catholic weekly announced with growing concern that only two major parties and candidates had emerged a month before elections— Sánchez Cerro's Unión Revolucionaria and Haya de la Torre's Apra. Even though it was known that Sánchez Cerro favored legalizing divorce and establishing the right to civil marriage, *La Colmena* exhorted Arequipeños to choose sides: either for Apra, which represented the "fiercely antireligious tide" and threatened to plunge the country into "chaos," or for Sánchez Cerro, who represented the peoples' traditional "faith and customs."[2]

The most frequently cited "proof" that Apra was antireligious was, of course, Haya de la Torre's leadership of the May 23, 1923, protest movement. In October, 1931, the polemical Catholic weekly *Verdades* reminded its readers that Haya de la Torre was an "enemy of the Heart of Jesus" and of God.[3] In 1933 *El Amigo del Clero* warned Catholics not to associate with Apra because Haya de la Torre had always fought "in-cessantly against . . . all Catholic action," beginning with his attempt to stir up the students and workers against the conse-cration of Peru to the Sacred Heart in 1923.[4] Even the cofounder of the Communist party, Eudocio Ravines, found Apra's claim

139

not to be antireligious hypocritical in light of its origins: "Even the rocks in Peru know that the *caciques* [chiefs] of Aprismo had their debut on May 23, 1923 as rabid standardbearers of an anti-clerical and anti-Catholic movement."[5]

Besides the May 23, 1923, affair, the sweeping reformist program of Apra convinced many that organized religion was facing the greatest threat to its existence in Peruvian history. Depending upon which model of religious persecution awakened the greatest fears, critics warned that Apra would unleash in Peru the religious persecutions of Russia, Mexico, or Spain. *El Amigo del Clero* explained to its readers that in spite of appearances, Apra was really a Communist movement:

> Haya de la Torre has developed a new party which is not called communist, but rather panamerican: his Popular Revolutionary Alliance of America, or *Apra,* founded in December, 1924, espouses part of the program of Moscow, especially the antireligious part.[6]

Aware that Haya had founded Apra in Mexico, the editors of *Verdades* summoned the people to rebel if Apra attempted to introduce the religious persecutions of Mexico in Peru: "If they intend to imitate the Calles of Mexico, our people will know how to fight back, suffer martyrdom and triumph like the noble Aztec people."[7] The diocesan newspaper of Puno, *El Heraldo,* saw no difference between leftists in Spain in their treatment of the church and Apra in Peru.[8]

Apra's Ambiguous Stance

Much of the uncertainty about the intentions of the Apra stemmed from the ambiguous stance of the Apristas themselves on the religious issue. For every official repudiation of anticlericalism, an incident or a statement of an Aprista leader served to nullify the denials and confirm the suspicions. In the edition of *La Tribuna* commemorating the protest of May 23, 1923, for example, the editors insisted that that protest had been purely political with no anticlerical intent. But in the same edition the editors also reproduced the highly anticlerical Declaration of Principles that summed up the students' demands.[9] In the same edition two caricatures appeared that also belied the anticlerical disclaimers of the editors. In one a drunken priest is portrayed prostrate on the floor of a wine cellar, and in the other a priest is shown on his knees courting a pretty young girl. The captions accompanying the caricatures were of the same taste.[10]

Much more significant than these anticlerical broadsides in the Aprista press, however, were the pronounced anticlerical tendencies and resolutions of the regional Aprista congresses, especially that of Huancayo in the department of Junín. In July the delegates to the Huancayo congress proposed the following resolutions to be considered in the national congress in Lima in August: separation of church and state; confiscation of the goods of religious houses and monasteries for the construction of schools; expulsion of all foreign priests from Peru; nationalization of the clergy and the limitation of their number; obligatory closing of churches during working hours; limitation of the number of feast days prescribed by the church; and finally, complete religious toleration.[11]

Here was confirmation of the worst fears about Apra's real intentions. Upon learning of the Huancayo resolutions, *Verdades* declared: "To support Apra is a crime against the nation and against religion."[12] Two years later the *indigenista* writer, Dora Mayer de Zulen, cited the Huancayo congress as unmistakable proof of Apra's aim to extirpate not just the clergy but religion itself from Peru.[13]

In light of this growing fear of Apra, Aprista leaders took measures to reassure Peruvians that the statements or actions of individual party members should not be mistaken for the official stand of the party. In preparation for the national party congress Luis Alberto Sánchez and Manuel Seoane weeded out almost all of the anticlerical proposals of the regional congresses.[14] The only reference to the church in the final draft of the party's "Minimum Program" of September 20, 1931, was a relatively modest clause: "We will separate the Church from the State and we will guarantee the neutrality of the State in religious matters."[15]

Nevertheless, the Apristas never entirely freed their assurances from the overtones of González Prada anticlericalism. When Manuel Seoane presented the official party line on the religious question before the Aprista national congress in Lima, he declared: "Aprismo is neither religious nor antireligious. It is a political movement and therefore a lay movement." But in another speech before the same body, the Aprista leader condemned clerical interference in politics and called for the total separation of the church from the state. After reassuring his audience that under no circumstances did Apra intend to raise an antireligious banner as in Mexico, Seoane stated that the party aimed to use church wealth to "raise schools in front of convents."[16]

The Presidential Campaign

On August 23, before some 40,000 Apristas in the bullring of Acho, Lima, Haya de la Torre accepted the candidacy for the presidency. His lengthy address touched upon a wide range of proposals to effect the political, social, and economic regeneration of Peru, but it never mentioned the church. Those who feared that Apra really intended to do no more than merely separate the church from state, which for many Catholics was radical enough by itself, could find little consolation in Haya's declaration at the end of his speech that "We are the heirs of the magnificent thought of Manuel González Prada."[17]

In spite of the Apristas' official repudiation of González Prada's anticlericalism and their stated desire to stick to strictly economic and political issues, their continual references to the founder of Peruvian radicalism and to Marxist concepts kept the religious issue alive during the campaign. Haya found himself frequently called upon to explain away a statement made by another Aprista or to allay fears over the Huancayo congress. In September in Huánuco he declared that Apra had no intention of "destroying churches, expelling religious, persecuting priests or seizing Church goods." He stressed that Apra had nothing to gain by persecuting the religion of the majority of Peruvians.[18] Later, in Arequipa, in answer to the charge that he was anti-Catholic, he responded by pointing to the devout Catholicity of his parents. After noting that Arequipa was almost totally Catholic, the Aprista leader declared that not only would Apra not persecute religion but that it would prevent the religious struggles then occurring in Spain from happening in Peru.[19] Finally, hoping to put all fears to rest, the Aprista candidate affirmed: "We believe that religion is an affair of the interior kingdom of each one; we do not intend to loot churches or hang religious as some have said."[20]

But the bishop of Puno, where Haya was scheduled to speak after Arequipa, was not moved by these assurances. In a pastoral letter to his diocese, he "conjectured" that Haya's reference to the "interior kingdom" meant that he wanted to do away with external worship and religious education and restrict religion to internal worship alone. The bishop based his "conjecture" on Haya's leadership of the May 23 protest movement.[21] In other parts of Peru clergymen sounded a cry of alarm as election time neared. In Arequipa a pastor announced to his faithful that he had personally heard Haya de la Torre say, " ¡Apra sí; Cristo no!" In Huaraz some clergymen placed large posters in their churches in which Aprismo appeared as one of the signs of the Final Judgment.[22]

These apocalyptic forebodings were not fulfilled, however, at least for the moment. According to the hotly disputed election results, Sánchez Cerro won 152,062 votes to Haya de la Torre's 106,007, while two other candidates won a combined total of 41,574 votes.[23] With relief, *El Heraldo* of Puno stated that Sánchez Cerro's victory signified the triumph of "the Right over the Left, of order over disorder."[24]

APRISTA OR CATHOLIC?

But the time of trials for Peru had only begun with the election. Instead of dissolving, Apra seemed to grow in numbers, and in the minds of its opponents, in belligerency. The fact that a vast number of Peruvian Catholics had supported and continued enthusiastically to embrace Aprismo was a cause for grave concern among many clergymen in Peru. In late October, 1931, the bishops of Peru issued a pastoral letter in which they defended the union of church and state, the right of foreign clergy to work in Peru, religious education, and church property. Although some of the subjects dealt with were probably directed at Sánchez Cerro, such as civil marriage and divorce, the greater proportion of themes raised corresponded almost exactly to the anticlerical proposals of the Aprista Huancayo congress.[25] And in 1933 and 1934, a second stage in the minor war between the Catholic press and the Aprista party took place in an exchange of polemical tracts over whether a Catholic could be an Aprista.

This "battle of the pamphlets" was initiated by Luis Alberto Sánchez, who from his exile in Ecuador composed an essay to answer charges from Ecuadorians and especially *El Comercio* in Lima that Apra was fundamentally antireligious and anticlerical. Though Aprismo is Marxist, Sánchez argued, Marxism itself is a philosophy of history and not a new religion, and therefore religious belief and Aprismo were compatible. The real target of Apra's criticism, said Sánchez, was not religion, but the unholy alliance between the church and the state to the detriment of

the church, as in the case of Archbishop Lisson's close and unfortunate relationship with President Leguía.[26]

Furthermore, Sánchez criticized the upper clergy, arguing that
because it came from the upper class or from foreign congregations it served the interests of Peru's oligarchy and foreign imperialism. He claimed that Apra would protect the Peruvian-born
lower clergy, which he said strongly sympathized with Apra. To
underline this point, the Aprista intellectual revealed that one
evening in December, 1931, a group of Peruvian priests came to
his house to discuss with Haya de la Torre points in common.
Among other things, the priests asked Apra to take a stronger
stand against foreign clergymen, whom they accused of sending
out of the country a great deal of the contributions they received and of preempting parishes in the highlands where the
national clergy would be better suited.[27]

Unimpressed by these arguments, the Jesuit historian Rubén
Vargas, S.J., fired off his own countertract ¿Aprista o Católico?,
in which he contended that Aprismo and Catholicism were totally
incompatible. Vargas observed that Marxism is based upon a materialistic conception of the world in which there is no room for
God or spiritual values. While the Jesuit author admitted that
Apra was not the same as communism in its methods, he insisted
that its ultimate goal was the same—to establish a socialist society in which religion is excluded from public life. Even if
Apristas expressly repudiated antireligious persecutions, Haya
de la Torre's leadership of the May 23 movement was reason
enough to doubt Apra's claims. Finally, Vargas found it difficult to believe that priests "educated and conscious of their
duty" would have made the proposals to the Aprista party leader
that Sánchez mentioned.[28]

The Jesuit historian's tract was soon answered by the third
pamphlet in the series, Catolicismo y Aprismo. Signed by "Catholic Apristas," it aimed to show that Catholicism and Aprismo
were quite compatible.[29] The author argued that Marxism, and
therefore Aprismo, were opposed not to religion but only to a
type of religiosity that legitimatized systems of exploitation.
After admitting that there were, indeed, some anticlericals among
Aprista leaders, the author went on to emphasize the official
neutrality of the party toward religion. But more important than
this neutrality was the fact that both Catholics and Apristas
shared an identical mission to work for social justice in Peru.

The author cited the various papal social encyclicals to justify the presence of so many practicing Catholics in the ranks of Apra. Finally, the author accused the detractors of Aprismo of fearing Apra not because it might be anti-Catholic but because it stood for social justice.[30]

Four weeks after the essay by the "Catholic Apristas" appeared, *Verdades* published the fourth of the polemical tracts, *Aprismo-Anticatolicismo*. In answer to their question of why so many Catholics fought for Apra, the authors responded that those Catholics who joined Apra were ignorant of both the atheistic premises of Marxism and the real, antireligious intentions of their leaders. The authors pointed once again to the May 23 protest and the Huancayo resolutions as proof that the Aprista leaders intended to follow the same road of religious persecutions as in France, Mexico, and Spain.[31]

APRISMO AND POPULAR CATHOLICISM

While Apristas and conservative Catholics hurled hostile broadsides at each other, a far more important drama was taking place within the Aprista movement itself. The debate over whether or not an Aprista could be a Catholic was carried on at a level of abstraction that probably had little meaning for the vast number of rank-and-file Apristas who turned out to vote for Apra in spite of the dire warnings from churchmen.[32] Unable to find an outlet for their newly awakened social and political consciousness within the traditional church, which was largely unresponsive to the call for radical social change, many Apristas without formally renouncing membership in the church sought to express their religious sentiments within the Aprista movement. On the less intellectual but equally important level of feelings, values, and basic loyalties, they began to transfer the symbols and images of their traditional Catholicism to the Aprista movement. The result was a continuation and even an accentuation of the mixing and blending of political protest and popular religiosity within the Aprista party that had begun in the Popular Universities in the twenties.

One factor that favored this transference of religious symbolism to a secular movement was that Apra continued to foster the cultural mission of the Popular Universities within the party. When the Apristas returned from exile, one of their first acts was to resurrect the Popular Universities in every city or town where the party was

strong. Even during the lengthy periods of persecution the Popular
Universities continued to operate as basic party cells in the homes
of Apristas at night time.[33]

This strong commitment to personal and group cultural and educational self-improvement, which Apristas envisioned as a preparation for the regeneration of all of Peru, conditioned party members to see Apra not as a mere political party but as a combination
of neighborhood family club, civic reform group, cultural circle,
fraternity and charitable organization. For many Apristas the party
fulfilled many of the functions of an active neighborhood church.
The spirit of this cultural mission is exemplified in this propaganda
insert, which appeared in an Aprista newspaper in 1934: "Aprista:
Raise your cultural level, educate yourself, prepare yourself, im-
prove yourself. The work of our party must magnify itself in order to save this country."[34] The emphasis on the party as a family
is illustrated in a propaganda exhortation: "Aprista: Your party is
a great family in which whoever knows, teaches and whoever does
not know, learns. Do what you can to teach him who does not
know."[35]

A second important factor was the persecution unleashed against
the Apra during the thirties. Under the impact of bloody repression
the Apristas developed a quasi-religious cult to the Aprista "martyrs"
and to the party itself, which was frequently likened to the crucified Christ. This cult was less the work of a conscious ideological
design on the part of party leaders than of a spontaneous reaction
of rank-and-file party faithful who had been raised in the atmosphere of traditional popular Catholicism. The political repression of
the largest reform movement in Peru produced a result almost
totally the opposite of what had occurred in revolutionary Mexico.
There a reformist elite persecuted the traditional Catholic church,
which acquired a martyr status in the eyes of its followers. But in
Peru it was the Aprista party, not the church, that acquired a
martyr status. One consequence of this reversal of roles was that
unlike the symbols of the conservative reaction of the church in
Mexico, and especially the Cristero movement, the popular religious symbols and imagery that arose out of the Apristas' struggle
were infused with a leftist and revolutionary sense. The Cristero's
cry to defend tradition—"Long live Christ the King!"—was matched
by the Apristas' slogan challenging tradition—"Christ alone will
save my soul; *Apra* alone will save Peru!" This accentuation of
messianic and political fervor corresponds to the second period

of Aprista history, the so-called Aprista martyrdom, from late
1931 until 1945.

THE CULT OF MARTYRDOM

On the evening of December 8, 1931, the day on which Sánchez Cerro assumed the presidency, Haya addressed the downcast
Apristas of Trujillo. The Aprista leader called upon his followers
to raise their spirits because even though a new "period of trials"
had begun for the party, the movement would emerge stronger
than ever. Haya announced that in reality Apra had not been defeated because the object of the Aprista movement was not merely
to acquire political power but to transform the conscience of the
country. "To govern is to lead, to educate, to give good example,
to redeem," he affirmed. "The mission of Aprismo was to reach
the conscience of the people before reaching the Palace."[36] In a
rhetorical challenge that must have proved irritating to the followers
of Sánchez Cerro, Haya declared: "While those who seized power
with gold and guns think they rule from the Palace, we will continue to govern from the people." Then Haya sounded the note of
messianic suffering which would characterize most of his major
addresses and Aprista propaganda for the next fourteen years:

We will not be driven to act out of force; much Aprista blood
will flow, the immortal list of our martyrology will expand,
terror will reinitiate its opprobrious campaign, but Aprismo
will grow deeper in the conscience of the people.[37]

After referring to his eight years of exile, Haya described Aprismo
as a "son" born of the sorrows of the people. Finally, he declared
that he would never abandon "his post," for "Aprismo is the religion of justice" that would one day be implanted in Peru only
at the cost of great sacrifices. He ended his speech with the characteristic Aprista slogan, "Apra alone will save Peru!"
During the next several months Sánchez Cerro escalated his repression against the Aprista party. In December, 1931, agents of
the dictator assaulted various party headquarters throughout the
country. In February, 1932, the government closed down the
Popular Universities, arrested many Aprista leaders, and expelled
the twenty-three Aprista members of parliament. Haya himself
went into hiding. On March 6 an ex-Aprista attempted unsuccess-

fully to assassinate Sánchez Cerro in Miraflores. On May 6 Haya
was captured and imprisoned. The following day pro-Aprista
sailors in Callao rebelled, but they were summarily executed a
few days later.

The Trujillo Uprising, 1932

The most important event that transformed secular loyalty into
near religious allegiance within the Aprista party was the Aprista
uprising and subsequent massacre in Trujillo. On the morning of
July 7, 1932, a group of Apristas, without the full approval of
the local party leaders, stormed the military headquarters of Fort
O'Donovan, and after a four-hour battle seized control. That day
the Apristas of Trujillo rose up and turned the city and department government over to Agustín Haya de la Torre, the younger
brother of Víctor Raúl. Within a few days Aprista uprisings broke
out in Huaraz and many other points in the north. By July 10,
however, government troops had advanced on the Aprista strong-
hold while the air force bombed the suburbs. After most of the
Aprista leaders had fled inland, unknown parties murdered the
officers and soldiers held prisoner in Fort O'Donovan. In revenge,
Sánchez Cerro ordered the summary trial and execution of many
Apristas in the pre-Inca ruins of Chan Chan outside of Trujillo.[38]
Haya de la Torre himself was ordered to be shot on at least one
occasion but was saved only through the intercession of influential world figures who wrote on his behalf to the Peruvian government.

While imprisoned, Haya wrote a letter, in somewhat faulty English, which was smuggled out to English Protestant friends in Lima.
In it, he announced that in the future the party must be more
than a political movement; it was destined to become a "spiritual
force" as well.

Our party needs a great leading work yet. We have to clean it
of passions, ignorance and indiscipline. We have to make of it
a colossal spiritual force in which convictions and faith, reason
and emotions, experience and energy, science and vision, should
be harmoniously combined. . . . Yet I believe that it shall bring
to this country and to Latin America the solution of many
problems not only economical and political, but moral and
spiritual, for we are not merely sentimental and religious as

Gandhi nor merely social and economical as communism. We
have the best of both sides, and we must value the importance
of each but without losing the fundamental significance of
humanity.[39]

The assassination of Sánchez Cerro by an ex-Aprista on April 30,
1933, ended the first period of anti-Aprista persecution. In early
August General Oscar Benavides, who had assumed power after
Sánchez Cerro, proclaimed a general amnesty, and on August 10
he released Haya de la Torre after the latter had spent 500 days
in prison.

The Aprista Calvary

On November 12 Haya addressed a mass Aprista assembly for
the first time since his imprisonment. In his message, which
abounded with the biblical images of blood and resurrection, he
exhorted the 40,000 party faithful in Lima to remain strong and
to learn from the past. He declared that it was necessary for Apra
to have suffered so that it could regenerate Peru. "It was necessary
that we wash ourselves with the blood of our blood because we
are not infallible." The Aprista leader compared the task of the
party to that of Christ attending to Lazarus: "The legacy which
we received from this blood-stained and oppressed Peru is like
Christ receiving Lazarus, already dead, so that he could raise him
up."[40]
But the ritual consecration of the cult of Aprista martyrdom
was not fully enacted until a month later when Haya de la Torre
returned to his native Trujillo, eighteen months after the mass
executions. After a pilgrimage to the grave sites in Chan Chan,
he addressed the Apristas of Trujillo on December 18 in the Popular theater. Aware that there was hardly an Aprista family in
the audience that had not lost a father or a son in the uprising,
Haya delivered a combination funeral oration and an exhortation
of encouragement. This address, which contained few ideological
or programmatic statements, was a model of Haya's ability to
sense the mood of repressed sorrow of his audience and to make
use of symbols and images held in reverence by his listeners.
After his greeting, in which Haya proclaimed that Aprismo had
arisen like a "spirit wrapped in glory, a glory which is never lost
because it continues to live in the midst of death," he went on

to envision a new mission for the party. He reminded his listeners that Apra is not a mere political party but a "great fraternity" that is called to perform a role in history far beyond that which is "merely human." The Aprista martyrs and the collective suffering of all Apristas dictated what this new mission was to be:

> *Compañeros,* this is the great lesson which I owe to the dead, to the martyrs, because they tell me from their graves: "We are your teachers. Go even further than this. Take your party to where we wanted to go. Make of your party a religion. Make of your party an eternal path through history."[41]

Reminiscing on his long period of solitude in prison, Haya declared that from the depths of the suffering of all Apristas he sensed a mandate to discover a "more religious . . . more spiritual" meaning in the party. He went on to draw a parallel between the party and the crucified Christ:

> The hour of struggle has arrived. The hour of Calvary, of sweating blood has arrived. Our Golgotha is here. The Third Hour still has not come. We must wait, in the Calvary of our hearts for death to surrender, for our sorrows to be buried and for the Promised Life of the Peruvian people to arise, glorified and all-powerful.[42]

After a lengthy narration of the sufferings of Apristas throughout Peru, Haya compared the enemies of the party to the darkness that tries to destroy the light. "They fear the light because they love the darkness." Haya exhorted his followers to bear the cross of redeeming Peru:

> We all bear a redeeming cross. We have all suffered by falling down and being whipped. We were placed on a throne and crowned with thorns. They carried us to Golgotha and exclaimed with irony: "Aprismo alone will save Peru!" And they placed above our heads: "This is Aprismo: King of Peru" with the same sarcasm with which they said to Christ two thousand years ago: "This is your kingdom. You are the king of the Jews."[43]

Finally, after announcing that he had already said his prayer before the "altar of my land," Haya summoned his followers to "continue to believe in me" because he had not deserted them in the hour of need. In a peroration abounding in metaphors that seemed to be drawn from the literature of the Sacred Heart devotion, Haya declared that he had a wound that would never heal:

My wound always bleeds, because it is the wound of sorrow of the people, sorrow which is strength, sorrow which is creation, sorrow which is hope, sorrow which is energy, sorrow which will be victory.[44]

Carlos Philipps

If the tragedy of Trujillo gave rise to the cult of Aprista martyrdom, it was the uprising in Huaraz that provided the movement with its cultic slogan. On July 13, unaware that Trujillo had already capitulated, a young army officer, Major Raúl López Mindreau, organized a pro-Aprista uprising of soldiers, policemen, and civilians in Huaraz. Even though he had not participated in the seizure of power, the Aprista party secretary of Caraz, Dr. Carlos Alberto Philipps, was named subprefect of the province of Huaylas. By August 3 Mindreau and most of the Aprista leaders had been captured, and on August 4, Mindreau, Carlos Philipps, and three others were shot by a firing squad. According to a later popularized Aprista version, Philipps cried out, before being shot: "May Christ save my Soul; Aprismo alone will save Peru!"

In many ways Philipps was a typical representative of the lower echelon of Aprista leaders in the thirties. Born into a middle-class family in Caraz in the Callejón de Huaylas, he studied dentistry at San Marcos in Lima. After finishing his studies, he returned to his home town, married and had one son. At the age of thirty he joined the Aprista party and soon became a fervent apostle of the new movement. He helped found the first Popular University of Caraz, in which both he and his wife gave classes. In his spare time he wrote poetry in his private diary, much of which was highly religious in nature. Though he did not regularly practice his Catholicism as his wife did, he considered himself a committed Christian, and his family and friends were impressed by his idealism. He held frequent lengthy conversations on philosophy and politics with his friend, Father Alfonso Ponte, the rector of the seminary of Huaraz.[45]

During the four brief days in which he exercised control over the northern province of the Callejón de Huaylas, Philipps worked zealously to maintain discipline among the Apristas and to prevent acts of violence. When government forces moved on Caraz, he and a group of companions were captured while fleeing toward the *Cordillera Negra*. He and the others sentenced to be executed were held incommunicado for fifteen days, then brought to San Francisco Church in Huaraz, where Philipp's wife had been summoned to see her husband for the last time. After hearing Mass and receiving communion with his wife, Philipps and the others were driven away to the cemetery to be executed. Before being shot, Philipps turned to the priest who said the Mass and accompanied the prisoners and declared: "Father Echevarría, with my feet on the edge of my grave and my eyes fixed on eternity, I believe that God will save my spirit and that Aprismo will save Peru."[46]

APRISTA RELIGIOUS PROPAGANDA

The defiant words of Philipps, the massacre of Trujillo, and the collective sufferings of Apristas in the thirties gave birth to numerous songs, slogans, and legends, which formed the body of Aprista folklore. Aprista propaganda served the same function that apocalyptic literature did for the early Christians—to encourage the faithful to stay firm and to resist in the face of adversity. Much of the propaganda, such as Haya's Trujillo speech and Philipp's words, was shrouded in symbols and images drawn directly from the popular Catholicism of the people. In particular, the image of the suffering Christ, which enjoys enormous popularity among lower-class mestizos and Indians in Latin America, was frequently used as a symbol of the party's martyr status and determination to resist the regimes in power. At the same time, the old radical anticlerical slogans tended to fade quietly into the background.

Many Apristas consciously compared themselves to the early Christians. One Aprista newspaper claimed that like the early Christians the party was persecuted for its idealism:

Only in the age when the Roman Caesars persecuted the Christians is there a parallel to the sublimity of this struggle of a young party against an entrenched and decrepit oligarchy.[47]

In 1934 Alcides Spelucín wrote an article on the anniversary
of the Trujillo massacre in which he likened the martyrdom of
the Apristas to that of the early Christians; in both cases "the
supreme contribution of blood" was a necessary condition for
ultimate victory.[48] The novelist Ciro Alegría even saw Apra itself as a quasi-religious movement:

> Under oppression, in the face of bullets, before the rifles
> of the firing squad, in daily activities, before the daily spec-
> tacle of misery, in memory of the heroes and martyrs,
> Aprismo does not just think. Aprismo feels, believes and
> waits. Aprismo is a new kind of religion. It has a profound
> mystical vibration. . . . A mystical vibration is created
> around a cause only after it is thoroughly understood.
> This is what has happened to all the great *avant garde*
> movements of humanity.[49]

Many Aprista songs and marches of the thirties exalted Apra's
struggle in religious terms. In a song commemorating the Trujillo
uprising, the Aprista author Serafín Delmar wrote from his prison cell in Lima:

> Oh holy nation of men who fought
> for us and the new Aprista religion,
> upon your blood-stained protest
> the foundations of a new and generous society
> without petty hatreds will be laid.[50]

The Aprista lexicon during this period abounded with words
such as *faith, redemption, morality, apostle,* and *martyrdom.* In
a letter to Aprista prisoners, Haya wrote:

> The Aprista Faith is more powerful than all bitterness and
> more ennobling than any liberty without greatness. . . . I
> recommend that you do not forget that each Aprista pris-
> oner is a true apostle of his ideal. I founded Aprismo to
> redeem my people. . . . Because of that, Aprismo is a task
> of apostolate, of education, of example and energy.[51]

An Aprista propaganda flyer in 1941 contained these two messages for all Aprista youth:

Do not forget, Peruvian youth: Haya de la Torre has opened
for us the road of spiritual, material, and intellectual redemption!

But we the youth of Peru are resolved to follow the path of
the 6,000 martyrs of the North before tolerating any new
abuses! [52]

Inevitably, Haya himself was compared to Christ on a number
of occasions by ecstatic followers. To dismiss fears that Haya's
assassination would destroy the party, one Aprista wrote that as
in the case of Christ, Haya's death would actually accelerate the
triumph of the party.[53] Scandalized by the fact that in taking his
oath as a senator in parliament, Luis Heysen swore "by Haya de
la Torre," Dora Mayer de Zulen accused Apra and other leftist
movements of creating "a religion without an ecclesiastical cult."[54]

At times Aprista propagandists overtly appropriated Catholic
formulas and symbols for their own purposes. An extreme example of this was a propaganda booklet written by an Aprista in
exile in Ecuador. The booklet contained an "Aprista Examination
of Conscience," an "Aprista Act of Contrition," an "Aprista Med-
itation," an "Aprista Prayer," and even an "Aprista Litany." The
first line of the "Aprista Prayer," which bore the Latin title *Salus
Populi Suprema Lex Esto* ("Let the Salvation of Your People be
Your Supreme Law"), is representative of this somewhat strained
mixture of Biblical allusions and current political realities:

Aprismo: save your people, saddened and broken by that circle
of Iscariots and Pilates of Civilist Judah; your pure and honor-
able life will be the mighty ground swell of your aspirations to
pull in all those Peruvians who have drifted away because they
have come into contact with Civilist leprosy.[55]

JUSTICE AND THE PEOPLE'S FAITH

Apra's appeal to the religious sentiments of the people did not
limit itself to mere propaganda rhetoric intended to win support
and inspire faith in a partisan cause. Many young Aprista intellectuals went far beyond the *indigenistas* in their exaltation of
popular religiosity, which they frequently identified with the cause
of social justice. During the thirties Aprista writers and poets
formed their own special group within the party, the League of

Revolutionary Writers of Peru (Liga de Escritores Revolucionarios del Perú), which included such notable authors as Alberto Hidalgo, Magda Portal, Serafín Delmar, Ciro Alegría, and Estéban Pavletich.

Serafín Delmar

The most overtly political poetry and novels of the period were composed by Reynaldo Bolaños, who was better known by his pseudonym, "Serafín Delmar." A native of Huancayo, Delmar wrote in *Amauta* and *La Sierra* in the twenties, and after a three-year exile under Leguía, he returned to Peru in 1930. He became a member of the first Aprista committee in Lima and directed the Aprista magazine *Apra*. In March, 1932 he was arrested for alleged complicity in the first assassination attempt on Sánchez Cerro and was imprisoned until 1940. In this verse of a poem written while he was in prison in Lima, Delmar directly identifies Christ with the revolutionary events occurring in Peru:

> The winds carry messages to and fro:
> Forgive, now that you are strong;
> The hour of justice will arrive for all.
> Ah! Love one other.
> Christ, the invincible revolutionary, will not
> return to Heaven,
> Without first making men happy on Earth,
> Thus says the new Religion.[56]

A frequent motif of Delmar's novels is the contrast between the people's new revolutionary faith and their older traditional faith which fails to speak to them. In one of his novels on the Trujillo uprising, he depicts the women of Trujillo praying for their husbands and sons in the cathedral but finding little consolation in the cold, waxy-eyed saints who symbolize another age. In a prayerful trance, one young girl announces to the other women that Christ has returned to the earth to join them in the revolution.[57] In another novel, a youth exclaims to his mother that the church "profanes the sweet and invincible revolutionary figure of Jesus Christ." The boy's mother, a new convert to Aprismo, responds by replacing the saint's image over her son's bed with a portrait of Haya de la Torre. With pride, she exclaims to her son that Haya is the new "redeemer" who will teach the people the "Religion of the new man."[58]

Ciro Alegría

José Carlos Mariátegui once noted that the master work of *indigenismo* was still to be written. The honor of fulfilling that task fell to Ciro Alegría, whose novel, *El Mundo es Ancho y Ajeno*, translated into English under the title *Broad and Alien is the World*, attracted worldwide attention to the plight of the Peruvian Indians. Born and raised on haciendas in the jungle-mountain country near Huamachuco in the department of La Libertad, Alegría was a firsthand witness of the life and traditions of the Indians and peons who worked on the haciendas. Nearly every character who appeared in his later novels was based upon a real-life Indian or white exploiter whom he remembered from his youth.

Sent by his family to school in Trujillo, he soon exhibited talent as a writer. He attracted the attention of Antenor Orrego, the director of the newspaper *El Norte*, who had influenced Haya de la Torre earlier and who was one of the guiding philosophers of Aprismo until his death in 1960. While working as a reporter for *El Norte*, Alegría joined the new Aprista party in 1931 and soon became one of its main organizers in the north. He was imprisoned by Sánchez Cerro in December, 1931, but was liberated during the uprising of July 7, 1932. After participating in the uprising, he managed to flee inland but was captured and imprisoned again, this time in Lima. After Sánchez Cerro's death he was freed, but under the new persecutions of Benavides he was deported to Chile along with many other fellow Apristas. In Chile, where he lived until 1941, he composed his three famous novels, *La Serpiente de Oro*, *Los Perros Hambrientos*, and *El Mundo es Ancho y Ajeno*.

Although his novels possess literary qualities that give them a universal value beyond that of a particular political cause, they reflect many of the themes and attitudes of the Aprista party in the thirties, particularly its views of the Indians and religion. Alegría's works also brought to fulfillment the literary *indigenismo* of the twenties, which in its romanticization of the Indians frequently failed to enter their real world and bring to light their authentic values and traditions. By way of contrast, in Alegría's novels the world is seen through the eyes of the Indians themselves. Their beliefs, customs, and superstitions become incarnated in concrete individuals whom the reader can readily identify as real people, who are both good and bad but all of them human.

In one respect, however, there is a direct continuity between Alegría and the entire *indigenista* movement, and that is the stark contrast that he draws between the simple, innocent faith of the people on the one hand and the venality and moral perversity of the rural Andean priest on the other hand. In the forty years or so that elapsed between Matto de Turner's *Aves sin Nido* and Alegría's novels, hardly a change occurred in the portrayal of the priest who works among the Indians. He is invariably bent upon exploiting the people and exacting exorbitant stipends from them for Masses and sacraments. Though his own cultural level is not much higher than the people, he wields his position of authority to maintain them in their state of ignorance. When he is not drinking, he is harboring evil designs on the young girls of the region. And he is frequently a Spaniard.

In his first novel, *La Serpiente de Oro* (*The Golden Serpent,* 1935), which deals of the fatalistic influence of the jungle and the Marañón river on the destinies of men, Alegría describes the visit of the priest Don Casimiro to the small town of Calemar to help celebrate the annual feast of the town's patroness, Our Lady of Perpetual Help. The townsfolk are quite proud of their Virgin, whom they believe to be more miraculous than the Virgins of surrounding towns. "It must be," one townsman piously explains, "because our Virgin is *gringa*, rosy-cheeked, with sad blue eyes, and this must be pleasing to God." When not saying Mass or performing other functions expected of him by the people, the priest spends most of his time drinking or dancing with the young girls of the town. To their dismay, however, the people discover that the priest, who had consumed even the Mass wine, has been consecrating *cañazo*, the local home brew. Instead of offering an explanation to the commission sent to discuss the matter with him, the priest angrily demands immediate payment for all his Masses. Sensing a swelling of anger among the people, he hurridly sneaks away for his safety. To the cries of "death to the swindler-priest!," the people send a hunting party after the fleeing clergyman. Though momentarily disconcerted, they soon discover that they can celebrate their feast without the presence of the obnoxious priest. In the midst of merry singing and dancing, the townsfolk drink to the health of their Virgin.[59]

In his master work, *El Mundo es Ancho y Ajeno* (1940), Alegría tells of the losing struggle of a small Andean community, Rumi, to preserve its lands against the encroachments of an hacienda landlord, who is supported by the local government officials. Throughout the novel Alegría records with sympathy many of the popular religious beliefs and practices of the mountain dwellers. The people of Rumi believe that their community lives under the special protection of Saint Isidore. So great is their faith in Saint Isidore that when the saint's image mysteriously "moves" to a nearby hill three nights in a row, the entire community moves to the new site. Even the outlawed bandit leader Fiero Vásquez, who comes to the defense of Rumi, seeks the consolation of religion. He carefully commits to memory the lengthy prayer to the "Just Judge," a compendium of popular beliefs, which he confidently recites to ward off his enemies.[60]

In contrast to the great faith of the people in their saints and devotions is the aloof pomposity of the priest of the region, Don Gervasio Mestas. As depicted by Alegría, Mestas is "white, Spanish, obese and loquacious." He speaks a sophisticated Spanish that even the educated people of the region have difficulty understanding. When the old mayor of Rumi, Rosendo Maqui, seeks the counsel of the priest in the struggle against the landlord, Mestas exhorts him to "obey the designs of God and have faith." God alone, counsels the priest, will judge who is to be rich or poor on earth, and no one should question his judgment.[61]

The model of religious piety and rectitude is the old Indian, Rosendo Maqui, wise man and spokesman for the community. Alegría describes Rosendo's religious world view as a mixture of Catholicism, pantheism, and superstition. He treats all things in the world—animals, rocks, the land, and the people—with great reverence. He is faithful to the devotion to Saint Isidore, but that does not prevent him from meditating on many occasions before the hill of Rumi, which he believes to be inhabited by the spirits of his ancestors. As Alegría explains, "Rosendo's way of understanding all things is to love all things."[62]

Finally, the image of the crucified Christ is invoked as a justification for the community's rebellion against the authorities. As one of the Indian leaders exclaims just before the people take up arms: "The Indian is a Christ nailed to a cross of abuse!"[63]

APRA: THE INDIAN AND THE CHURCH

Ironically, even though Alegría's novels expressed the pro-Indian and anticlerical attitudes of many Apristas, the reality was at times quite the opposite. During the thirties Apra proved

to be considerably less anticlerical than its enemies feared, and
for all the *indigenismo* associated with it, Apra enjoyed relatively
little support from the Indians. This contrast between propaganda
and reality is illustrated by an incident that occurred during the
uprising in Huaraz. Fearful for their lives, several Aprista leaders
in the nearby town of Caraz sought refuge in the local parish
priest's house. But many Indians, in the belief that the priest,
Father Augusto Soriano, was endangered by the Apristas, came
down from the hills every day to make sure that he was not
harmed.[64] The Aprista press itself revealed the detail that several
Indians had led the government troops to Major Mindreau's hide-
out after he fled Huaraz, and Carlos Philipps also seems to have
been exposed by an Indian.[65] The *indigenista*, Dora Mayer de
Zulen, accused "Apro-Communism," as she termed it, of being
"as far distant as a great many rightists" from understanding the
Indians, especially their religious beliefs.[66] Undoubtedly, the re-
puted anticlericalism of Apra had much to do with the indifference
or hostility which many Indians felt toward the Apristas.[67]

But the Apristas are much more easily cleared of the charge of
being anticlerical, at least in their actions if not in their statements. In his *Manifiesto* of 1933, Haya stressed the fact that for
the few days that the Apristas had been in control of large sections of the north, they never once committed an act of violence
against the church.[68] Even more convincing was the fact that
many Apristas in Trujillo requested and attended an outdoor
Mass on July 9, the day before the government offensive.[69] During the attack and the dark days of the mass executions, Aprista
women prayed daily in the churches of Trujillo.[70] In late November, 1934, the Apristas and allied factions rose up in the interior
departments of Ayacucho and Junín and seized control of several
cities and towns. During the uprising a priest, Ambrosio Ruiz, was
killed in Huancavelica.[71] Despite the attempts of the anti-Aprista
press to use the incident as clear proof of Apra's anticlericalism,
more impartial observers noted that the leader of the uprising in
Huancavelica who killed the priest, Cirilo Cornejo, was not an
Aprista but a member of an allied group, La Alianza Nacional.[72]
A final irony of the 1934 uprising was that as the Aprista leaders
prepared to flee Ayacucho after controlling it for four days, they
offered to turn the city government over to the bishop, who was
none other than Fidel Olivas Escudero, the conciliator between
Atusparia and the citizens of Huaraz forty-nine years earlier. The
elderly prelate refused.[73]

THE CHANGING APRA

As a result of this second aborted revolution, the Aprista party was once again placed outside of the law and its leaders were deported or forced underground. But even as the party fortified itself in preparation for a long period of resistance, some non-Apristas began to wonder whether it was the same old Apra, at least in religious questions. Although the Catholic press continued its holy crusade of exposing the real intentions of Apra, *Verdades* noted in 1934 that it seemed to be an "obsession" of Apra to demonstrate that it was not anti-Catholic.[74] In an article in 1939 entitled "Is Apra Changing?" *Verdades* observed with satisfaction that *La Tribuna* had published a manifesto in which, among other points, Apra reaffirmed its respect for the Catholic religion, which, *La Tribuna* added, "is that professed by the immense majority of [the party's] members."[75]

The shift away from an earlier unofficial anticlericalism was formally and officially sealed in a resolution unanimously passed by the clandestine National Aprista Convention of 1942 which abrogated the church-state–separation clause of the party's program. The resolution also clearly reflected Apra's pro-allied stance during the war.

> Having adhered to the principles of the Atlantic Charter and the Declaration of the Four Freedoms, and finding it imperative to reaffirm our inalterable democratic convictions, the Aprista citizens of Peru declare null and void the clause in our great party's Plan of Immediate Action referring to the separation of Church and State . . . recognizing that the immense majority of Apristas, who at the same time form a majority within the nation, are Catholics.[76]

In the spring of 1945, after eleven years of underground existence, Apra emerged triumphant and larger than ever. The party formed part of a coalition government under President José Luis Bustamante y Rivero, which managed to survive only until October, 1948, when General Manuel Odría, fearful of growing Aprista strength, overthrew President Bustamante and forced Apra to submerge underground once again. Haya himself sought asylum in the Colombian embassy, where he remained for the next five years until he received a safe conduct from the Odría regime to leave the country. But in the meantime, several notable Apristas such as Ciro Alegría, Magda Portal, and Alberto Hidalgo began leaving the party in the belief that it had lost its old revolutionary fervor. Even President Bustamante, who had his hands full trying to manage the Apristas in his government, noted that Apra had largely lost its "anti-imperialist phobia and its anticlerical bias."[77]

Whether or not Apra had changed in its new politics of reconciliation with middle- and upper-class groups is a topic of continuing debate. What is more certain, however, was that with the first signs of social Christianity in Peru in the postwar years, the increase of secularization among middle-class Catholics in general, and Apra's strong stand against communism, membership in Apra no longer represented the bold, quasi-religious act that it had been in the thirties. Indeed, when the Aprista party exhorted Peruvian Catholics to protest the arrest of Cardinal Mindzenty in 1949, Apra began to appear more like a traditional Catholic party than a movement that traced its origins to a public act of defiance against the archbishop of Lima.[78]

The coming together of the reformist elite and large sectors of the lower classes in the Aprista movement effected a profound transformation in the social and religious history of Peru. By reason of its sheer size as well as the enthusiastic militancy of its members, Apra posed the most serious challenge to the church in Peruvian history.[79] Correctly or incorrectly, many churchmen feared that in the Aprista movement the liberalism of Vigil and the radicalism of González Prada would become the creed of thousands of lower-class traditional Catholics. But instead of converting the religious issue into a case of conscience as in many other Latin Catholic countries, particularly Mexico, the Aprista leaders, aware of the enormous strength of popular religiosity among lower-class Peruvians, deliberately courted the religious sentiments of their followers. Although Apra never entirely freed itself from the charge of being anticlerical, it did create the necessary psychological conditions within the party whereby Peruvian Catholics could be militant Apristas without abdicating their Catholicity or forsaking their religious convictions.[80]

As an outgrowth of Apra's cultural mission, and especially under the impact of political persecution, membership in the Aprista party acquired a quasi-religious significance for both leaders and rank and file members. At the same time, the symbols and images of the popular Catholicism of lower-class Apristas acquired a new, revolutionary sense, unlike the conservative overtones of similar symbols associated with the Catholic Right in other Latin American countries. By identifying their traditional Catholicism with the cause of social justice, Aprista Catholics anticipated and paved the way for the emergence of a social Christianity long before most Peruvian churchmen began to think in these terms.

The demise of González Prada's anticlerical liberalism did not signal immediately the appearance of a new, secularized politics that went beyond the "religious question." On the contrary, religion and politics were never more overtly and passionately interlaced in modern Peruvian history than in the stormy thirties. Indeed, the Apristas' realization that while their followers were willing to fight for a social, economic, and political revolution, they were not disposed to discard their traditional religious beliefs, was a key psychological insight which they exploited to the fullest. By joining religious to political emotions, the Apristas created a near messianic movement which grew in adversity and weakened only in triumph.

On May 20, 1945, five days after Apra became legalized again, Haya de la Torre addressed some 200,000 Apristas and sympathizers in the Plaza San Martín in downtown Lima. In his speech, which had the statesmanlike ring of one who already governed the country, Haya sought to conciliate the enemies of Apra. He reminded his followers that they had all suffered a "martyrdom," but every "authentic martyrdom knows how to forget the suffering and the one who caused it." Haya urged party members to forgive their enemies because "in every genuine Golgotha there is a pardon for those who do not know what they do." The Aprista leader ended his address with an Aprista slogan from the thirties: "In the struggle, brothers; in suffering, brothers; in victory, brothers."[81]

The Aprista Calvary had ended, and with it the first stage of the great experiment in populist politics. In the Aprista party, the elite and the masses, the reformers and the people ended a century of separation. New forces and new personalities would emerge in the next several decades to challenge Apra's nearly total dominance of the coastal lower classes and to widen the process of national integration that the San Marcos University students and factory workers had begun in the Popular Universities in the twenties and that the Apristas accelerated in the thirties and forties. The most important of these new forces that succeeded Apra as major catalysts of national integration are the new military and the new church.

8: LONG LIVE CHRIST THE KING!
THE CHURCH AND THE MILITARY, 1945-76

THE MILITARY COUP OF 1968

At approximately 2:20 in the morning of Thursday, October 3, 1968, a column of army tanks surrounded the presidential palace in downtown Lima and smashed open the massive wrought-iron gate that separated the courtyard of the palace from the Plaza de Armas. A contingent of officers and soldiers marched through the palace and rather ungraciously hustled the shoeless and disheveled president of the republic, Fernando Belaúnde Terry, out of his quarters and set him on board an airplane headed for Bueno Aires. Thus, the eighth successful military coup of the twentieth century unceremoniously ended the little more than five years of Peru's most ambitious reform government up until then.

Few Peruvians were surprised when they learned of the coup some hours later, and few raised a voice in protest; the army's move had been long expected and even desired by many. Scattered, half-hearted demonstrations organized by the deposed president's party, Popular Action (Acción Popular), could not hide the deep disillusionment shared by many Peruvians over Belaúnde's failure to put into effect the sweeping social reforms he had promised in the elections of 1962 and 1963. In the wake of his overthrow, Popular Action virtually faded out of existence. Héctor Cornejo Chávez's Christian Democratic party, which had formed an alliance with Popular Action, continued to exist and even to exert considerable intellectual influence over the new military government, but it was too small numerically to have much popular impact. This left only three major institutional forces to fill the political vacuum: the armed forces, which had seized power, Apra, which

164

continued to be the party of the opposition, and the Roman Catholic church.

Apra was a familiar force, both at home and abroad. During the decades following the Second World War, it had maintained, but not expanded, its great constituency, which by and large had moved up the social scale from lower to middle and lower-middle class. The great population explosion and the massive migrations from the *sierra* to the coast following World War II had given rise to a new, restless urban proletariat that was largely ignored by Apra. Content to champion the cause of the more established and conservative lower-middle classes, Apra had also seriously tarnished its image as a reform party by its policy of entering into alliances with the oligarchy in order to regain legality and win respectability. What was far less familiar to most Peruvians and foreign observers, however, were the other two forces, the newly socially sensitized army and the newly updated church.

The first several years of military rule witnessed the unprecedented spectacle in Peruvian history of the military and the church overtly courting, and at times competing for, the favor of the newly politicized lower classes. The winner, or winners, of this all important ideological contest will be assured a permanent role in determining the course of events in the next several decades as Peru accelerates and consolidates its revolution. Although the military regime that took power in 1968 has effected profound and in many cases irreversible reforms, it has conspicuously failed to create a broad base of popular support for itself. While most lower-class Peruvians support the revolution with varying degrees of enthusiasm, they merely tolerate the military regime that executes the reforms. Of the three forces, the church alone has successfully penetrated the reserves of Peru's restive lower classes. Especially in the *pueblos jóvenes* ("young towns," formerly known as *barriadas*) surrounding the coastal cities and in the *sierra,* the new church has managed to identify itself convincingly with the aspirations of the lower classes, a factor that makes it either a valuable ally of the reformist military government or a potential threat. The generally quiet and gradual transformation of the army and the church into socially conscious forces, in retrospect the most important phenomenon in Peruvian social history since the rise of Apra in the thirties, was little noticed by most Peruvians, who quite naturally focused their attention on the more visible and clamorous reform parties that arose in the middle fifties to challenge the hegemony of Apra.

THE QUEST FOR REFORM 1945-68

José Luis Bustamante y Rivero's short-lived government (1945–
48) represented the first attempt to offer a reformist alternative
to Apra. Bustamante, a lawyer from Arequipa and a practicing
Catholic, was supported by many other like-minded intellectuals, professionals, and businessmen, who desired reform but
eschewed the violent tactics and laicizing tendencies of many
Apristas. But because Apra had so effectively preempted reformist sentiment, Bustamante and his independent supporters saw
little possibility of establishing a new political force. Bustamante
believed, moreover, that a political party created and directed
from the presidential palace would never become a popular, grass-
roots movement.

Cooperation with Apra proved just about impossible for the
mild-mannered jurist, however, and by early 1948 Bustamante
had replaced all his civilian ministers with military in the hopes
of containing Apra. In early October of that year, lower-ranking
army and navy officers, supported by cadres of Apristas, precipitated an armed uprising in Callao as part of a general plan to
overthrow the government. Although the president acted swiftly
to put down the uprising and place Apra outside the law, the
military commander of Arequipa, General Manuel Odría, convinced that Bustamante could not long control the situation, came
out against the central government in late October and seized
power.[1]

Among General Odría's first measures upon assuming the presidency were to drive Apra underground and to force Haya de la
Torre to seek asylum in the Colombian embassy, where he remained until 1954 when he received a safe-conduct pass to leave
the country. For most rank and file Apristas, the Colombian embassy became a sort of rallying symbol of resistance during the
first repressive years of Odría's dictatorship. But for a few Apristas,
and many non-Aprista Peruvians, the meager social reforms that
Apra had sponsored or put into effect when it dominated the parliament under Bustamante confirmed their belief that the grand
old party of reform had definitely lost the revolutionary visions
of its youth.

Odría's eight-year dictatorship (1948–56) reaffirmed the conservative landowning oligarchy's hold over the country. At the
same time, Odría also spent considerable sums on primary education, public housing, hospitals, and certain charities in order to

curry the favor of the rapidly growing lower classes. But the dour and uncharismatic dictator failed to generate much enthusiasm, and when the time for the 1956 elections came, which he himself had convoked, Odría stepped down in favor of Manuel Prado, who was elected for his second term. Head of one of the leading land-owning and banking families in Peru, Prado won the election mainly because Apra threw its support behind him in order to win legality. Like the pact with Bustamante in 1945, Apra accepted legal recognition on the condition that Haya de la Torre not run for the presidency. The noncandidacy of Haya served not only to ease competition for Prado but also to focus the electorate's attention on the debut of two new reform parties, Fernando Belaúnde Terry's Popular Action and Héctor Cornejo Chávez's Christian Democracy.

Belaúnde and Cornejo Chávez

A professional architect, Fernando Belaúnde began his political career as a deputy from Lima in 1945, while his father, Rafael, served as prime minister under President Bustamante. Both father and son cooperated on a number of occasions with Apra, an inevitable consequence of Apra being the only reform party in the country. It was understandable, furthermore, that many features of Belaúnde's program for the 1956 elections resembled Apra's program. For example, Belaúnde stressed grass-roots community action among the lower classes for building roads, schools, and houses. Yet, there were differences that made him more acceptable to the middle classes: his pragmatic bent, his winning idealism, and, of course, his youth. Moreover, the Catholicity of his family—his uncle was Víctor Andrés Belaúnde, Peru's leading Catholic conservative philosopher—forestalled accusations of being a communist from the Catholic Right. Belaúnde did so well for a newcomer in the 1956 elections that he immediately set his sights on the 1962 elections.

In 1956, a small group of intellectuals, businessmen, and journalists in Arequipa brought into existence the Christian Democratic party of Peru. The main architect and spokesman was Héctor Cornejo Chávez, a young lawyer who had served as Bustamante's personal secretary during his stay in power. Inspired by the Christian Democratic parties of Europe and elsewhere in Latin America, especially Chile, the young idealists of Arequipa applied the

modern social teachings of the Catholic church to Peruvian realities. Among Christian thinkers who influenced them the most were
Jacques Maritain, Emmanuel Mounier, Nicolas Berdyaev, Ignace
Lepp, and the French Dominican priest, Louis-Joseph Lebret.[2] In
their programs, the Christian Democrats were far advanced over
the hierarchy and clergy of the Peruvian church, which were only
beginning to recognize the existence of the social encyclicals,
much less their social and political implications.

The young party suffered from two liabilities from the onset.
First, the Christian Democrats never overcame their somewhat
elitist, "intellectual" image, which prevented them from capturing the imagination of the lower classes. Though well-intentioned,
they did not understand that lower-class Catholics were more
often than not confused or bored by the legalistic and stilted
language of papal encyclicals. Secondly, Popular Action preempted
much potential support from among Peruvians who saw little
difference, all ideological distinctions aside, between Belaúnde's
tacit Christian idealism and Cornejo Chávez's explicit Christian
idealism. The Christian Democratic party always remained a
small movement, although it had a considerable impact on middle-
class professionals, intellectuals, and many university students.

The Elections of 1962–63

For many young Peruvians, aroused by the spectacle of Castro's
Cuba, Hugo Blanco's peasant campaigns in Cuzco, the Alliance
for Progress, and the general momentum of thirty years of revolutionary rhetoric, the decade of the sixties promised to spell
the end of the oligarchy and the triumph of the middle and
lower classes. Unfortunately for them, however, the election of
1962 did not offer such well-defined alternatives. The three major
candidates were Fernando Belaúnde, Haya de la Torre, running
for the first time since 1931, and Manuel Odría, the former dictator. Héctor Cornejo Chávez ran for the Christian Democrats,
and several small leftist parties competed for attention. Although
Odría most clearly represented the conservative sector, he also
won votes from barriada settlers who remembered his patronage
when he was in power. Haya de la Torre by 1962 had become an
ambiguous figure, representing an older reformist liberalism, which
to a new generation of Peruvians seemed little different from
staid, old-fashioned capitalism. Belaúnde was most clearly the

reform candidate, although Cornejo Chávez held more advanced positions on agrarian reform and economic imperialism. In one sensitive area, however, the candidates all appeared alike, and that was the care with which they measured their words and actions in dealing with the religious sentiments of the electorate.

The religious issue was just as potentially volatile as in the thirties because the electorate now included women, who since had received the right to vote, and a vastly increased *barriada* population. *El Comercio,* the leading voice of the conservative oligarchy and inveterate enemy of Apra, tried rather unsuccessfully to resurrect the religious issue as material against the Apristas. In several editorials, *El Comercio*, which pointedly avoided mentioning Apra by name, warned Catholics not to vote for "enemies of the Church," particularly parties which advocate lay education and fascist regimentation of the youth.[3] Church-going Apristas simply ignored the charges, and other Peruvians dismissed them as overworked and empty themes from the past. Manuel Odría, however, aware of the potential impact of such charges upon lower-class Catholics, published full page campaign ads in the newspapers listing Haya de la Torre's "crimes" and his alleged acts against religion.[4] The ex-dictator's electoral machine, , Unión Nacional Odriista, also announced that a Mass would be said in honor of General Odría in order to seek the intercession of the Sacred Heart for his victory.[5] Though above such overt exploitation, Belaúnde too made several explicit references to Christ, usually in order to stress Popular Action's conformity with the Social Gospel.[6] None of the candidates came close, however, to Father Salomón Bolo Hidalgo's bizarre mixture of traditional Catholicism and left-wing politics.

Popularly known as "Cura Bolo," Father Bolo was a secular priest belonging to the diocese of Huaraz. His mercurial personality and passionate public oratory frequently incurred the censure of his religious superiors, who finally suspended him from the exercise of his priesthood for his involvement in politics in the 1962 election. Bolo was one of the founders of the National Liberation Front, a communist-supported party which sympathized with Castro's revolution and called for a similar sweeping revolution in Peru. The party's presidential candidate was General César Pando Egúsquiza, with Bolo as the vice-presidential candidate. Always appearing at party assemblies in cassock, even after his suspension, Bolo ended his vitriolic diatribes, full of allusions to the Gospel and the writings of Marx and Lenin, with the cry,

"Long Live Christ the King! Long Live Peru!"[7] Lacking the support of the institutional church, however, Bolo amused rather
than aroused most ordinary practicing Catholics who heard
him.

The far Left did poorly in the elections anyway, as did the
Christian Democrats. Although Haya came in first, none of the
three major candidates captured a clear plurality, and the outcome was to have been decided by parliament. Fearing a possible
Aprista victory, the army used Belaúnde's charge of massive electoral fraud as a pretext to overthrow President Prado in July,
1962, and annul the elections. New elections held a year later
under the watchful eyes of the interim military *junta* (1962–63),
finally brought Belaúnde to victory, with the aid of the Christian
Democrats and the Left, who chose to cast their votes for the
Popular Action candidate rather than facilitate a possible Aprista
victory.

Guerrilla War in the Andes, 1965

While Belaúnde set about to translate campaign promises into
reality, certain young dissidents of the Communist and Aprista
parties took up arms in the Andes in 1965 in order to accelerate
the day of the revolution. Inspired by Castro's movement based
in the Sierra Maestra, Luis de la Puente, a former Aprista youth
leader and cofounder of the Movement of the Revolutionary Left
(movimiento de la Izquierda Revolucionaria, or Mir), established
his base of operations in La Convención valley not far from
Cuzco, while Héctor Béjar and other members of the National
Liberation Army, a left-wing group that had been expelled from
the Communist party, began their campaign near Ayacucho.
Both groups were hunted down by Peruvian rangers and by September, 1965, virtually wiped out. But some of the guerrillas
survived to reflect on their experiences, including why they
failed.

Héctor Béjar, for example, criticized his fellow guerrillas for
their failure to study thoroughly local customs and to learn the
language of the people. As a result of this failure, the Quechua-
speaking Indians frequently looked with suspicion on the armed
and bearded men from the coast, and some peasants even dis-
closed the guerrilla's positions to the pursuing army troops.[8]
This experience stands in contrast to that of Hugo Blanco, the
young Trotskyite student leader who successfully unionized

many of the peasants in the Cuzco area in the late fifties and early sixties. Before beginning his campaign, however, Blanco thoroughly mastered Quechua and lived the life of a peasant for a period. With some justification, the guerrilla leaders also criticized the local church for serving as an instrument of oppression by deadening the social consciousness of the peasants. At the same time, however, Béjar's dismissal of Catholicism and Protestantism as religions "full of myths and fantasies" reveals an enormous insensitivity to the very cultural traditions of the Indians that he had resolved to defend.[9] In general, the angry young leftists of the sixties seemed to have learned little from an earlier generation of *indigenistas* and Apristas about the undercurrent of revolutionary sentiment latent in the people's popular religiosity.

The guerrilla outburst in the Andes was but symptomatic of the general failure of Belaúnde's government to deal effectively with the mounting social crises. Paralyzed by an Aprista-dominated parliament, Belaúnde continually fell short of producing effective solutions to the land problem, Standard Oil's irksome monopoly of Peruvian oil, inflation, political corruption in the government, and the rising swell of newcomers to the *barriadas*. The army's move in October, 1968, was not directed so much against Belaúnde personally as it was against the Peruvian political system itself, which somehow had bottled up real reform in the name of parliamentary democracy.

THE PERUVIAN REVOLUTION

The generals and colonels who seized power under General Juan Velasco Alvarado's leadership quickly set into motion what they termed the Peruvian revolution. Their first act was to expropriate Standard Oil of New Jersey's holding in northern Peru. But it soon became apparent that the military government intended to do far more than liberate Peru from foreign monopolies. During the next few years the government enacted an agrarian reform law that broke the back of the landed oligarchy, an industrial community law that placed a good deal of power into the hands of the workers, and a social property law that provided for collective ownership by the workers of new firms and enterprises. The generals resisted moving in the direction of a full socialism, however, preferring to experiment with models tried out earlier in Yugoslavia and Israel. For example, the government has recognized four types of property: private, reformed private, social (joint worker-management), and state. Basically, the military aimed to steer a middle course between rugged individualistic capitalism and regimented totalitarian communism. In frequent addresses and pronouncements, the military defined the Peruvian revolution as an experiment in revolutionary humanism, inspired by Christian ideals, which sought to create a pluralistic society of full participation for all Peruvians in the political and economic life of the country.[10]

The unique features of the Peruvian revolution were its proclaimed commitment to seek a third way, neither communist nor capitalist, and its accent on revolutionary humanism. Unlike the highly anticlerical Mexican revolutionary leaders, the Peruvian military pointedly courted the church and sought its counsel from the onset, and unlike the Cuban revolutionaries, the Peruvian generals avoided Marxist rhetoric, stressing instead the Christian and humanistic nature of their revolution. Perón, of course, had also proclaimed a third way, *Justicialismo,* but never with the passionate tenacity and intellectual thoroughness of the Peruvian military. For many skeptics and critics, the third way of the Peruvian revolution is at best ambiguous and at worst totally contradictory. The apparently indiscriminate lumping together of "revolutionary humanism" and Christianity in the same revolution may reveal either intellectual confusion over the meaning of the two terms or an imaginative insight into their intrinsic compatibility. In any case, what seemed most original about the new military was their determination to construct the revolution within tradition, a course of action advocated a generation earlier by José Carlos Mariátegui.

THE NEW MILITARY

The men who made up the revolutionary government soon became household names in Peru. General Velasco, although lacking somewhat in charismatic appeal, was soon recognized as the author and leader of the revolution. General Jorge Fernández Maldonado, the brilliant minister of mining and energy, very early became identified as the spokesman for the leftist faction in the military. General Francisco Morales Bermúdez, minister of finance, became a familiar figure as the exponent of the government's ambitious economic reforms. General Ernesto Montagne, the prime minister and brother-in-law of the cardinal, lent an aura of respectibility and moderation to the regime. The refined and distinguished-looking minister of foreign affairs, General Edgardo Mercado Jarrín, was largely responsible for achieving for Peru a leading role among the nonaligned Third World nations. Generals Alfredo Arrisueño in education, Javier Tantaleán in the new ministry of fisheries, Leónidas Rodríguez de Figueroa as head of Sinamos, and others presented a convincing picture of a talented team dedicated to the social reconstruction of Peru.[11]

Though varying in personalities and ideological orientations, these men fairly typified the new military elite in Peru: well-educated, pragmatic, nationalistic, anti-Communist but deeply concerned over social justice, and team-oriented in their approach to government and reform. Most had spent a period at Caem, the Center for Higher Military Studies, where they studied military strategy within the larger context of national, social, and economic problems. Generals Montagne and Morales Bermúdez had received valuable experiences serving as ministers in Belaúnde's cabinets. Most were from the middle and lower classes and had no political or personal ties with the great landowning oligarchy. As loyal soldiers, they had executed orders to wipe out the guerrillas in the mid-sixties, but at the price of a bad conscience. Though unsympathetic to communism, they did sympathize with the guerrilla's cry for justice for the landless and politically voiceless peasants of Peru. While the politicians wrangled endlessly over proposed reforms in Belaúnde's parliament, these officers were quietly but busily versing themselves in the economic and social problems of the country.[12]

Cultural Catholics

The somewhat indeterminate mixture of revolutionary and Christian humanism in the ideology of the same revolution reflected to a great extent the different backgrounds of the men behind the reforms. A few of the generals, like Velasco himself, who was probably more typical of the majority of lower-echelon officers, had been raised in the atmosphere of cultural Catholicism. Cultural Catholicism is the reception of certain sacraments of the church or the observance of certain rituals of popular religiosity more because they are family or social traditions, and less because of the religious truths behind them. The ordinary cultural Catholic in Latin America may be critical of the church as an institution, but he is usually too indifferent to submit religion itself to a similar critical analysis. Although the military who fell into this classification were not conspicuously practicing Catholics, most were cautiously respectful toward the church, which they recognized to be a powerful political force. Many of these officers came from the middle or lower classes and, like Velasco, products of Peru's state school system, where the obligatory religious education programs have been, until recent times, notoriously unimaginative and superficial. The cultural Catholicism of the home, where the forms of Catholicism and popular religiosity were honored without any deeper commitment to Catholic Christianity itself, extended into army life.

On different occasions, for example, soldiers, cadets, and officers are expected to escort the patron saint of a town or village in a procession, attend a Mass inaugurating a civic program, or honor their own patron saint. These are practices common to all branches of the armed forces and the Guardia Civil, the paramilitary police force. Each year in August, for example, members of the Guardia Civil escort through the streets of the capital an image of their patroness, St. Rose of Lima, and on at least one occasion the government has even awarded the saint a special decoration. The custom of honoring saints and images of Christ with civil or military awards seems to have grown in popularity in spite of the secular drift of the times. As though vying with one another, the army, the navy, and the air force have all at one time or another formally decorated Our Lady of Mercy, the patroness of the armed forces.[13] Shortly after the military took power in 1968, the head of the air force, General Alberto López Causillas, presided at a ceremony in which the Lord of Miracles was awarded the Great Peruvian Cross of Aeronautical Merit.[14]

Middle-class civilians in Lima, whether nonbelievers or practicing but secularized Catholics, may dismiss such public displays of martial piety as quaint customs left over from an age when patriotism and religion were but two sides of the same coin. But most officers who attend and preside over such rituals of popular piety are more attuned to the sentiments and traditions of Peru's lower classes than are their civilian counterparts. Many soldiers, who are drafted from remote villages and towns in the Andes, are far more at home marching in the Lord of Miracles procession than attending an updated Mass in one of the suburbs in Lima. Whether he is from the lower class itself or has been stationed in the provinces or is simply sensitive to the traditions of his men, the average Peruvian officer is aware of the great importance attached by the lower classes to their popular devotions. This realization, and the need to legitimize their unprecedented revolution in the eyes of the church, accounts in great part for the care with which the new military regime continued to observe traditional acts of piety, a concern unheard of in the Mexican or Cuban revolutions.

Each year on July 28, Independence Day, the president, his cabinet, and all important government officials attend a Te Deum sung in the Cathedral. When Raúl Castro, a professed nonbeliever, visited Peru in 1974, a few Catholics raised eyebrows at his presence among the military at the annual Te Deum. But Peru is not Cuba, and the military are well aware of the importance of such acts in the eyes of Catholic Peruvians. Also, each year when the Lord of Miracles procession passes through the Plaza de Armas, the president of the republic customarily makes some gesture of respect or recognition. In October, 1970, for example, Velasco and his entire military cabinet greeted the procession from a balcony in the presidential palace on bended knees and with heads bowed.[15]

Committed Christians

Within the military government, however, there were other officers whose Christianity went far beyond cultural Catholicism. Several of the generals, such as Leónidas Rodríguez Figueroa, Alfredo Carpio Becerra, and Jorge Fernández Maldonado, had made the *Cursillos de Cristiandad*, the short but intensive indoctrination retreats in Christian life that became popular in Latin America in the fifties and sixties. Several of the generals, particularly those of middle-class backgrounds, had graduated from schools run by religious orders. General Montagne studied under the Sacred Heart Fathers in La Recoleta colegio, General Mercado Jarrín studied under the Marist brothers, and General Morales Bermúdez graduated from La Inmaculada, the Jesuit colegio of Lima.[16] General Fernández Maldonado, the left-leaning minister of mining and energy, was perhaps the most explicit in the expression of his Christian idealism, which he frequently cited as the source of his commitment to the revolution.[17] The imprint of this idealism on the revolution, as well as the ambiguous blending of secular and Christian humanism, is particularly evident in three key documents: the *General Educational Reform Law,* the *Ideo-logical Basis of the Revolution,* and the *Policy Guidelines on Pop-ulation.*

THE DOCUMENTS OF THE REVOLUTION

The educational reform law, enacted in March, 1972, called for a massive overhauling of the entire educational system and the in-fusion of the new, revolutionary idealism into all levels and areas of the renovated system. The authors of the law were highly in-fluenced by the educational theories of Paulo Freire, who had been so successful with adult literacy programs in Brazil. One of the prime objectives of the law, for example, was to create a critical sense of participation among the lower classes in the so-cial transformation of Peru. The members of the commission chosen to compose the law were mainly civilian educators, includ-ing one Jesuit priest, who reflected the same diverse humanistic tendencies found among the military. Article five, for example, states that the purpose of Peruvian education is the "integral for-mation of the human person in his immanent and transcendental projections."[18] The adjective, "transcendental," was included only after considerable debate and at the insistence of the Peruvian bishops, who had studied the reform before its enactment. The somewhat vague adjective, "immanent," was added to balance the formula and to placate the secular humanists.[19]

The *Ideological Basis of the Revolution,* promulgated in Feb-ruary, 1975, was strongly influenced by the philosophy behind the educational reform law. In fact, some of the authors of the latter contributed to the *Ideological Basis,* notably the ex-Aprista Carlos Delgado.[20] The document defined revolutionary humanism as a nondogmatic, nontotalitarian socialism that views man as the end and not as a means, of the revolution. The three historical sources cited for this revolutionary humanism are socialism, lib-ertarian philosophies, and Christian social thinking. The Christian contribution to the revolution, not sharply distinguished from the other sources, is its emphasis on the equality of men, its rejection of systematic violence, and its call for social justice as a precondi- -tion for constructing a more human community.[21] One of the principal authors of the references to Christianity was Héctor Cornejo Chávez, who developed many of these same themes in the pages of *El Comercio,* of which he was the government-appointed editor after its expropriation in 1974.[22]

Cornejo Chávez and the Christian Democrats also strongly influenced the formulation of the industrial community and social property laws, both of which expressed concepts that they had advocated since the early sixties. The Christian Democrats differed from the Velasco regime, however, in several important areas. They believed that the military government accorded a dangerously preponderate role to the state in the new industrial communities and enterprises, and they rejected as contrary to the pluralistic nature of the revolution the desire on the part of some members of the government to create a monolithic, government-sponsored political party. Somewhat disillusioned by the government's unwillingness to effect more rapidly the proposed transfer of the press to representatives of the people, Cornejo Chávez resigned his post as editor of *El Comercio* soon after Velasco's removal from power in August, 1975.[23]

In September, 1976, the government approved a major policy statement outlining its philosophy on population planning.[24] Far more than previous documents, this statement coincided almost entirely with the official position of the bishops, who had issued a pastoral letter on family and population planning in 1974.[25] Indeed, a Jesuit priest working in the National Planning Institute, Father Juan Julio Wicht, and a special church commission invited to examine the government's document, virtually composed the principal sections referring to the morality of state population programs and planned parenthood in general.[26] The general thrust of the document, clearly reflecting the church's thinking, was that state and family population planning must be placed within the larger context of social justice, and that overpopulation was the result of underdevelopment and not vice versa.

THE REVOLUTION FALTERS

The key ideological commitment of the government behind all of these laws and documents was to bring into existence a "fully participatory Social Democracy." Yet, participation, in the narrower sense of political support or enthusiasm for the government, seemed to be the military's Achilles' heel. The military, of course, understood participation in the wider sense of creating the conditions by which millions of Peruvians would be included in the economic and social life of the nation. Obviously, this process will take generations. Still, even given the necessity of patient waiting, the military at times so blatantly contradicted the high-minded Christian and libertarian principles enshrined in the documents of the revolution that they themselves were often responsible for fostering an attitude of skepticism and apathy toward the government. On a number of occasions, for example, the short-tempered Velasco peremptorily deported journalists, politicians, and union leaders who criticized his regime. In July, 1974, he expropriated all major newspapers. This last measure was intended to be a step toward transferring the press from the hands of the oligarchy to spokesmen who would be more truly representative of the majority of Peruvians. But the immediate result was a further stifling of free expression and a widening of the gulf between the government and the people. In the absence of elections, certain other signs pointed to this mood of apathy and even hostility toward the government.

In February, 1975, while the city police were on strike, a major riot broke out in Lima, and unruly crowds looted the downtown stores. Politically motivated arsonists burned down one of the government newspapers, gutted the assembly hall of the new civic center, and severely damaged the military club in La Plaza San Martín. Another telling sign came when General Velasco himself was removed from power in August of that year by his fellow officers, who replaced him with the prime minister, General Francisco Morales Bermúdez. The removal of the man who had engineered the revolution from the beginning and guided it through its first seven years produced hardly a ripple in Lima or elsewhere, much less a clamor of protest against the move. Middle- and upper-class suburbanites in Lima, of course, approved the change because they disliked Velasco's methods and feared his leftist measures. A year later, after a brief period of relaxation of tensions, President Morales announced a drastic devaluation of the Peruvian *sol*, a measure dictated by certain economic setbacks and decreased foreign investments resulting in part from the revolution. Minor riots broke out and many Limanian bus drivers went on strike. Fearing a recurrence of the events of February, 1975, Morales immediately suspended constitutional guarantees, placed Lima under an indefinite curfew and soon afterwards closed down all magazines. Clearly, the military government had not won the confidence of large sections of the citizenry eight years after the beginning of the revolution.[27]

But the apathy had deeper roots than the heavy-handed tactics of Velasco and his successor. The military had attempted to create a revolution from above in a country that had already

produced a mass popular movement from below, the Aprista party.
Velasco in different addresses refuted the frequent charge that the
military were copying Aprista reforms proposed forty years earlier.[28]
It appeared to many that the military were trying to create a type
of corporative society in which the state mediates between the different classes, a concept not unlike that which Apra proposed much
earlier. But the charge was partially false too because Apra had never
proposed a radical land reform.[29]

But more important than specific reform measures were the dynamics of rapport between leaders and followers and the sense of
participation of the people in the decision-making process. Although
the military consulted widely with civilians before enacting their
reforms, and many generals conscientiously traveled around the
country to explain the reforms and sound out local opinion,
their efforts fell far short of generating the same intense and passionate loyalty that bound Apristas to their party in the heroic
thirties and forties. The fact that the military have already put
into effect some of its party's reforms diminishes in nothing the enthusiasm of thousands of loyal Apristas, who still fill the party's
great hall to hear "Víctor Raúl" discourse on the state of the
nation each February 22, his birthday. But the military seem not
to have taken to heart the vital lesson from Aprista history, that
to suffer with the people is more important for establishing credi-
bility and inspiring loyalty than to issue idealistic statements in
favor of social justice. Although the military government officially
ignored the Aprista party, it could not afford to ignore the one
other major national institution in Peru, the Catholic church.

THE NEW CHURCH

The new church was far more successful than the military in
projecting a positive image of itself and in assuming a leadership
role among the lower classes in their struggle to win greater economic and political participation. In the late sixties and early
seventies the church pursued a two-fold strategy in order to encourage reform within a Christian context: on the one hand, it
aimed to influence government and military leaders so that they
would incorporate Christian ideals into their reform plans; and
on the other hand, it actively sought to identify itself with the
marginal classes. Since 1968 the Peruvian church has produced a
number of inspiring documents urging the military to remain

faithful to the Christian humanism expressed in the documents of the revolution. Onis, the progressive priests' group founded in 1968, has taken the avant-garde in numerous statements pressing bishops and military leaders to place the plight of the oppressed majority above their fears of communism. Moreover, priests and Christian laypersons within the government, have sought to influence planners and policy-makers with a Christian vision of society. This elitist, power-oriented strategy has been balanced by the church's populist-pastoral strategy of going out to the people and entering their life situation.[30] In the long run, this second strategy may prove to be of greater significance because it has resulted in winning for the church a degree of moral legitimacy and acceptance among the lower classes which it has rarely enjoyed in Peruvian history.

The populist-pastoral approach has also had the effect of awakening the political and social consciousness of the church far more than papal or episcopal documents could ever have. In the quest to identify itself with the people, the church has also come to look more positively upon popular religiosity. Like some Apristas in the thirties, churchmen in the seventies began preaching the message of social justice in the language of popular religiosity. In so doing, the church helped to ease the transitional crisis of the lower classes, which saw themselves threatened by the reforms and by change in general. At the same time, the church provided moral support in their fight for justice. In the church, more than in the army or Apra, the lower classes have found a secure and familiar forum in which they can more easily assimilate the new idea of revolution into their traditions.

A Slow Awakening

The Peruvian church was late in addressing itself seriously to the social question, but when it finally did, it moved forward at an ever accelerating pace. Certain groups of national and foreign clergy had, of course, long anticipated the bishops in adopting modernized approaches to their apostolic work or in preaching the Social Gospel. The small group of Peruvian clergy who favored the Aprista cause in the thirties foreshadowed the politicized clergy of the sixties. The Maryknollers, who had arrived in Peru in 1943, led the way in modernization by establishing a radio network in Puno in order to evangelize and catechize more effectively the distant villages of the *altiplano*. The Maryknoll priest, Father Daniel McClellan, won fame for the credit unions he founded among the peasants, and in Arequipa toward the end of the fifties, the Jesuit priest, Carlos Pozzo, created "Catholic Circles" (Círculos Católicos), a self-help organization aimed to encourage *barriada* dwellers to construct their own homes, schools, and other facilities.[31]

In 1958 the bishops held their first "Social Week," during which former president Bustamante y Rivero lectured the churchmen on the different social classes in Peru, and Bishop José Dammert urged his fellow bishops to give top priority to the social doctrines of the church.[32] While "Cura Bolo" spoke at National Liberation Front meetings, the Jesuit, Father Romeo Luna Victoria, attracted attention for his public lectures applying the social message of the church to Peruvian realities.[34] In 1969, a year after the Latin American bishops gathered in Medellín, Colombia, to apply the message of Vatican II to the Latin American church, Cardinal Juan Landázuri Ricketts gave symbolic expression to the call for a simpler church by moving from the archbishop's palace to a modest home in La Victoria, a lower-class district of Lima.

Onis, 1968

While the bishops called for change in general terms, a group of priests, mostly Peruvian, gathered in Cieneguilla outside Lima in March, 1968, and issued a declaration condemning specific unjust social conditions in Peru. The priests also invited laypeople, other priests, and the bishops to join them in their indictment of the social evils listed in the document. With this declaration, Onis, National Office of Social Investigation, came into being. The normally cautious cardinal surprised many when he expressed approval at the general orientation of the declaration a short while later.[35] Onis has since played a key role in influencing the church's positions on social and political questions. This can be explained in part by the fact that one of Onis's founders, Germán Schmitz, later became one of the auxiliary bishops of Lima, and another of the auxiliary bishops, Luis Bambarén, though not a member of Onis, is highly sympathetic to its stands. Most importantly, Cardinal Landázuri, while never publicly endorsing all of Onis's positions, listens carefully to its spokesmen and to his bishops.

The priests who founded Onis were mainly of middle-class background, highly educated and articulate. Some had studied in Europe or the United States, and all were thoroughly versed in both the social teachings of the church and modern social theories, including Marxism. A few Onis priests worked among university students, while others had had extensive contact with factory workers and *barriada* dwellers. A few of the more outstanding spokesmen for Onis's positions and the new church in general have been Gustavo Gutiérrez, Jorge Alvarez Calderón, Ricardo Antoncich, Alejandro Cussiánovich, and Romeo Luna Victoria. Luna Victoria, who led the way in the early sixties in pressing the church to speak out on social and political issues, was largely instrumental in setting Onis into motion. Gustavo Gutiérrez, a Limanian diocesan priest, soon won fame throughout the Americas as the leading exponent of liberation theology, a theological current which criticizes unjust social structures from the perspective of biblical faith.[36] Later, Father Gutiérrez formed a team and founded a center of theological reflection in Lima, Centro Bartolomé de las Casas, in order to continue rethinking his theological positions in the light of new political and social developments.

Optimism Amidst Crises

The new image of a progressive and socially sensitive church, however, could not entirely obscure the fact that the priests, nuns, and laypersons who pushed for change were still a minority within a generally conservative and tradition-laden church. In the fifties, José Dammert, later bishop of Cajamarca, was nearly a solitary figure among the other members of the hierarchy for his outspoken social views. In the seventies, only a few new bishops, such as the two auxiliary bishops of Lima, have distinguished themselves as champions of social justice. The rest of Peru's more than fifty bishops, while far from opposing social change, have been at best cautiously slow in implementing the recommendations either of Vatican II or of Medellín in their dioceses. A minority, including three bishops belonging to the right-wing Opus Dei, have continued to preach an other-worldly and individualistic Christianity.[37] Even Onis, which numbers about 200 priests, is a minority among the clergy.

Another serious obstacle in the way of the new church has been continued scarcity of native vocations and the reliance on foreign missionaries. Of the 2,459 priests in Peru in 1973, some 1,513, or 61 percent, were foreign born. By way of contrast, in 1953 only 44 percent of the clergy were foreign born. Native vocations have not only not increased, moreover, but they have been steadily declining since World War II.[38] The situation is most poignant in the *pueblos jóvenes* of Lima, where out of approximately twenty-five parishes in 1976, there was only one native Peruvian pastor.[39] The seminaries, which reflect more the mentality of the conservative bishops, have not fostered the formation of a progressive clergy. In 1974 several religious superiors began pulling their students out of Santo Toribio Seminary in Lima because of the poor quality of studies and the conservative orientation of some of the professors. Besides this larger crisis, there have been many individual personal crises typical of the entire church in the wake of Vatican II. In 1969, the young and promising auxiliary bishop of Lima, Mario Cornejo, left his post and married shortly afterwards, and that same year the Maryknoll innovator, Daniel McClellan, also left the priesthood and married. In 1972 the popular bishop of Puno, Julio González, was obliged by the Holy See to resign his position because of his allegedly scandalous conduct, which included, among other accusations, dancing with the peasants on feast days.

In spite of these institutional crises and liabilities, the church entered the period of the revolutionary government with great optimism. With the cardinal as a sympathetic supporter, the younger and more progressive bishops and priests continued to set the pace in speaking out on social issues. Four days before the promulgation of the agrarian reform, Onis issued a statement defining its position on land reform, and in his speech announcing the reform, President Velasco made pointed and favorable reference to the Onis statement.[40] From then on the pattern of official church-military relations was established. Before enacting any major reform, especially in the sensitive areas of education or population planning, the military carefully consulted the church first, and the church and Onis have frequently influenced government policy with their pastoral letters and declarations. The church's commitment to support the humanistic thrust of the revolution led it at times to endorse specific reforms or actions of the government. The cardinal, for example, strongly supported the expropriation of Standard Oil, as did the majority of American missionaries working in Peru.[41] In 1972 Cardinal Landázuri and Cardinal Muñoz Vega of Ecuador seconded their governments' claims to jurisdiction over 200 miles of territorial waters.[42] In the first few years of the revolution, the pastoral letters of the bishops and the official declarations of the military created the impression of unruffled, harmonious relations between church and state. The accentuated pastoral concern of the church, however, increasingly produced tensions between itself and the military, and on a few occasions precipitated near head-on collisions.

A New Pastoral Approach

During the sixties and early seventies, many priests and women religious submitted their pastoral methods and degree of identification with the people to a critical reevaluation in the light of the Gospel and the church's social teaching. Their reflection led them to redirect many of their activities and to readapt their lifestyles more in harmony with that of the poorer classes. As one Maryknoll priest declared in 1968: "We must really become part of the people, participating in their sorrows and joys with a profound disposition of the spirit, which implies more than mere external adaptation."[43] In 1969 the Maryknollers closed down their minor seminary in Puno and dedicated themselves to training lay leaders in the villages.[44] Many groups of religious imitated the cardinal's gesture by moving out of their centrally located convents or schools in order to live in poorer districts of the city. As a sign of the church's concern for the marginal classes, in 1968 the cardinal converted the *pueblos jóvenes* into a special pastoral area and placed them under the care of the new Jesuit auxiliary bishop, Luis Bambarén. Commenting on these changes within the church, the new bishop observed:

> Although the Peruvian Church had been aware for some time of the problems of social injustice in the country, it was between 1968 and 1970 that it acquired a critical consciousness of that reality and committed itself, as a Church, to those who suffer the consequences of that injustice.[45]

The effort to go out to the poor frequently had the effect of radicalizing many church groups. A case in point is the experience of Fe y Alegría. Modeled on the original Fe y Alegría ("Faith and Joy") schools founded in 1956 in Venezuela by Father José María Vélaz, S.J., Fe y Alegría of Peru had some 19,500 students in twenty-four different educational centers in *pueblos jóvenes* throughout Peru in 1976. The Fe y Alegría schools are private schools for children in the *pueblos jóvenes* run under the administration and guiding philosophy of the Jesuit fathers. Although the government pays the teachers' salaries, the schools must resort to raffles and campaign drives to raise funds for their maintenance. In the middle sixties one argument advanced to potential donors for contributing was that their donation would help "contain the expansion of communism in Latin America."[46] By the middle seventies, however, this somewhat uncritical view had long since faded away and been replaced by a more politicized and populist one inspired by Paulo Freire's notion of education as an instrument of political and social liberation. The Jesuit directors of Fe y Alegría regularly hold *cursillos* in order to reeducate their teachers in the methods of Freire and the ideas of Ivan Illich on community-oriented education. Furthermore, the Jesuits and their teachers envision their schools as centers for awakening the social awareness and sharpening the political consciousness of the surrounding community. An indication that this approach has been partially successful is that on a few occasions the parents of the school children have organized delegations to protest to the Ministry of Education for failing to pay the teachers' salaries.[47]

The new political-pastoral concern of the church soon produced minor clashes within the church and with the military. In March, 1969, some fifty seminarians committed the unheard of act in modern Peruvian church history of taking over the seminary in Trujillo and holding eight of their priest-professors as "hostages." The seminarians' move was directed against the bishop of Trujillo, Carlos María Jurgens, whom they believed to be about to replace their well-liked "hostages" with a new group of more conservative professors. But the seminarians also protested against Jurgen's decision to expel from the diocese three Spanish priests who had supported a steel workers' strike and picketed the opening of an exclusive country club. When sixteen other priests of the diocese declared their solidarity with the three Spaniards, the bishop backed down.[48] During a nationwide teachers' strike in 1972, Onis supported the strike and severely criticized the government for deporting two foreign priests along with many leaders of the teachers' unions.[49] These incidents were but skirmishes, however, compared to the first major test of wills between the church and the military, the celebrated confrontation between Bishop Bambarén and the minister of the interior, General Armando Artola.

THE BAMBAREN-ARTOLA AFFAIR

Background

The background of the clash was the increased concern of both the church and the new military government over the ever-expanding squatter settlements, where by the early seventies close to one-third of Lima's roughly 3,000,000 inhabitants lived.[50] Symbolic of the government's desire to create a more positive image for these settlements was the official sanctioning of the term *pueblo jóven* ("young town"), instead of *barriada* ("slum"). Although the term was somewhat euphemistic because most of the settlers lived in conditions of near misery, it did convey the optimism and forward-looking attitude of the settlers, who were beginning a new life and literally creating "new towns." Many of the settlers came directly from the *sierra,* but the majority were recent migrants who had spent some time living with friends or relatives in Lima before moving out. Some were simply long-time Limanian residents in search of more adequate housing. In either case, the religious culture of the settlers was a continuation of the same religious subculture of highland dwellers and the lower classes of Lima. In the fifties, the "invaders," as they are popularly called, occupied barren public lands, usually hills, around Lima. But in the seventies, pressured by a housing shortage and land scarcity, many of the invaders were willing to risk confrontation with the police by attempting to seize private property. By the time of the military takeover, the search for land was creating a potentially violent situation.

The military government's immediate response was to establish a new national office to deal with the problems of the *pueblos jóvenes.* As the cardinal's delegate to the *pueblos jóvenes,* Bishop Bambarén was appointed a member of the new office. The government also sought to establish lines of communication with the settlers in order to gain their confidence. The man chosen to perform this task was General Armando Artola, whose position as minister of the interior (police) hardly seemed to qualify him for the job. But Artola's extroverted personality, down-to-earth language, and crowd-amusing antics quickly set him apart from the rest of the military cabinet as the "people's man."

Artola launched his campaign to win the settlers over with gusto and enthusiasm. He made several trips by helicopter out to the *pueblos jóvenes,* delivered speeches, and gave many the impression that he was running for an elective office. On one occasion, the minister delighted his audience by dancing for them, and on another he drove an earth-clearing tractor.[51] But the gesture that became most associated with him was his practice of distributing used clothing and food, especially large sweetened rolls called *panetones.* Artola claimed that, among other sources, the food and clothing came from a local Adventist charity.[52]

In May, 1969, Bishop Bambarén interjected a discordant note in Artola's campaign when he expressed his opinion in a press conference that "social problems are not solved with bread (*panetones*) and used clothing." By this statement, the young bishop obviously intended to criticize Artola's somewhat paternalistic approach to the problem of the *pueblos jóvenes.* In Bambarén's opinion, more substantial changes were called for, such as the construction of homes and roads and the creation of new jobs.[53] Bishop Bambarén's statements caused a public stir because it was the first time that an influential churchman had directly criticized the military since they had taken power seven months earlier. A much-offended Artola retorted that he was only doing what Cáritas, the Peruvian Catholic relief service, did on a normal basis.[54] The exchange between the minister and the bishop delighted the journalists, who played one against the other in their newspaper columns.[55] Neither Artola or Bambarén wished to provoke a church-state confrontation, however, and the incident soon faded away from public attention. But the grounds for a second and more serious clash had been prepared.

In late April, 1971, some 200 families furtively "invaded" government-owned property in an area called "Pamplona," not far from the Jesuit colegio in the southeast section of Lima. Members of the Guardia Civil soon showed up to detain the flow of newcomers, and on May 3 the police turned on the settlers themselves in an effort to drive them out. In the meantime, the settlers sought out the aid of the Maryknoll priests in the nearby parish in Ciudad de Dios, a suburb of Lima. The priests and the parish council helped organize a commission to present the settlers' case to the Ministry of Housing.

While negotiations between the commission and the ministry were in progress, the police attempted to dislodge the settlers again. Finally, in the early hours of Wednesday, May 5, the police advanced for a third time, but this time the settlers counterattacked with rocks, sticks, and other homemade weapons. When the pitched battle was over, one of the settlers lay dead and some fifty policemen and other settlers had been wounded. That evening, the parish council addressed a letter to the president of the republic protesting the police's action. At the same time the council announced that a Mass would be said the following Sunday for the dead and wounded. In the meantime, hundreds of land-hungry newcomers continued to pour into the area.[56]

A Mass for the Invaders

On Sunday morning, May 9, Bishops Bambarén and Schmitz and four priests who worked in the area celebrated Mass in the midst of the Pamplona settlers. In his sermon Bishop Bambarén sought to console the settlers and to pacify aroused tempers. He assured them that they were not "invaders," but in reality the "founders of a new town." He urged the people not to "walk with heads bowed," since in truth they were "living Christs who are suffering another Calvary." The bishop also implored them not to harbor hatred toward the police because many of the police lived in *pueblos jóvenes.* Finally, he optimistically predicted that their example would stimulate the government to assign top priority to the housing needs of the poor.[57]

An irate Artola found the words of the bishop neither consoling or pacifying. In the belief that Bambarén had exacerbated an already inflammatory situation, Artola ordered his detention the following day. For thirteen hours Bambarén was held and shifted from the prefecture of Lima to the Ministry of Justice, and finally to El Sexto city prison. When President Velasco, who had just delivered the inaugural address to a meeting of the Inter-American Development Bank, heard of his minister's action, he immediately ordered Bambarén's release. But the damage had already been done, and both church and state found themselves forced into the unwanted situation of either defending their man or backing down.

While Artola defended his action in news conferences, a much-perturbed cardinal suddenly departed from a meeting of the

Latin American bishops in Costa Rica in order to return home. In the meantime, different religious groups, including Onis, fired off declarations protesting the detention of Bambarén. When the cardinal arrived in the evening of May 11, several hundred priests, religious, and laypeople were on hand to hear his word. The counsel of his private secretary not to make public statements seemed only to upset further the normally mild-mannered prelate. Instead of speaking to the awaiting journalists in the press room, he directed himself to the middle of the airport's great entrance hall. In a brief message, he announced his support for his bishop and ended with a cry not heard in Latin America since the Mexican revolution, "Long Live Christ the King!"[58]

The government heard the cardinal's message, and in a meeting a couple of days later, Velasco assured Landázuri that Artola's action was strictly his own and not that of the government. Artola and Bambarén exchanged conciliatory notes, and both the cardinal and the president repeatedly assured the public that there did not exist any friction between church and state. But the church's aggressive response had already dictated what the denouement of the drama was to be, and a week after the cardinal's return, Artola resigned his post.

PAMPLONA: LESSONS AND AFTERMATH

The Pamplona incident was not a church-state conflict in the narrow sense because neither the government nor the church willed it to happen. But in a wider sense, the Pamplona affair was a church-state confrontation because it brought to the fore the underlying ideological struggle that the two had been waging for the loyalty of the people. Artola had actively courted the people in the name of the government and had won a considerable number of supporters. It has even been suggested by some that he was attempting to build a power base for himself among the *pueblo jóven* dwellers in order to further his own ambitions. Whether this was true or not, it seems clear that he did not welcome the competition to his efforts to capture the loyalty of the *pueblos jóvenes* that the church in the person of Bishop Bambarén represented. On the other hand, Bishop Bambarén's action of saying a Mass and preaching a sermon in the midst of a socially volatile situation had the effect of imparting a political connotation to his presence and the ceremony. By interpreting the settlers' aspirations through references to the hallowed and venerated metaphors of the Crucified Christ, he wove social justice and tradition together into a familiar fabric. For all his momentary popularity, Artola could not counterbalance the combined weight of tradition and the prestige of the new church.[59]

Pamplona also put to the test the revolutionary humanism of the government. The violent attempt to dislodge the settlers seemed to belie the military's professed intention of seeking a better life for the marginal classes. Also, the government's generally bureaucratic approach to organizing the *pueblos jóvenes* often had the effect of smothering local initiative and reducing political participation to a government monologue. This became particularly evident in the example of Sinamos (National System for the Support of Social Mobilization), the organization which became the principal government representative in the *pueblos jóvenes* after the Pamplona affair. Although Sinamos aimed to "mobilize" the people, it ended up alienating so many sectors of society that the military finally had to announce in 1975 that Sinamos was in a state of "reorganization." The virtual demise of Sinamos was symptomatic of the military government's failure in general to generate a widespread sense of participation in the revolution. More and more, participation became the main point of tension between the government and the church.

The immediate outcome of the Pamplona invasion was renewed good relations between the church and the military and an increased government effort to meet the needs of the *pueblos jóvenes.* Within a few weeks after the invasions, the government had relocated thousands of settlers to a new site, Villa El Salvador, which by 1973 had a population of some 50,000.[60] Apparently, Bishop Bambarén's Mass had set a new style for future invasions. In January, 1976, a group of families invaded deserted property by the banks of the Rimac River. Their first action was to invite nearby priests to offer a Mass of thanksgiving for the founding of their new community.[61]

The church's growing identification with the marginal classes contrasted with the growing distance between Velasco's increasingly arbitrary regime and the general population. In December, 1975, the bishops issued a pastoral letter urging the government to speed up the process of transferring power from the military to representatives of the people.[62] This was the first official declaration of the church in which it clearly criticized the military for not fulfilling the expectations of the revolution. Later,

in early 1976, Bishop Bambarén challenged the government to
render account for the disappearance of several union and political leaders.[63]

THE CHURCH AND POPULAR RELIGIOSITY

While the church criticized the military in the name of their
own revolutionary humanism, many within the church began re-
examining their attitudes toward popular religiosity. In the fifties
and sixties, many modernized churchmen were offended by what
they considered to be infantile and alienating forms of worship.
Some pastors stripped their churches of saints and images in
order to focus the attention of the people on the central mystery
of the liturgy, the sacramental presence of Christ. Many young
priests associated the "superstitious" practices of the lower
classes with the general state of economic and political oppression in which they lived. But the new concern to share the life
of the people has tended, in many cases, to engender a new sympathy for the people's ways.

In a lecture on popular religiosity delivered to the bishops
in 1972, Father Manuel Marzal, a Jesuit anthropologist, stressed
the necessity of evangelizing by using the forms of the popular
religiosity of the people. At the same time, Father Marzal warned
that some forms of popular religiosity stand in opposition to
Christian humanism because they do not conduce to an increase
of liberty, maturity, or personal capacity to love.[64] In different
seminars and study groups, churchmen, anthropologists and catechists who work in the Andean region have all concluded that
the church must speak its message of social justice within the
context of the people's traditional practices. To do otherwise,
the church would risk alienating the people against both the
church and the Social Gospel. Some pastoral teams, for example,
have formed reflection groups with village leaders in order to
discuss ways and means of fostering a greater sense of social
responsibility during the annual feast day. Both churchmen and
leaders want to use the feast day as an occasion to encourage the
participants to reallocate some of the money they would have
normally spent on *chicha,* the local brew, for the maintenance
of the village school or clinic.[65] The day of the highland priest
who exploits the people is largely past. In 1968 Cardinal Landázuri publicly urged the faithful to consider offering donations to

a charitable institution instead of spending the money on flowers for the Lord of Miracles procession.[66] In the *pueblos jóvenes* and elsewhere, most clergy are conscious of the need to speak to the people in the cultural medium of popular religiosity in which most of them have been raised.

In the meantime, the military continue to search for the elusive formula that will enable them to speak the people's language. In a renewed effort to spark enthusiasm for the revolution, President Morales set off to visit different parts of the country in the first part of 1976. He seemed particularly anxious to seek the support of the church and even of the Apristas. To symbolize the new spirit of dialogue characteristic of the "Second Phase," which the post-Velasco period has been termed, President Morales visited Trujillo in late April and early May and called upon the citizens there to lay aside lingering bad memories over the massacre of 1932. The president's appeal was especially moving because his own father had been assassinated in 1939, allegedly by Apristas, while serving as a military commander in Trujillo. In Lima a week later, a still vigorous Haya de la Torre, now in his eighty-first year, presided over Apra's fifty-second anniversary. The Aprista chieftain welcomed Morales's gesture of reconciliation, although he also touched off rebellious cries of enthusiasm among younger Apristas when he demanded a quick return to a democratic form of government.[67]

Later, in June, the president visited Huaraz, Ayacucho, and other cities in the interior. In all of these places his public acts of piety drew attention. In Huaraz, he stood in reverence for a few moments before the image of Our Lord of Solitude, and in Ayacucho he meditated before the monument to the battle of Ayacucho.[68] In late July, on the feast of Saints Peter and Paul, popularly known in Peru as the "Pope's Day," the president and all high-ranking government officials attended a Mass in the cathedral. Far more than any previous president, Morales made explicit references to Christianity in almost all of his official addresses. After his trip to the North, he delivered a speech in Lima reaffirming the Christian nature of the revolution. In a peroration sprinkled with Pauline metaphors, he declared: "We are honest, we are patriots, we are Christians. We are armed with the sword of faith and defended by the shield of truth."[69] While no one questioned the sincerity of Morales, who is a practicing Catholic, it did seem as though he were making a studious effort to identify himself with the religious sentiments of the people.[70]

In the late seventies, the Peruvian revolution continues to be full of paradoxes. A party which has never been fully in power still commands the loyalty of thousands of Peruvians, while the military, who are implementing many reforms, fail to elicit much enthusiasm from the thousands who are intended to benefit from them. Older Apristas do not look favorably upon the radical leftists in the Catholic church, while young Peruvian Catholics view the Aprista party as a conservative force standing in the way of change. In the middle stands the church, committed to both tradition and change. In the meantime, millions of newly politicized lower-class Peruvians are beginning to forge the common national identity that has eluded Peru for so long.

CONCLUSION

The American philosopher Josiah Royce defined a true community as one in which the members share a common past and future. In many ways Peruvian history from the time of independence in 1824 on has been the story of culturally disparate communities struggling to overcome the liability of very different pasts in order to create a common future.

One lens through which to study this process of community building is that of religion, which was practically the only important cultural element that all Peruvians, whether they were upper-class white creoles or lower-class Indians and mestizos, held in common. In reality, however, religion itself served as an example of the profound psychological and cultural gap that separated the educated ruling minority from the politically marginal lower classes. For more than a century after independence most Peruvians who belonged to the cultural elite looked with indifference, scorn, and even hostility on the popular religious beliefs and practices of lower-class Indians, mestizos, and Negroes.

Even the minuscule group of enlightened Peruvians who made up the reformist elite and sought to close this cultural gap displayed similar attitudes toward the popular religiosity of the lower classes. Many of their negative attitudes can be traced to the reformist theories of the founding fathers of Peruvian liberalism, especially Manuel Lorenzo de Vidaurre, Francisco de Paula González Vigil, Francisco Javier Mariátegui, and Manuel González Prada.

Immersed in the philosophies of the Enlightenment and Gallicanism, Vidaurre, Vigil, Mariátegui, and other first-generation liberals defined national reforms principally in terms of curbing the power of the church. Influenced by three hundred years of the Patronato Real, these reformers barely distinguished between the institutional church and religion itself. For them, religion was

194

primarily an element of stability and order in man and society. In their mind, to subordinate the church to the interests of the new republic necessarily implied harnessing the religious instinct in all men for the benefit of society.

Disillusioned by the failure of first-generation liberalism to liberate Peru from the bondage of its colonial past, especially after Peru's defeat by Chile in the War of the Pacific, Manuel González Prada challenged his predecessors' notion that either the church or religion was useful for building up the new nation. Although he was fascinated by the positivist's emphasis on science and the anarchist's vision of the future, González Prada spent most of his time and energy exposing the evils of the past. In his negative critique of society, however, he made a positive contribution to the advance of ideas by sharpening the distinction between church and religion and by placing religion in the context of Peru's social problems. Although he aimed to direct the attention of fellow Peruvians away from the legal fixations of the earlier liberals to the real social problems of the country, González Prada himself fell short of fully understanding the cultural world of the Indians and lower-class mestizos, especially in the area of religion.

While reformers debated the possible good or bad influences of the church and religion on the lower classes, the Indians themselves provided evidence on the matter in the many uprisings that they staged during the nineteenth and early twentieth centuries. Two fundamental phenomena remained constant in most of the major recorded Indian uprisings that occurred between 1850 and 1900. In the first place, the church continued to exercise its traditionally enormous influence over the Indians, to the extent that in some cases the government even viewed the church as a major threat to its control over the Indians. In the second place, the Indians remained faithful to their popular religious practices during and after the uprisings. In the case of Atusparia's uprising in Huaraz in 1885, religious fervor even seemed to increase during the rebellion.

The conclusion to be drawn from these phenomena is that loyalty to a conservative church and traditional popular Catholicism did not in any significant way inhibit the Indians from fighting against social and political abuses in republican Peru. The liberals' notion of religion as an inherently stabilizing, and hence conservative, instinct in man made them incapable of observing this compatibility between revolution and religion that the Indians experienced.

Rising concern over the plight of the Indians gave rise to the *indigenista* movement after the War of the Pacific. The *indigenistas* applied González Prada's social revisionism to the interior provinces, where the Indian problem was the greatest, and they also forged the principal link between nineteenth-century liberalism and the twentieth-century social-reform movements. From the appearance of Clorinda Matto de Turner's *Aves sin Nido* in 1889 until Ciro Alegría's *El Mundo es Ancho y Ajeno* in 1940, *indigenista* literature aimed to expose the evils that the Indians suffered, particularly clerical exploitation, and to glorify Indian traditions and customs. Although many early *indigenistas* looked unsympathetically on the Indian's religious beliefs and practices, later *indigenistas* came to realize that they must study and take seriously popular religiosity if they were to remain consistent with their belief that national reform must take into account all important elements of Peruvian culture.

The *indigenistas* made two key discoveries that influenced other social thinkers in Peru. The first was that there was such a phenomenon as popular religiosity, which existed alongside of the official, clerical-dominated religion, and the second was that popular religiosity was an integral part of the people's culture. Although most *indigenistas* continued to be unsympathetic to many aspects of popular religiosity, others came to see in the people's religious practices and beliefs a positive source of strength for the coming revolution.

José Carlos Mariátegui, Peru's first great Marxist thinker, formally articulated the relationship between popular religiosity and social revolution. Raised in a traditional Catholic, lower-class home, he was always personally sympathetic to the popular religiosity of the lower classes. During his European stay, he was strongly influenced by the evolutionary vitalism of Henri Bergson and the revolutionary voluntarism of Georges Sorel, who proposed early Christianity as a model for socialists in their struggle against Western capitalism. Mariátegui rejected liberal anticlericalism because it failed to address itself to underlying social problems and because it conceived of religion in too narrow a fashion. Mariátegui saw religion as a dynamic element in man which inspires him to act and to create. Politics for him was in reality a secular extension of the religious instinct.

Under the notion of "myth," Mariátegui identified the coming social revolution as the religion of the future. In his *Siete Ensayos* and other writings, he expressed his belief that the popular religiosity of the lower classes would itself be the source of the new myth of the revolution. Mariátegui called for other social thinkers to study religion calmly and objectively as an integral part of national culture and not to dismiss it too quickly as a pernicious influence as many positivists had done. Mariátegui's sympathetic treatment of religion as a potential source of inspiration for social revolution strongly influenced many leftist humanists and a later generation of Christian social thinkers.

The task of testing the reformist theories and insights of the liberals, González Prada, the *indigenistas,* and Mariátegui fell to the Peruvian Aprista party, which spearheaded the cause of leftist reform in the thirties and forties in Peru. In the Popular Universities which Víctor Raúl Haya de la Torre and companion San Marcos University students founded to close the gap between the middle-class and lower-class workers, the reformist elite and the lower classes intermingled in intimate and sustained contact for the first time in modern Peruvian history. One result of the Popular University experiment was that González Prada radicalism and traditional popular Catholicism were brought together into a state of ambivalent coexistence, foreshadowing a similar mixing of anticlericalism with popular Catholicism in the Aprista party in the thirties. In the protest movement of May 23, 1923, against the consecration of Peru to the Sacred Heart, Haya de la Torre and other Popular University leaders applied their newly learned insights into the compatibility of religion and reform by successfully appealing to both the religious sentiments and the political frustrations of middle- and lower-class Peruvians.

The Popular University experiment convinced future Aprista leaders that only a populist amalgamation of many different classes and groups could win power in Peru and bring about a sweeping social revolution. This populist approach explains in great part Apra's flexibility in changing strategies and adapting to new situations. It also explains the reversal within the party from an initial official neutrality toward religion, with undertones of an unofficial anticlericalism, to an open appeal to the religious sentiments of Apristas during the thirties and forties. Two special circumstances favored this conversion of the Aprista party into a quasi-messianic movement. One was the party's fundamental cultural orientation, which aimed to transform the whole man; and the other was the series of persecutions to which the party was subjected. This mixing and blending of social reform and popular Catholicism, more than the explicit ideology of the party, explains to a great extent the enormous popularity of Apra among lower-class Peruvians during the years of the "Aprista Martyrdom" from 1931 to 1945.

Furthermore, the debate between Apristas and conservative Catholics over whether or not a Catholic could be an Aprista was less significant than the major shift in religious and political values among lower-class Apristas. Within Apra, Aprista Catholics found it possible to advocate social reform without rejecting their traditional religious beliefs, unlike the situation in some other Latin American countries where the Catholic Right monopolized the symbols of religious belief.

On a minor scale, the Aprista party symbolized the end of the century-long quest of the reformist elite to rediscover and understand the politically and socially marginal lower classes of their country. But Apra failed to include within its orbit the great majority of Peruvians who lived in the *sierra* or who began migrating to the coast after World War II. New personalities and forces that arose in the next several decades competed for the right to speak in the name of the newly emerging lower classes. For a brief period Fernando Belaúnde's star aroused the hopes of a new generation of reform-minded Peruvians. In the wake of the failure of the new reformist movements of the fifties and the sixties, the military who took power in 1968 appeared destined to break the impasse in the way to Peru's social transformation.

The new military regime proclaimed the beginning of a revolution inspired by the noblest ideals of Western humanism and Christianity. Whether they were cultural Catholics or convinced Christian idealists, the new military leaders were careful to cultivate the good will of the church and to respect the popular traditions of the lower classes. Certain Christian thinkers have exerted considerable influence in formulating the general philosophy of the revolution and several of its reform laws. Although the revolution itself is well received by the lower classes, the military regime has failed to create a mass-based movement in support of the revolution. The fundamental reason for this failure is that the military, unlike Apra, have not undergone the experience of building a movement from below in solidarity with the lower classes.

The Catholic church, which had always enjoyed a vital contact with the lower classes from colonial times, became the new forum in which the lower classes sought to integrate their popular traditions with their new expectations of radical social change. The church aimed to bring about change in the sixties and seventies by influencing the government elite and by identifying itself with the marginal poor. When churchmen began entering the life situation of the lower classes, they themselves became politicized and socially awakened in the process. From the vantage point of settlers in the *pueblos jóvenes* or peasants in the *sierra*, the church has criticized the military for failing to live up to their own message of revolutionary humanism.

Taken together, the *indigenistas*, Mariátegui, the Apristas, the military, and churchmen have all contributed to create the necessary psychological and intellectual climate in which religion and revolution could be viewed as harmonious and complementary realities in Peru. In another sense, however, these thinkers and leaders have only discovered and affirmed what has always been true among the Peruvian lower classes. In the process of searching, both the reformers and the lower classes substantially altered their respective religious and political world views. In so doing, they have also begun to create a community of shared symbols and expectations.

NOTES

NOTES TO THE INTRODUCTION

1. Fredrick B. Pike, *The Modern History of Peru* (New York: Frederick A. Praeger, 1967), p. 14.

2. Manuel Marzal, S.J., "Investigación e Hipótesis sobre la Religiosidad Popular," *Pastoral y Lenguaje, Colección del Instituto Pastoral Latinoamericano* (Bogotá: Indo-American Press Service, 1973), 18:20-22.

3. For two articles on the suffering Christ image in Latin America, see Leo T. Mahon, "*Machismo* and Christianity," *Catholic Mind* 63 (February, 1965): 4-11; and, Miles Richardson, Marta Eugenia Pardo, and Barbara Bode, "The Image of Christ in Spanish America as a Model for Suffering," *Journal of Inter-American Studies and World Affairs* 13 (April 1971): 246-57.

4. For a history of the devotion and procession, see Rubén Vargas, S.J., *Historia del Santo Cristo de los Milagros*, 3d ed. (Lima, 1966).

5. Manuel González Prada, *Presbiterianas* (Lima: Imprenta "El Olimpo," 1909), p. 10.

NOTES TO CHAPTER 1

The Great Temple of the Law

1. Karl Mannheim, *Ideology and Utopia: An Introduction to the Sociology of Knowledge*, trans. Louis Wirth and Edward Shils (New York: Harcourt, Brace and World, Inc., Harvest Books, n.d.), pp. 192-96.

2. Jorge Basadre, *Historia de la República del Perú, 1822-1933*, 6th ed. (Lima: Editorial Universitaria, 1968), 1:19.

3. For a study of the shift of the clergy to the conservative side, see the article by Fredrick B. Pike, "Heresy, Real and Alleged, in Peru: An Aspect of the Conservative-Liberal Struggle, 1830-1875," *Hispanic American Historical Review* 47 (February 1967): 50-74. Another study which places the blame for the increase of conservative ultramontanism more on the action of Rome, see the article by Antonine Tibesar, "The Peruvian Church at the Time of Independence in the Light of Vatican II," *The Americas* 26 (April 1970): 349-75.

4. Basadre, *Historia de la República del Perú*, 6:42-44. See also Raúl

Ferrero Rebagliati, *El Liberalismo Peruano: Contribución a una Historia de las Ideas* (Lima: Biblioteca de Escritores Peruanos, 1958), p. 25.

5. In his work on the subject, Richard Herr observes that in Spain "Jansenism" was frequently used interchangeably with "regalism" and that the reformers in Spain did not accept the doctrinal aspects of French Jansenism. *The Eighteenth Century Revolution in Spain* (Princeton, New Jersey: Princeton University Press, 1969), pp. 11–36, 398–434. For a complementary work that emphasizes the impact of these ideas on the ruling elite in Spain, see Jean Sarrailh, *La España Ilustrada de la Segunda Mitad del Siglo XVII* (Mexico, D.F.: Fondo de Cultura Economica, 1957).

6. José Ignacio Moreno, *Ensayo sobre la Supremacía del Papa, Especialmente con respecto a la Institución de los Obispos* (Lima: Imprenta de José Masías, 1831). For a further study of the influence of the Abbé de Pradt on Latin America, see Manuel Aguirre, *El Abate de Pradt en la Emancipación Hispanoamericana (1800–1830)*, Analecta Gregoriana, vol. 25 (Rome: Typis Pontificiae Universitatis Gregoriannae, 1941).

7. The only comprehensive study of Vidaurre is Jorge Guillermo Leguía's psychological portrait of the somewhat erratic and excessively scrupulous Peruvian jurist, *Manual Lorenzo de Vidaurre: Contribución a un Ensayo de Interpretación Sicológica* (Lima, 1935). A bibliography of Vidaurre's works is also included, pp. 211–31.

8. *Diccionario Enciclópedico del Perú*, 3: 352.

9. *Plan del Perú* (Philadelphia: Juan Francisco Hurtel, 1823), pp. 52–58. The *Plan* was originally written as a *fidelista* apology. The 1823 version included many new additions, influenced in part by Vidaurre's visits to France, England, and the United States. Also, Vidaurre was completely committed to independence by that time.

10. Ibid., pp. 94–95. In his condemnation of the sensuality of some nuns and their alleged illicit affairs, Vidaurre seems to revel in his own moral indignation, a curious reaction from one who later lamented his own sins of "pride" and "passion."

11. Ibid., p. 89.

12. *Proyecto del Código Eclesiástico* (Paris: Imprenta de Julio Didot, 1830), p. 169. Other legal works by Vidaurre concerning the church are his *Proyecto de Reforma de la Constitución Peruana* (Lima: Imprenta de J. M. Masías, 1833), in which he called for an end to church *fueros* and his *Proyecto del Código Civil Peruano*, 3 vols. (Lima, 1834–1836). Other more minor speeches and tracts related to the church are mentioned in Leguía's bibliography, pp. 211–31. Articles by Vidaurre may also be found in the following Limanian publications: *El Discreto* (1827); *El Revisor* (1827); *El Peruano* (1827); *El Fénix* (1834); and the *Triunfo de la Libertad* (1831) of Cuzco.

13. *Plan del Perú*, pp. 59–86.

14. *Vidaurre contra Vidaurre* (Lima: Imprenta del Comercio, 1839), p. 143.

15. *Escritos Políticos* (Lima: Imprenta del Estado por J. González, n.d.), p. 29.

16. *Proyecto de un Código Penal* (Boston: Hiram Tupper, 1828), p. 223.

17. Ibid., pp. 147–50, 223.

18. *Cartas Americanas, Politícas y Morales*, 2 vols. (Philadelphia: Juan F. Hurtel, 1823), 1:194–95.

19. *Escritos Políticos*, pp. 29–30.

20. *Vidaurre contra Vidaurre*, pp. 63–69.

21. Ibid., p. 120.

22. Unwilling to accept the condemnation of his work without a fight, Vidaurre unsuccessfully appealed for a court action to remove the ban. See *Informe Pronunciado en la Illma. Corte Superior de Justicia por el Promotor Fiscal de este Arzobispado, Sr. D. Pedro de Benavente* (Lima: Imprenta de J. M. Masías, 1840). Mariátegui's rebuttal appeared under the pseudonym, Marca-Martillas, *Defensa Católica del Primer Tomo del "Curso de Derecho Eclesiástico" del Sr. Vidaurre contra las Censuras del Presbitero D. José Mateo Aguilar y del P. F. Vicente Seminario* (Lima: Imprenta de Eusebio Aranda, 1840).

23. A good short biography of Vigil, including a comprehensive bibliography of his works, is contained in Jorge Guillermo Leguía, *Estudios Históricos* (Santiago de Chile: Ediciones Ercilla, 1939), pp. 34–62. A much longer biography with a highly positive but uncritical view of Vigil is that by Alberto González Marín, *Francisco de Paula González Vigil, El Precursor, El Justo, El Maestro* (Lima, 1961). Rubén Vargas's highly unfavorable portrait of Vigil is found in his *Historia de la Iglesia en el Perú*, 5 vols. (Burgos, Spain: Imprenta Aldecoa, 1962), 5: 228–236. González Prada's essay on Vigil is based upon Vigil's unpublished autobiographical sketch which he composed in 1867, "Apuntes acerca de mi Vida." González Prada, *Pájinas Libres* (Lima: Fondo de Cultura Popular, 1966), 1:83–97.

24. (Lima: Imprenta José Huidobro Molina, 1848–49), 1:22–23.

25. Ibid., 1:108–73; 6:230–31.

26. Ibid., 1:23.

27. Ibid., 6:219.

28. Ibid., 6:51–60.

29. Ibid., 6:142.

30. Ibid., 6:161–64.

31. Ibid., 6:243.

32. Vigil, *Cartas al Papa Pío IX con Varios Documentos al Caso* (Lima: Imprenta de "El Comercio," 1871). Although Vigil recognized papal primacy within the church, he did not accept the dogmatic definition of Vatican I on papal infallibility. For more on Vigil's public controversies with different churchmen, see Pike, "Conservative-Liberal Struggle," pp. 50–54.

33. Vigil, *Los Jesuitas Presentados en Cuadros Históricos*, 4 vols. (Lima: Imprenta de Manuel A. Reyes, 1863).

34. *Manual de Derecho Público-Eclesiástico para el Uso de la Juventud Americana* (Lima: Imprenta del "Pueblo," 1863).

35. *Roma: Opúsculo sobre el Principado Político del Romano Pontífice* (Lima: Imprenta de "El Comercio" por J. R. Sánchez, 1871).

36. *Diálogos sobre la Existencia de Dios y de la Vida Futura* (Lima: Imprenta del "Pueblo," 1863), p. 98.

37. "La Religión Natural," unpublished manuscript (Lima: National Library).

38. *De la Libertad de Cultos sin Religión del Estado* (Tacna, Perú: Imprenta de "El Porvenir" por José Huidobro Molina, 1961), p. 3. For a list of Vigil's other tracts on religious toleration, see Basadre, *Perú: Problema y Posibilidad* (Lima: Casa Editorial E. Rosay, 1931), p. 86.

39. *Manuel de Derecho Público-Eclesiástico*, pp. 182–83.

40. *Importancia de las Asociaciones; Importancia de la Educación Popular*, Alberto Tauro (Lima: Ediciones Hora del Hombre, 1948), pp. 119–20.

41. *Opúsculos Sociales y Políticos Dedicados a la Juventud Americana* (Lima: Tipografía de Guillermo Guerrero, 1862). See also, Vigil's *Catecismo Patriótico para el Uso de las Escuelas Municipales de la Ciudad del Callao* (Callao: Imprenta de Estéban Danino, 1859). Other political writings of Vigil may be found in the liberal newspaper that he, Mariátegui, Laso, José Gálvez and others published in Lima, *El Constitucional.*

42. Francisco Javier Mariátegui, *Refutación al Papel Titulado Abuso del Poder contra las Libertades de la Iglesia, Escrita por un Verdadero Católico* (Lima: Imprenta de Manuel Corbal, 1831).

43. Supra, note 22. In another polemical tract Mariátegui defended civil marriage: *Vindicación que la Mayoría de los Vocales de la Comisión de Códigos Presenta al Público contra las Imputaciones que se le Hacen por el S.D.D. Manuel Pérez de Tudela en la Nota con que Pasó al Ministerio El Proyecto del Código Civil, Escrita por uno de Ellos* (Lima: Imprenta de Eusebio Aranda, 1847).

44. Francisco Javier Mariátegui, *Reseña Histórica de los Principales Concordatos Celebrados con Roma* (Lima: Impreso por José María, 1856), pp. 4-5.

45. Patricio Matamoros [pseud.] , *Manual del Regalista, con la Agregación de la Carta Escrita al Sr. D. Francisco de Paula G. Vigil sobre la Infalibilidad y el Entredicho de Puno* (Lima: Imprenta del Universo, 1873).

46. Ibid., pp. 12-16.

47. Ibid., pp. 223-24.

48. Ibid., p. 269.

49. Vidaurre, *Proyecto del Código Eclesiástico*, pp. 3-9.

50. Vigil, *De la Libertad de Cultos sin Religión del Estado*, pp. 12-13, 28.

51. Mariano Amezaga, *Los Dogmas Fundamentales del Catolicismo ante la Razón* (Valparaiso, Chile: Tipografía de Justo Fierro, 1873), p. 2. Another writer of the period noted for his anti-Catholic diatribes was the Chilean-Peruvian, Francisco Bilbao. See, for example, his *La América en Peligro* (Santiago de Chile: Ediciones Ercilla, 1941).

52. Amezaga, *Los Dogmas Fundamentales*, p. 125.

53. Benito Laso, *El Poder de la Fuerza y el Poder de la Ley* (Lima: Ediciones Hora del Hombre, 1947), p. 61. This essay first appeared in *El Constitucional*, Lima, 1858. See also the series of debates between Laso and Bartolomé Herrera in *Artículos Editoriales del Correo Peruano Escritos por El S.D.D. Benito Laso* (Lima: National Library, n.d.). Other articles by Laso appeared in *El Censor Eclesiástico*, Cuzco, 1825, and *La Revista de Lima*, 1859-62.

54. Basadre, *Perú: Problema y Posibilidad*, pp. 100-105.

55. It is instructive in this regard to observe the negligible impact of the liberals on later Christian social thinkers. In Gustavo Gutiérrez's *A Theology of Liberation*, trans. Sister Caridad Inda and John Eagleson (Maryknoll, New York: Orbis Books, 1973), perhaps the most representative expression of social Catholicism in recent times, the only Peruvian before World War II who is cited as a precursor of social Catholicism is José Carlos Mariátegui.

NOTES TO CHAPTER 2

González Prada's Anti-Catholic Knee

1. Luis Alberto Sánchez, *Don Manuel*, 4th ed. (Lima: Populibros Peruanos, n.d.), p. 205. On another occasion González Prada referred to his "heretical knee." Private interview with Luis Alberto Sánchez, Lima, August 14, 1974.
   2. A few of the more commonly cited guides to González Prada's life and thought are: Luis Alberto Sánchez, *Don Manuel*, 4th ed. (Lima: Populibros Peruanos, n.d.); Adriana González Prada, *Mi Manuel* (Lima: Editorial Cultura Antártica, 1947); Eugenio Chang-Rodríguez, *El Pensamiento Político de González Prada, Mariátegui and Haya de la Torre* (Mexico: Ediciones Andrea, 1957). González Prada as a literary figure is studied in Luis Alberto Sánchez, *La Literatura Peruana* (Lima: Ediciones de Ediventas, 1965) 3:1050–68, and in Rufino Blanco Fombona, *Crítica de la Obra de González Prada* (Lima: Fondo de Cultura Popular, 1966). For a view of González Prada as a humanist, see Martin S. Stabb, *In Quest of Identity: Patterns in the Spanish American Essay of Ideas, 1890–1960* (Chapel Hill, North Carolina: University of North Carolina Press, 1967), pp. 102–45.
   3. Adriana González Prada, *Mi Manuel*, p. 135.
   4. Felix del Valle, "Nuestros Grandes Prestigios," *Revista de Actualidades* (July 14, 1917): 31–32.
   5. Manuel González Prada, *Baladas Peruanas* (Lima: Ediciones de la Biblioteca Universitaria, 1966), p. 77. In recognition of the indissoluble unity of content and form in poetry, the verses of González Prada selected in this chapter will hereafter be presented in the original Spanish, with a literal, "non-poetical" translation included in the notes to aid in capturing some of the poet's meaning and "feeling."

> Death to the Inca, death to the Inca!
> If you're afraid and hesitate,
> Give me the pen:
> I will sign the sentence.

6. Ibid., p. 111.

> But the priest, before the cadaver.
> Kneels in holy peace,
> And humbly prays
> The Office of the Dead.

7. Ibid., pp. 114–15.

> Goodbye my hut!
> Goodbye my fields!
> Goodbye! I am leaving
> To follow my loved one
> . . . .

You are silent, O my spouse,
You march in silence . . .
Cursed be the war!
Cursed be the white men!

8. González Prada, "Impresiones de un Reservista," *El Tonel de Diógenes* (Mexico City: Fondo de Cultural Económica, 1945), pp. 31-39.

9. Jorge Basadre, *Historia de la República del Perú* 6th ed. (Lima: Editorial Universitaria, 1969), 9:114-34.

10. González Prada, *Pájinas Libres* (Lima: Fondo de Cultura Popular, 1966) 1:60-67.

11. *La Integridad,* Lima, October 22, 1892, p. 1. *La Integridad* became the main organ of the Unión Nacional after the newspaper intended to be the principal organ of the party, *Germinal,* folded in 1899 after only eight editions. Another radical newspaper of the period which published González Prada's Politeama address and other essays in spite of official censure was *La Luz Eléctrica,* which appeared in Lima between 1886 and 1897. See also the organ of the Club Literario, *La Revista Social,* which appeared in Lima in 1885, and *El Radical,* Lima, 1889.

12. *La Integridad,* Lima, October 22, 1892, p. 1.

13. González Prada, *Horas de Lucha* (Lima: Fondo de Cultura Económica, Ediciones "Futuro," 1964), p. 27.

14. Jorge Basadre, *Historia de la República del Perú,* 9:234.

15. Luis Alberto Sánchez, *Antología del Pensamiento Democrático Americano: Manuel González Prada* (Mexico: Imprenta Universitaria, 1945), p. xi.

16. Felix del Valle, *Revista de Actualidades,* p. 32.

17. González Prada, *Horas de Lucha,* pp. 47-55.

18. The most important anarchist organs in Peru were *Los Parias,* which appeared in Lima from 1904 until 1910, and *La Protesta,* Lima, 1911-26. The most well-known contributor was González Prada, who frequently wrote under the pseudonym of Luis Miguel. A brief outline of anarchism in Peru and its publications may be found in Hugo García Salvatecci, *El Anarquismo Frente al Marxismo y el Perú* (Lima: Mosca Azul Editores, 1972), pp. 114-26. See also the work by one of Peru's anarchists, Juan Manuel Carreño, *La Anarquía en el Perú* (Callao, 1915).

19. Augusto Salazar Bondy, *Historia de las Ideas en el Perú Contemporáneo* (Lima: Francisco Moncloa, Editores, 1965), 1:10-37.

20. Hugo García Salvatecci, *El Pensamiento de González Prada* (Lima: Editorial Arica, 1972), p. 17.

21. Jorge Basadre, *Perú: Problema y Posibilidad* (Lima: Editorial E. Rosay, 1931), pp. 156-70.

22. González Prada, *Pájinas Libres,* 2:267-77.

23. González Prada, *Grafitos* (Paris: Tipografía de Louis Bellenand et Fils, 1937), p. 196. González Prada only published two prose works while living, *Pájinas Libres,* 1894, and *Horas de Lucha,* 1908. He also only published two works of poetry *Exóticas,* 1911, and in 1909, *Presbiterianas,* which appeared anonymously. Most of his other essays and poetry that appeared in different anarchist and freethinking publications were collected and published posthumously by his son, Alfredo González Prada, or by his biographer, Luis Alberto Sánchez.

24. González Prada, *Exóticas* (Lima: Tipografía de "El Lucero," 1911), p. 151.

25. Ibid., p. 51.

> Before the iniquitous drama of life
> My justice-seeking heart protests:
> I forgive my sorrows, but I will not forgive
> The eternal universal crucifixion.

26. González Prada, *Grafitos*, p. 202.

> In all things and beings
> There is a hidden pain,
> In death and in life
> There is a hidden suffering.
> What can a soul believe
> In this field of horror?
> What invisible planter
> Crosses the firmament
> Spilling in the wind
> His seeds of sorrow?

27. González Prada, *Trozos de Vida* (Paris, 1933), p. 46.

> Let us not imagine a Father
> Moved by cries of sorrow,
> A good Father soothing
> Wounded hearts.
> If there is an Omnipotent Being,
> A King of ants and coins
> Perhaps he is just as unjust
> As us men.

28. Ibid., p. 105.

> Happiness everywhere; not a cry
> Do earth, sea and wind hear;
> Peace everywhere: wolves and lambs
> Walk always together.
> Who worked this miracle?
> With the passage of time,
> God has become more human,
> At last he was merciful and good.

29. González Prada, *Libertarias* (Paris: Tipografía de Louis Bellenand et Fils, 1938), p. 117.

> But if today the Gods of Christian Faith
> Walk decrepitly toward their death
> Who will enlighten our way tomorrow?
> Science, the only God of the future.

30. González Prada, *Pájinas Libres*, 1:121.
31. González Prada, *El Tonel de Diógenes*, p. 199.
32. Ibid., pp. 234, 150-51.
33. González Prada, *Propaganda y Ataque* (Buenos Aires: Ediciones Imán, 1939), pp. 130-31.
34. González Prada, *Nuevas Páginas Libres* (Santiago de Chile: Editorial Ercilla, 1937), p. 58.
35. González Prada, *Horas de Lucha*, p. 217.
36. González Prada, *Nuevas Páginas Libres*, pp. 17-41.
37. González Prada, *Grafitos*, p. 182.
38. González Prada, *Horas de Lucha*, p. 217.
39. González Prada, *El Tonel de Diógenes*, pp. 133-34.
40. González Prada, *Nuevas Páginas Libres*, p. 51.
41. González Prada, *El Tonel de Diógenes*, p. 171. In other passages, however, González Prada found Protestant ceremonies just as "ridiculous" as the Catholic Mass. "The same thing can be said about religions as about diseases," he stated, "None are good." *Prosa Menuda* (Buenos Aires: Ediciones Imán, 1941), p. 51.
42. González Prada, *Nuevas Páginas Libres*, p. 53.
43. González Prada, *Anarquía* (Santiago de Chile: Editorial Ercilla, 1936), pp. 12-29.
44. Ibid., p. 125.
45. González Prada, *Propaganda y Ataque*, p. 93.
46. González Prada, *Horas de Lucha*, pp. 43-44.
47. Ibid., pp. 107-9.
48. González Prada, *Propaganda y Ataque*, p. 29.
49. González Prada, *Horas de Lucha*, p. 170.
50. Ibid., p. 98.
51. González Prada, *Propaganda y Ataque*, p. 47.
52. González Prada, *Horas de Lucha*, pp. 166-70.
53. González Prada, *El Tonel de Diógenes*, p. 42. An interesting remembrance of his Spanish sojourn is González Prada's collection of popular antireligious refrains. Ibid., pp. 87-112.
54. González Prada, *Nuevas Páginas Libres*, p. 59. At the same time, however, González Prada included among his favorite authors Cervantes and Quevedo, and he greatly admired Miguel de Unamuno, whom he honored by sending one of the few answers to letters he received. Luis Alberto Sánchez, *La Literatura Peruana*, 3:1063-65.
55. González Prada, *Horas de Lucha*, p. 162.
56. González Prada, *Propaganda y Ataque*, pp. 85-89.
57. Ibid., p. 118.
58. González Prada, *Horas de Lucha*, pp. 57-60.
59. González Prada, *Prosa Menuda*, p. 55. This was apparently not a threat in his own household, for his wife, Adriana, had renounced her faith after the death of their second child in 1890 and joined her husband as a freethinker. Adriana González Prada, *Mi Manuel*, pp. 163-64.
60. González Prada, *Horas de Lucha*, p. 68.
61. González Prada, *Prousa Menuda*, p. 156.
62. Most of González Prada's ideas on the Indians are found in his essay, "Nuestros Indios," *Horas de Lucha*, pp. 199-213.

63. Ibid., p. 211. Other impressions of González Prada on the disorientation of the Indians toward the War of the Pacific are found in Adriana González Prada, *Mi Manuel*, p. 83.

64. González Prada, *Prosa Menuda*, p. 156.

65. González Prada, *Horas de Lucha*, pp. 212-13.

66. González Prada, *Pájinas Libres*, 1:63-64; see also *Prosa Menuda*, p. 80.

67. González Prada, *Horas de Lucha*, pp. 137-38.

68. Ibid., p. 207; *Los Parias*, November, 1906, p. 1.

69. See especially his poems in *Presbiterianas* (Lima: Imprenta "El Olimpo," 1909), "En una Procesión," p. 10, and, "Milagro Excesivo," pp. 41-42. Such derision of popular piety was common in the Masonic or anarchist press. One author referred contemptuously to the Lord of Miracles procession as the people's funeral march for a "Dead God." *La Integridad*, November 26, 1892, pp. 2-3.

70. The articles from *La Lucha* were later collected and published in book form by Alfredo González Prada, *Bajo el Oprobio* (Paris: Tipografía de Louis Bellenand et Fils, 1933).

71. Luis Alberto Sánchez, *La Literatura Peruana*, 3:1063.

72. Luis Alberto Sánchez, *Don Manuel*, p. 191.

73. Felix del Valle, *Revista de Actualidades* (July 14, 1917): 34. Another character portrait of González Prada may be found in Alfredo González Prada's preface to *El Tonel de Diógenes*, pp. 11-18.

NOTES TO CHAPTER 3

Holy Week in Huaraz, 1885

1. *Plan del Perú* (Philadelphia: Juan Francisco Hurtel, 1823), p. 37. For the views which the liberal precursors of independence, such as José Baquíjano and Hipólito Unánue had of the Indian, see Felipe Barreda, *Vida Intelectual del Virreinato del Perú*, 3d ed. (Lima: Universidad Nacional Mayor de San Marcos, 1964), pp. 223-34, 247-50.

2. An exception among the first generation of liberals was Benito Laso, the liberal prefect and deputy from Puno who spoke out for the Indian on numerous occasions. See his *Exposición que Hace Benito Laso Diputado al Congreso por la Provincia de Puno* (Lima: Imprenta Republicana Administrada, 1826), p. 13, and his article in *El Constitucional*, April 15, 1858, pp. 38-39.

3. Jorge Basadre, *Historia de la República del Perú, 1822-1833*, 6th ed. (Lima: Editorial Universitaria, 1968), 4:98-99.

4. Thomas R. Ford, *Man and Land in Peru* (Gainesville: University of Florida Press, 1955), p. 12.

5. *Censo General de la República del Perú Formado en 1876* (Lima: Imprenta del Teatro, 1878), 6:364; 7:734. These figures must be taken as a general index only and not as a precise description because of the deficient census-taking techniques of the time as well as the ambiguous criteria for distinguishing Indians from mestizos and mestizos from whites. For a critique of the 1876 census, see the study by Alida Díaz, *El Censo General de 1876 en el Perú* (Lima: Seminario de Historia Rural Andina, 1974).

6. Ford, *Man and Land in Peru*, pp. 63-68. See also Emilio Romero,

Historia Económica del Perú (Buenos Aires: Editorial Sudamericana, 1949).

7. Ford, *Man and Land in Peru*, pp. 72–102. Though dated, the works of Hildebrando Castro Pozo are still valuable guides to the complex agrarian social structure in Peru, especially *Nuestra Comunidad Indígena* (Lima: Editorial "El Lucero," 1924), and *El Yanaconaje en las Haciendas Piuranas* (Lima: Compañía de Impresiones y Publicidad, 1947). A few of the more modern studies that help to clarify social relationships in the highlands are the works of the Instituto de Estudios Peruanos—Robert Keith, Fernando Fuenzalida et al., *La Hacienda, la Comunidad y el Campesino en el Perú* (Lima: Moncloa-Campodónico, Editores Asociados, 1970); and Fernando Fuenzalida, Enrique Mayer, et al., *El Indio y el Poder en el Perú* (Lima: Moncloa-Campodónico, Editores Asociados, 1970).

8. For an overview of republican legislation on Indians, see José Varallanos, *Legislación Indiana Republicana* (Lima: 1947), and Thomas M. Davies, Jr., *Indian Integration in Peru: A Half Century of Experience, 1900-1948* (Lincoln, Nebraska: University of Nebraska Press, 1970).

9. A Castro y Luna Victoria, *Relaciones Históricas sobre la Guerra y la Paz en el Perú* (Lima: Imprenta del Universo, 1884), p. vii.

10. Pascual Ahumada, *Recopilación Completa de Todos los Documentos Oficiales, Correspondientes y demás Publicaciones referentes a la Guerra que Ha Dado a Luz la Prensa de Chile, Perú y Bolivia*, 9 vols. (Valparaiso: Imprenta del Progreso, 1884), v, 5:404.

11. Javier Prado y Ugarteche, *Estado Social del Perú Durante la Dominación Española* (Lima: Imprenta de El Diario Judicial, 1894), pp. 161–62, 189.

12. Federico Amat, *Memoria Elevada por el Subprefecto de la Provincia, D. Federico Amat, a la Prefectura del Departamento de Puno, Mayo 25, 1898* (Lima: Biblioteca Nacional), pp. 3–4.

13. Ibid., pp. 13–17.

14. Mario Castro Arenas, *La Rebelión de Juan Santos Atahualpa* (Lima: Imprenta Editora Atlántida, 1973), pp. 9–18.

15. Boleslao Lewin, *La Rebelión de Tupac Amaru y los Orígenes de la Independencia de Hispanoamérica*, 3d ed. (Buenos Aires: Sociedad Editora Latinoamericana, 1967), pp. 229–75, 408–9. See also the studies by Daniel Valcárcel, *La Rebelión de Tupac Amaru*, 2d ed. (Mexico City: Fondo de Cultura Popular, 1973), and *Rebeliones Indígenas* (Lima: Editorial P.T.C.M., 1946).

16. For a brief history of banditry in Peru, see José Varallanos, *Bandoleros en el Perú* (Lima: Editorial Altura, 1937).

17. *El Comercio*, Lima, December 11, 1866, p. 2.

18. Ibid. See also the *Comercio's* editorial on the events of Huancané, December 12, 1866, p. 3, and Juan Bustamante, *Los Indios del Perú* (Lima: Imprenta dirigida por J. M. Monterola, 1867). This latter work contains many newspaper articles from *El Comercio* and other dailies on the uprising as well as a *Representación* by Bustamante in favor of the Indians.

19. *El Comercio*, Lima, February 22, 1868, p. 3. Born in the department of Puno, Bustamante was the son of a Spaniard and an Indian woman. A self-educated man, he attained the rank of colonel in the

battle of May 2, 1866, against Spain. He won distinction as a world traveler and as an exponent of Indian rights. While serving as Puno's deputy to congress, he was instrumental in having Huerta named as the first bishop of Puno, and he even helped defray the bishop's traveling expenses from Lima to Puno. His advocacy of Indian's rights and the mysterious disappearance of his body caused him to become the object of veneration by the Indians of Puno. His death helped inspire the formation of one of the first groups in Peru dedicated to the rights of Indians, La Sociedad Amiga de los Indios. See *El Comercio*, Lima, March 4, 1868, p. 3. For data on Bustamante, see Basadre, *Historia de la República del Perú*, 4:93-95; Alfonso Torres Luna, *Biografía de Juan Bustamante* (Lima: Imprenta "Lux," 1941).

20. *El Comercio*, Lima, January 19, 1868, p. 2.

21. Although Huerta wrote many notable pastoral letters while he was bishop of Puno and Arequipa, he made no reference to the Indian rebellion of 1866, at least in his known writings. Nevertheless, his pastoral letters, directed mainly against Masons, rationalists, and anticlericals, with whom he clashed on a number of occasions, provide an insight into the mentality of the Catholic hierarchy in nineteenth century Peru. See for example, his *Instrucción Pastoral que, sobre el Syllabus Publicado por Nuestro Santísimo Padre el Sr. Pío IX el 8 de Diciembre de 1864 Dirige a sus Amados Diocesanos el Iltmo. Obispo de la Diócesis* (Puno: Imprenta de D. Mariano C. Martínez, 1874); and his tract against Vigil, *Cartas del Illmo. y Rmo. Sr. D. D. Juan Ambrosio Huerta, Dignísimo Obispo de Puno al D. D. Francisco de Paula González Vigil, con motivo del Análisis que este Hizo de la Nota con que S. S. Illma. Contestó la Circular del Sr. Ministro del Culto sobre Supresión de las Comunidades Religiosas de la República* (Arequipa: Imprenta Seminario, 1873).

In 1869 Huerta and the regalista member of the Supreme Court, José Gregorio Paz Soldán, entered into a public debate over Huerta's rights to convoke a synod in his diocese and publish papal documents without the *pase*. For this controversy, see *Fundamentos en que se Apoya la Resolución Suprema Expedida el 20 del Actual sobre el Enjuiciamiento del Obispo de Puno y su Vicario General* (Lima: Imprenta del Estado, 1869). When the pastor of Lampa followed Paz Soldán's injunction not to adhere to the synod, Huerta placed Lampa under interdict. As a result of the storm created by the interdict, he was forced to resign in Puno, but later he was made bishop of Arequipa. For more details on Huerta, see Rubén Vargas Ugarte, S.J., *Historia de la Iglesia en el Perú* (Burgos, 1962), 5, 265-73.

22. *Documentos sobre la Destrucción de Fuerzas del Orden que a las Ordenes de los Subprefectos de las Provincias del "Dos de Mayo" y "Huamalíes," Marchaban a Restablecer la Tranquilidad en Aquellas Circunscripciones, Huánuco, Abril 21 de 1895* (Lima, Biblioteca Nacional), p. 3. See also *Informes Evacuados por el Jefe de la Expedición Pacificadora Enviada a Huánuco a Reestablecer el Orden, Huallanca, Junio 5 de 1895* (Lima, Biblioteca Nacional).

23. *El Comercio*, Lima, June 15, 1895, p. 3. The historian, José Varrallanos, also places much of the blame on Cacerists for stirring up

the Indians. *Historia de Huánuco* (Buenos Aires: Imprenta López, 1959), pp. 588-95.

24. Luis Cavero, *Monografía de la Provincia de Huanta* (Lima: Empreso Editorial Rimac, 1953), 1:245-50. See also Juan José Pino, *Las Sublevaciones Indígenas de Huanta* (Lima: Centro de Estudios Históricos y Militares, n.d.). See also the declaration by the people of Huanta disclaiming responsibility for the death of the bishop, Juan José Polo, *El Pueblo de Huanta ante la Opinión Pública* (n.p., n.d.).

25. *El País*, Lima, October 6, p. 2; October 21, p. 5, 1896; *El Comercio*, Lima, October 14, p. 1; October 29, p. 3; November 18, p. 1, 1896.

26. Cavero, 2:27.

27. *El País*, Lima, November 13, 1896, p. 2.

28. *El Comercio*, Lima, December 25, 1896, p. 2.

29. *El País*, December 25, 1896, p. 2; *El Comercio*, December 3, p. 1.

30. *El Comercio*, Lima, June 26, 1895, p. 2.

31. *Documentos sobre los Graves Sucesos Promovidos por los Indígenas de la Ciudad de Juli* (Lima: Biblioteca Nacional, November 12, 1896).

32. *Parte Elevada a la Subprefectura de la Provincia de Chucuito por el Comisario de Policía de la Frontera del Perú con Bolivia, informándole sobre los sucesos de Ilave. Ilave, Abril 10 de 1897* (Lima, Biblioteca Nacional), p. 3.

33. Ibid., pp. 1-2.

34. This can be said with certainty of Huerta, Betalleluz and Fidel Olivas Escudero in Huaraz. Although names may be deceptive, they are a helpful guide for determining social background. It is significant that the vast majority of the names of the priests listed in the *Guía Política, Eclesiástica y Militar del Perú* for the year 1873 were of Spanish origin and few Indian names appear. Pedro Cabello (Lima: Imprenta del Estado, 1873).

35. Antonio Raimondi, *El Departamento de Ancachs y Sus Riquezas Minerales* (Lima: Imprenta de "El Nacional," 1873), p. 19.

36. Ibid., pp. 35-40.

37. *Censo General*, 1:522.

38. Ibid., p. 524.

39. *El Comercio*, Lima, April 9, 1885, p. 1.

40. Manuel Reina Loli, "Causas del Movimiento Campesino de 1885," mimeographed (Lima, 1969), pp. 4-7. Ironically, in a letter to *El Comercio*, (April 10, 1885, p. 5) Noriega blamed the hacendados for instigating the Indians to revolt in order to avoid advancing the allotted tax for their Indians. But another writer refuted Noriega's contention by observing that it was precisely in the hacendados' interests to have the Indians further indebted to themselves. *El Comercio*, May 2, 1885, p. 3.

41. *El Comercio*, Lima, April 9, 1885, p. 1.

42. *El Comercio*, Lima, May 2, 1885, p. 3.

43. Noriega's ignominous flight stands in contrast to the first news dispatch of the uprising in *El Comercio*, which announced his total victory over the Indians. Lima, March 30, 1885, p. 2.

44. *Uchcu* means "tunnel" or "mine" in Quechua. It was also the name of the mine where Pedro Cochachín worked. Ernesto Reyna, *El Amauta Atusparia* 2d ed. (Lima, 1932), p. 47.

45. There are several chronicles of Atusparia's uprising that, although they vary in details such as exact dates, number of Indians involved, and certain

names, all agree on major people and events: Ernesto Reyna, *El Amauta Atusparia*, 2d ed. (Lima, 1932); Jorge Basadre, *La Multitud, la Ciudad y el Campo en la Historia del Perú*, 2d ed. (Lima: Editorial Huascarán, 1947), pp. 244–48; Santiago Antúnez de Mayolo, "La Sublevación de los Indios del Callejón de Huaylas," *Ediciones de la Revista El Luzuriaguino* (Lima, 1957); Artemio Angeles Figueroa, *Yungay, Tierra Mía* (Lima, 1963), pp. 106–22; Félix Alvarez Brun, *Ancash: Una Historia Regional Peruana* (Lima, 1970), pp. 199–208. None of these accounts, however, attempt to analyze the ways in which religion influenced the course of events.

    46. Quoted in *El Comercio*, April 9, 1885, p. 1.

    47. *El Bien Público*, Lima, May 5, 1885, p. 3.

    48. *El Comercio*, Lima, April 10, 1885, p. 2.

    49. Reyna, *El Amauta Atusparia*, pp. 34–36. Reyna was a socialist who wrote his chronicle of Atusparia as part of the socialist-*indigenista* movement of the nineteen twenties to glorify the Indian. He asked José Carlos Mariátegui to write the preface to the first edition, and Mariátegui's secretary, Ricardo Martínez de la Torre, to write the preface to the second edition in 1932. In the first preface (1929), Mariátegui himself notes that Reyna describes his characters somewhat romantically and that the chronicle is more of a "newspaper story than an historiographical essay." Ibid., p. 13. Nevertheless, Reyna's chronicle has great historical value because he went out to the *estancias* and villages around Huaraz to interview Indians who remembered Atusparia and the uprising. An indication of the general veracity of his chronicle is the fact that Reyna, known for his anticlerical tendencies, portrays the clergy of Huaraz rather favorably, an impression that he based upon the testimony of the Indians. Reyna later became an Aprista and served as the Aprista deputy from Casma, Ancash, in 1962. Other works by Reyna are *Los Tesoros de Huarmey* (Lima: Editorial Perú Actual, 1936), and *Fitzcarrald, el Rey del Caucho* (Lima: P. Barrantes Castro, 1942). These data on Reyna were obtained in a private interview with his nephew, Manuel Reina Loli, himself an historian of the department of Ancash, Lima, August 15, 1974.

    50. *El Comercio*, Lima, April 9, 1885, p. 1.

    51. *El Comercio*, Lima, May 28, 1885, p. 2.

    52. Fidel Olivas Escudero, *Curso de Geografía para Escuelas y Colegios de Instrucción Media Arreglado conforme al Programa Oficial*, 2d ed. (Lima: Imprenta Calle del Mascarón, 1889). The pages referring to the uprising are found only in the first edition of 1887, pp. 124-25. The *Geografía* of Olivas Escudero is of special value because it is one of the few works composed by an eyewitness that has not been lost or destroyed. For reasons unknown, Olivas Escudero deleted the section on the uprisings in the second edition, which appeared in 1889. Both editions are found in the private library of Manuel Reina Loli, Lima.

    53. Reyna, *El Amauta Atusparia*, pp. 41–42.

    54. Antúnez de Mayolo, "La Sublevación," p. 16.

    55. Reyna, *El Amauta Atusparia*, p. 52. Reyna also reports of a Mass of thanksgiving which Atusparia ordered to be said on the first Sunday after the seizure of Huaraz. Ibid., pp. 34–36.

    56. Alfonso Ponte, *Por la Senda* (Lima: Imprenta Gráfica "Stylo," 1943), p. 96. The "pesos" and the "óbolo" refer to the "widow's mite" offering for the poor. Father Ponte, currently a canon of the cathedral in Lima and director

of the cathedral library, was a parish priest in Sihuas and rector of the seminary of Huaraz in the twenties and thirities. He conversed with Olivas Escudero when the latter returned from his diocese of Ayacucho to visit Huaraz on different occasions. Also Ponte, a Quechua-speaker, gathered much of his information directly from the Indians of the region. Private interview, Lima, June 10, 1975.

57. Ibid., p. 96.

58. Manuel Reina Loli, "Monseñor Fidel Olivas Escudero," *Justitia et Pax: En Memoria de Mons. Fidel Olivas Escudero* (Lima, 1971), pp. 235-57.

59. Ponte, *Por la Senda*, pp. 96-97.

60. Reyna, *El Amauta Atusparia*, p. 47; Angeles Figueroa, *Yungay, Ancash*, pp. 109-113.

61. Olivas Escudero, *Curso de Geografía*, p. 125.

62. Ibid., p. 126.

63. Angeles Figueroa, *Yungay, Ancash*, pp. 116-17.

64. For the progress of the army as it advanced on Huaraz, see *El Comercio*, Lima, April 16, p. 1; May 20, p. 3, 1885. See also the official military reports from the field, *Oficio Dirigido por el Prefecto del Departamento de Ancash, al Ministro de Gobierno, Dándole Cuenta de los Sucesos que Han Tenido Lugar en esa Villa y las Incidencias de la Toma del Pueblo de Yaután, Casma, Marzo 29 de 1885* (Lima: Biblioteca Nacional).

65. There is some disagreement over why the Indians held the procession while fully conscious of the approach of the enemy. Ernesto Reyna claims that Atusparia wanted to build barricades but that he lost control of the Indians, who in their fear and confusion reverted to drinking and religious practices in search of "security." Reyna, *El Amauta Atusparia*, pp. 66-67. Manuel Reina Loli, however, is of the opinion that Atusparia wanted the procession to take place precisely as a means of calming the Indians and preventing mass looting of the stores. Private interview, Lima, August 15, 1974.

66. Olivas Escudero, *Curso de Geografía*, pp. 125-26; Alvarez Brun, *Ancash*, p. 207.

67. As late as June, 1885, Iraola confessed to the central government that the region was far from being pacified. He was referring to Uchcu Pedro's guerrilla activity. *Oficio Dirigido por el Prefecto del Departamento de Ancash al Director de Gobierno Haciendole Ver la Imposibilidad de la Salida de las Fuerzas de Policía de ese Lugar a Casma en el Tiempo que él Indica, para Hacer Frente a los Montoneros. Huaraz, Junio 11, 1885* (Lima: Biblioteca Nacional).

68. Alvarez Brun, *Ancash*, p. 208; Antúnez de Mayolo, "La Sublevación," pp. 12-13.

69. Olivas Escudero, *Obras de Monseñor Dr. Fidel Olivas Escudero, Obispo de Ayacucho* (Lima: Imprenta Comercial de Horacio la Rosa, 1911), 2:274.

70. See his six volume collected works cited above. In Ayacucho Olivas Escudero founded another newspaper, *El Estandarte Católico*, and wrote a history of the region, *Apuntes para la Historia de Huamanga o Ayacucho, con Motivo del Primer Centenario de la Batalla, 1824-1924* (Ayacucho: Imprenta Diocesana, n.d.).

71. A news item in *La Integridad* (September 28, 1889, p. 2) reported that the political club in favor of Nicolás de Piérola was headed by Fidel Olivas Escudero and several other leading citizens of the city, and composed of "forty Indians."

72. *El Comercio*, Lima, November 24, 1866, p. 4.

73. *El Comercio*, Lima, November 17, 1866, p. 4.

74. *Causa Celebre: Informe del Dr. Sr. Fernando Palacios ante la Excelentísima Corte Suprema de Lima, por la Combustión de la India Llamada Bruja Benigna Huamán en el Pueblo de Bambamarca* (n.p., n.d.).

75. *El Comercio*, Lima, October 19, 1896, p. 3. It is also interesting to note that a number of priests joined the Sociedad Amiga de los Indios. See, *El Perú Católico*, Lima, October 24, 1867, p. 1.

76. There were many more, little-studied Indian uprisings that took place in the early twentieth century. One of the most important was an uprising in the Puno region in late 1915 led by a mestizo army officer who renamed himself "Rumi Maqui." For accounts of the uprising, which resulted in a massacre of the Indians, see *El Comercio*, Lima, December 4 (morning edition), p. 1; December 6 (afternoon edition), p. 1; December 17 (morning edition), p. 1, 1915. See also Jorge Basadre, *Historia de la República del Perú* 12:251-53, 489-91.

NOTES TO CHAPTER 4

The Rediscovery of Peru

1. Luis Alberto Sánchez observes the distinction made by other literary critics between *indigenismo*, a literary-political movement aimed at liberating the Indian economically and socially, and *indianismo* ("Indianism"), a strictly literary movement that treats the Indian as an object of romantic curiosity. Luis Alberto Sánchez, *La Literatura Peruana* (Lima: Ediciones de Ediventas, 1965), 3:968. For a brief overview of the *indigenista* movement, see Jose Matos Mar, "El Indigenismo en el Peru," in *El Indio y el Poder en el Perú* (Lima: Instituto de Estudios Peruanos, Moncloa-Campodónico Editores Asociados, 1970), pp. 202-14. See also the survey by Jorge Basadre, *Historia de la Republica del Peru*, 6th ed. (Lima: Editorial Universitaria, 1970), 16:27-34. For a study of the *indigenista's* impact on legislation, see Thomas M. Davies, Jr., *Indian Integration in Peru: A Half Century of Experience, 1900-1948* (Lincoln, Nebraska: University of Nebraska Press, 1970), pp. 44-76.

2. For a fuller discussion of Narciso Aréstegui and the *costumbrista* school, see Luis Alberto Sánchez, *La Literatura Peruana*, 2:945-49; and, Mario Castro Arenas, *La Novela Peruana y la Evolución Social*, 2nd ed. (Lima: José Godard, Editor, n.d.), pp. 45-61.

3. In his *Tradiciones Peruanas*, Ricardo Palma, referring to Aréstegui's novel, relates of a priest, Eugenio Oroz, who murdered one of his penitents, Angélica Barreda, in Cuzco in 1836 (Lima: Editorial Cultura Antártica, 1951) 5:107-9.

4. Narciso Aréstegui, *El Padre Horán*, 2 vols. (Lima: Editorial Universo, n.d.), 1:230-37.

5. Ibid., 2:91-97.

6. Aréstegui wrote another novel, *El Angel Salvador* (Lima: "El Comercio," 1872) on the evil influence of the *beatas* of Cuzco on the youth of the city. Literarily, it made little impact.

7. Clorinda Matto de Turner, *Hima-Sumac* (Lima: Imprenta la Equitativa, 1892), pp. 18-19, 24, 53, 83. Another example of the romanticized image of the Indian is the drama, *¡Pobre Indio!*, produced by Juan Camacho and Juan Cossío in 1868. (Lima: Imprenta Liberal, 1868).

8. José Itolararres [Juan Torres Lara], *La Trinidad del Indio o Costumbres del Interior* (Lima: Imprenta "Bolognesi," 1885).

9. For a discussion of the role of the nineteenth-century literary clubs in politicizing artists and writers, see Augusto Tamayo Vargas, *Literatura Peruana* (Lima: Imprenta de la Universidad Nacional Mayor de San Marcos, 1954), 2: 169–74.

10. Clorinda Matto de Turner, *Aves sin Nido* (Buenos Aires: Ediciones Solar/Hachette, 1968), p. 48.

11. Ibid., pp. 48–49.

12. Ibid., p. 71.

13. Ibid., p. 61.

14. Ibid., p. 102. Matto de Turner's strong Christian sentiments led her to translate into Quechua for the American Bible Society the Gospels of Saint Luke and Saint John and a few epistles of Saint Paul, In her own words, she did the translations so that "with the Gospel, light and consolation will reach the homes of the Indians." *El Evangelio Según San Lucas en Quechua y Castellano*, 2d ed. (Lima: Imprenta El Progreso, 1912), p. 34. An anonymous spokesman for the Catholic press, however, found *Aves sin Nido* "immoral and irreligious" because it attacked a bishop and exposed the bad "customs" of priests. *Una Ojeada a la Novela 'Aves sin Nido'* (Cuzco: Tipografía de Propaganda Católica, 1891), p. 4.

15. Clorinda Matto de Turner, *Tradiciones Cuzqueñas* (Lima: Imprenta de Torres Aguirre, 1884), 1:191–95. Matto de Turner composed two other novels which failed to win the same acclaim as *Aves sin Nido: Indole,* 1891, and *Herencia,* 1895. *Indole* resembles Aréstegui's *El Padre Horán* because it deals with the attempts of a priest in the mountain-jungle region of Cajamarca to dominate women through the confessional. *Herencia* is a sequel to *Aves sin Nido,* but this time it is situated in Lima, thus losing the *indigenista* theme. Matto de Turner's criticism of the clergy as well as her strong pro-Cácerist stand led to her deportation from Peru in 1895 when Nicolás de Piérola seized power. She died in 1909 without ever returning to her native land. For more on the life of Peru's first great *indigenista,* see Sánchez, *La Literatura Peruana,* 2:1070-11 and, Castro Arenas, *La Novela Peruana,* pp. 105-12.

16. Dora Mayer de Zulen, *El Indígena Peruano a los Cien Años de República Libre e Independiente* (Lima, 1921), pp. 89-95.

17. Mercedes Cabello de Carbonera, "Una Fiesta Religiosa en un Pueblo del Perú," *El Ateneo de Lima* 3 (1887):185.

18. Ibid., pp. 185-86. For Cabello de Carbonera's religious views, see her tract, *La Religión de la Humanidad: Carta al Señor D. Juan Enrique Lagarrigue* (Lima: Imprenta de Torres Aguirre, 1893).

19. Alejandro Maguiña, *Informe del Delegado Maguiña,* in *La Raza Indígena en los Albores del Siglo XX* (Lima: Imprenta Calle de Filipinas, 1902), pp. 107-8.

20. Ibid., pp. 118, 120-21, 145-46.

21. Ibid., p. 94.

22. Pedro Irigoyen, *Inducciones acerca de la Civilización Incaica* (Lima: Imprenta "La Industria," 1909), pp. 108-9.

23. Luis Aguilar, *Cuestiones Indígenas* (Cuzco: Tipografía de El Comercio, 1921), p. 15.

24. Hildebrando Fuentes, *El Cuzco y sus Ruinas* (Lima, 1905), p. 186. Another author who described the religious customs of the Indians referred to

the "deviation of the religious sentiments" in the primitive Peruvians as the cause of the "superstitious beliefs" of contemporary Indians. Toribio Mejía Xesspe, *Algunas Costumbres y Creencias de los Indígenas* (Lima, 1922), p. 42.

25. Dora Mayer de Zulen, *El Indígena Peruano*, pp. 11-12.

26. Hildebrando Castro Pozo, *Nuestra Comunidad Indígena* (Lima: Editorial "El Lucero," 1924), p. 57.

27. Ibid., p. 206.

28. Ibid., p. 229. Other works of this period which refer to the work of the church among the Indians are Carlos Valdez de la Torre, *Evolución de las Comunidades de Indígenas* (Lima: Editorial Euforion, 1921), and Moisés Saenz, *Sobre el Indio Peruano y su Incorporación al Medio Nacional* (Mexico City: Publicaciones de la Secretaría de Educación Pública, 1933).

29. A "first generation" of pro-Indian newspapers besides *El Deber Pro-Indígena* and *La Autonomía* included *La Crítica* and *El Indio* in Lima and *El Volcán* and *El Ariete* in Arequipa. See Mayer de Zulen, *El Indígena Peruano*, pp. 98-99. A list of the principal *indigenista* publications in the twenties is provided in *La Sierra*, nos. 25-26, 1929, p. 1. For the membership and statutes of the Grupo Resurgimiento, see *Amauta* (January, 1927):37-38.

30. Luis Valcárcel, José M. Valega, Rafael Larco Herrera and Santiago Antúnez de Mayolo, *Hacia el Despertar del Alma India* (Lima: Southwell, 1929), p. 1.

31. Luis Valcárcel, *Tempestad en los Andes* (Lima: Editorial Universo, 1972), pp. 21-22.

32. José Uriel García, *El Nuevo Indio* (Lima: Editorial Universo, 1973), "Prolog to the First Edition." Both Uriel García and Valcárcel were students at the National University of Cuzco when they participated together in a strike to bring in a new rector in 1910. The new rector, fondly referred to by both Valcárcel and Uriel García, was the American-born economist and administrator Alberto Giescke, who thoroughly renovated the university and fostered the study of archeology and Cuzco's Indian past.

33. Luis Valcárcel, *De la Vida Incaica* (Lima: Editorial Garcilaso, 1925), p. 11.

34. José Frisancho, *Del Jesuitismo al Indianismo* (Cuzco: Talleres Tipográficos "Imperial," 1931), p. 121. For an earlier example of anti-Limanian sentiment among *indigenistas*, see the novel by Joaquín Capelo, *Los Menguados* (Madrid: Librería de Fernando Fé, 1912).

35. Emilio Romero, "Las Campanas Religiosas de Ayer y los Tiempos Nuevos," *La Sierra* (January, 1927): 27-30; and "El Cuzco Católico," *Amauta* (December, 1927):54. Romero's ideas are cited by José Carlos Mariátegui in his *Siete Ensayos de Interpretación de la Realidad Peruana*, 11th ed. (Lima: Empresa Editora Amauta, 1967), pp. 149-50, and by Uriel García, *El Nuevo Indio*, p. 128.

36. Emilio Romero, *3 Ciudades del Perú* (Lima: Imprenta Torres Aguirre, 1929), p. 7.

37. Ibid., p. 16. The *ayllu* was the fundamental social group in the highlands, based on kinship and ties to the land. See J. Alden Mason, *The Ancient Civilizations of Peru* (Baltimore: Penguin Books, 1957), pp. 170-75.

38. Romero, *3 Ciudades del Perú*, p. 17.

39. Ibid., p. 34. The colors of the rainbow were those that appeared on Inca banners, and the *quipus* were knotted cords used by the Incas to record quantities and transmit messages.

40. Ibid., p. 35.

41. Ibid., p. 39.

42. Ibid., pp. 24-25.

43. Uriel García, *El Nuevo Indio*, p. 142.

44. Ibid., pp. 128-29.
45. Ibid., pp. 126-27.
46. Ibid., pp. 167-68.
47. Ibid., pp. 168-69.
48. Ibid., p. 123.
49. J. Eugenio Garro, "La Iglesia y el Estado," *Amauta* (November-December, 1928):35-36.
50. Luis Valcárcel, *De La Vida Incaica*, p. 99.
51. Luis Valcárcel, *Mirador Indio* (Lima, 1937), p. 37. Valcarcel's view of the past was influenced in part by his own studies of pre-Inca and Inca religiosity with which he initiated his career. See, for example, his bachelor's thesis, *Kon, Pachacamac Virakocha* (Cuzco: Imprenta de "El Trabajo," 1912). For another romanticized view of the Inca religion dating from this period, see the novel by Augusto Aguirre Morales, *El Pueblo del Sol* (Lima: Imprenta Torres Aguirre, 1927).
52. Vicente Mendoza Díaz, "La Cuestión Religiosa Indígena en el Perú," *La Sierra*, no. 29 (1929):30-32.
53. *La Sierra* (May, 1927):35-39. See also a similar comparison by Ernesto Reyna, *La Sierra* (April-May, 1928):15-16.
54. Valcárcel, *Tempestad en los Andes*, pp. 85, 88-91, 123-24; *La Sierra*, (August, 1927):1-3.
55. Valcárcel, *Tempestad en los Andes*, pp. 161-67. José Carlos Mariátegui also believed that the Protestant missions in Latin America suffered because of their identification with North American imperialism. Mariátegui, *Siete Ensayos*, p. 167.
56. *La Sierra* (January, 1927):30. For a history of Protestantism in Peru, see "El Protestantismo Anglosajón en el Perú, 1822-1915" by María Elvira Romero San Martín (Ph.D. diss., Catholic University of Lima, 1974).
57. Alfonso Molina (ed.), *Cuentos Revolucionarios del Perú* (Lima: Ediciones América Latina, 1967), pp. 41-67. For another story of the same period depicting rather humorously the strength of popular Catholicism in the Andes, see "La Mula de Taita Ramún," by Enrique López Albujar, *Cuentos Andinos* 6th ed. (Lima: Editorial Juan Mejía Baca, 1971), pp. 117-39.
58. *El Tiempo*, Lima, April 12, 1917, p. 4. In the thirties Luis Valcárcel also composed a similarly sympathetic account of the great Limanian procession. *Mirador Indio* (Lima, 1937), pp. 76-77.
59. José Frisancho, pp. 131-45.
60. Uriel García, *La Sierra* (April, 1927):19-22.
61. Romero, *3 Ciudades del Perú*, pp. 90-101.
62. Ibid., pp. 98-101.
63. *La Puna*, Ayaviri, September 30, 1927, pp. 1-3.
64. Ernesto Reyna, *El Amauta Atusparia*, 2d ed. (Lima, 1932), pp. 35-36.

NOTES TO CHAPTER 5

Eulogy to an Ascetic Cell

1. See the two short biographies of Mariátegui by two of his close collaborators, María Wiesse, *José Carlos Mariátegui, Etapas de su Vida*, 3d ed. (Lima: Empresa Editora Amauta, 1971), and Armando Bazán, *Mariátegui y su Tiempo*

(Lima: Empresa Editora Amauta, 1969). See also Jorge Basadre's summary of Mariátegui's life and development in *Historia de la República del Perú*, 6th ed. (Lima: Editorial Universitaria, 1970), 13:321–37. The most recent and fullest bibliography of Mariátegui is that by Guillermo Rouillón, *La Creación Heroica de José Carlos Mariátegui*, 2 vols. (Lima: Editorial Arica, 1975). See also Guillermo Rouillón's *Biobibliografía de José Carlos Mariátegui* (Lima: University of San Marcos Press, 1963). For an overall survey of Mariátegui's thought, see Eugenio Chang-Rodríguez, *La Literatura Política de González Prada, Mariátegui y Haya de la Torre* (Mexico City: Ediciones de Andrea, 1957). Two works which study the sources and intellectual influences of Mariátegui are Diego Meseguer, *José Carlos Mariátegui y su Pensamiento Revolucionario* (Lima: Instituto de Estudios Peruanos, 1974), and Harry E. Vanden, *Mariátegui: Influencias en su Formación Ideológica* (Lima: Empresa Editora Amauta, 1975). See also the study by Jesús Chavarría, "José Carlos Mariátegui, Revolutionary Nationalist: The Origins and Crisis of Modern Peruvian Nationalism, 1870–1930" (Ph.D. diss., University of California, Los Angeles, 1967).

2. María Wiesse, *José Carlos Mariátegui*, p. 16.

3. *El Mercurio Peruano*, Lima, vol. 20, 1930–31, p. 206.

4. *El Amigo del Clero*, June, 1933, p. 124.

5. José Carlos Mariátegui, *El Alma Matinal y Otras Estaciones del Hombre de Hoy*, 4th ed. (Lima: Empresa Editora Amauta, 1972), p. 94.

6. Mariátegui, *La Novela y la Vida* 3rd ed. (Lima: Empresa Editora Amauta, 1967), pp. 154–55.

7. *La Prensa*, Lima, April 11, p. 2.

8. *La Prensa*, Lima, October 20, 1914, p. 3.

9. The entire sonnet consisted of four stanzas:

Elogio de la Celda Ascética

Piadosa celda guardas aromas de breviario,
tienes la misteriosa pureza de la cal
y habita en ti el recuredo de un Gran Solitario
que se purificara del pecado mortal.

Sobre la mesa rústica duerme un devocionario
y dice evocaciones la estampa de un misal;
San Antonio de Padua, exangüe y visionario
tiene el místico ensueño del Cordero Pascual.

Cristo Crucificado llora ingratos desvíos.
Mira la calavera con sus ojos vacíos
que fingen en las noches una inquietante luz.

Y en el rumor del campo y de las oraciones
habla a la melancólica paz de los corazones
la soledad sonora de San Juan de la Cruz.

The eulogy, which originally appeared in *El Tiempo*, Lima, August 28, 1916, p. 3, is reproduced in Wiesse, *José Carlos Mariátegui*, pp. 16–17.

10. *Colónida*, Lima, March 1, 1916, pp. 26–27.

11. Alberto Hidalgo, *Arenga Lírica al Emperador de Alemania* (Arequipa: Quiroz Hnos., 1916).

12. "Yo creo en Dios sobre todas las cosas y todo lo hago, devota y unciosa-

mente en su nombre bendito. Cual el emperador Constantino, yo acometo mis empresas por la señal de la santa cruz. Soy cristiano, humilde y débil y no puedo sentirme Luzbel. Y pienso que Dios me asiste y me consuela cuando lo invoco." *El Tiempo,* Lima, January 1, 1917, p. 10.

13. *El Tiempo,* Lima, February 17, p. 1.

14. *La Crónica,* Lima, April 10, 1917, pp. 12-13; *El Tiempo,* Lima, April 12, 1917, p. 4.

15. Ibid. For a history of the procession, see Rubén Vargas Ugarte, S.J., *Historia del Santo Cristo de los Milagros,* 3d ed. (Lima, 1966).

16. Luis Alberto Sánchez noted that Mariátegui preferred to discuss writers in touch with the revolutionary events of postwar Europe. Yet Sánchez does not accept the opinion of Mariátegui's son, Sandro, that his father had repudiated his pre-1919 essays and poems. Luis Alberto Sánchez, *Testimonio Personal* (Lima: Ediciones Villasán, 1969), 1:300-303.

17. On one occasion Mariátegui defended Haya de la Torre against the charge of having discovered arbitrarily a political significance in *Don Quijote.* Said Mariátegui: "But the case is that politics, which Haya and I feel to be elevated to the category of a religion, is, as Unamuno says, the very essence of history." *Amauta,* (October, 1926):47.

18. In a letter dating from his Marxist period, Mariátegui referred to his wife, Ana Chiappe, as "God's design." Mariátegui, *La Novela y la Vida,* p. 93.

19. Bazán, *Mariategui y su Tiempo,* p. 82.

20. Mariátegui criticized the church for its intransigence in the Mexican revolution in *Temas de Nuestra América* (Lima: Empresa Editora Amauta, 1960), pp. 43-46, and he accused some priests of fomenting religious fanaticism among the Indians in order to secure their dominion over them in *Ideología y Política,* 3d ed. (Lima: Empresa Editora Amauta, 1972), pp. 57-58.

21. *La Prensa,* Lima, "Voces," November 12, 1918, p. 2.

22. A study of the influences on Mariátegui during his European stay may be found in Meseguer, chapter 2 "Encuentro del Socialismo Revolucionario Europeo," *José Carlos Mariátegui y su Pensamiento Revolucionario,* pp. 61-147.

23. Mariátegui, *El Alma Matinal,* p. 24.

24. During his lifetime, Mariátegui only published the two books, *La Escena Contemporánea* and *Siete Ensayos.* His family published the great majority of his writings from 1923 to 1930 posthumously under titles drawn from one or another of Mariátegui's essays.

25. Mariátegui, *El Alma Matinal,* p. 24.

26. Ibid., pp. 20-21.

27. Ibid., p. 89; Mariátegui, *Cartas de Italia,* 2d ed. (Lima: Empresa Editora Amauta, 1972), pp. 139-40.

28. Mariátegui, *El Alma Matinal,* p. 27.

29. Ibid., p. 28.

30. For a study of Bergson's impact on Peru, see the relevant sections of Augusto Salazar Bondy, *Historia de las Ideas en el Perú,* 2 vols., 2d ed. (Lima: Francisco Moncloa, Editores, 1967).

31. Víctor Andrés Belaúnde's *La Realidad Nacional,* 3d ed (Lima, 1963), was written in 1930 as a refutation of Mariátegui's *Siete Ensayos.* Much earlier Mariátegui adverted to the division between followers of Bergson into rightists and leftists in *Historia de la Crisis Mundial* (Lima: Empresa Amauta, 1959), p. 199.

32. Henri Bergson, *L'Evolution créatrice*, in *Oeuvres*, ed. André Robinet and Henri Gouhier (Paris: Presses Universitaires de France, 1963), pp. 569–70. Bergson's *L'Evolution creatrice* was hailed by Mariátegui as a decisive intellectual weapon against idealism and "bourgeois rationalism." *Historia de la Crisis Mundial*, pp. 198–99.

33. Bergson, *L'Evolution créatrice*, in *Oeuvres*, p. 645.

34. Bergson, *Introduction à la métaphysique*, in *Oeuvres*, p. 1395.

35. Bergson, *L'Evolution créatrice*, in *Oeuvres*, p. 722.

36. Sorel was especially impressed by Bergson's distinction between the two selves that make up man: an exterior social self, subject to ephemeral psychological states and therefore largely unfree, and an inner self which alone unifies outer experience and "creates" the world in which man lives. It is this deeper, freer self (Bergson called it *le moi fondamental*) that makes religious commitments or, as Sorel wished to add, creates myths. Bergson develops his notion of the two "I's" in his *Essai sur les données immédiates de la conscience* (1888), *Oeuvres*, pp. 85–92.

37. Georges Sorel, *Réflexions sur la violence*, 3d ed. (Paris: Marcel Riviére, 1912), p. 180.

38. Ibid., pp. 177–78.

39. Ibid., pp. 36–37, 50.

40. Ibid., p. 33.

41. Georges Sorel, *La Ruine du monde antique*, 2d ed. (Paris: Marcel Riviére, Editeur, 1925), pp. 165–66.

42. Sorel, *Réflexions sur la violence*, p. 49. Other works by Sorel which Mariátegui cited were *Les Illusions de progrès*, 3d ed. (Paris: Marcel Riviére, 1921); *Matériaux d'une Théorie du Prolétariat* (Paris: Marcel Riviére, 1921); and *Introduction à l'économie moderne* (Paris; Marcel Rivière, 1922).

43. Mariátegui, *La Escena Contemporánea*, 4th ed. (Lima: Empresa Editora Amauta, 1970), p. 198.

44. Mariátegui was actually citing José Vasconcelos when he defended Marx. *Amauta* (September, 1926):3–4. Unamuno replied in a letter to Mariátegui that "Yes, Marx was a prophet, not a professor." *Amauta* (January, 1927):1.

45. Mariátegui, *Temas de Educación* (Lima: Empres Editora Amauta, 1970), pp. 21–23.

46. Mariátegui, *Temas de Nuestra América*, p. 46.

47. Mariátegui, *Siete Ensayos*, 11th ed. (Lima: Empresa Editora Amauta, 1967), p. 228.

48. Mariátegui, *Defensa del Marxismo*, 3d ed. (Lima: Empresa Editora Amauta, 1967), pp. 85–86.

49. Antonio San Cristóbal-Sebastián, C.F.C., *Economía, Educación y Marxismo en Mariátegui* (Lima: Ediciones Studium, 1960), p. 74. Another author, César Reinaga, asserts that Mariátegui's subordination of spirit to matter clearly separated him from orthodox Marxism and possibly even signaled his return to Christianity. *El Indio y la Tierra en Mariátegui* (Cuzco, 1959), p. 193.

50. Antonio Melis, Adalbert Dessau and Manfred Kossok, *Mariátegui: Tres Estudios* (Lima: Empresa Amauta, 1971), p. 89.

51. Mariátegui, *El Artista y la Epoca*, 4th ed. (Lima: Empresa Editora Amauta, 1970), p. 19.

52. Mariátegui did not fear the charge that he was a revisionist: "Heresy," he said, "is indispensable to test the health of dogma." He believed that Sorel

with his inspiration in Bergson salvaged Marxism from pedantic positivism and reformist socialism. *Defensa del Marxismo*, pp. 16-17. In *Ideología y Política*, he praised Sorel for completing and amplifying Marx, p. 112.

53. Mariátegui, *Defensa del Marxismo*, p. 56.

54. In his discussion of the means of the revolution, Mariátegui was closer to orthodox Marxism-Leninism. He very clearly accepted the class struggle as the fundamental explanation of contemporary history. Although he expressed admiration for Gandhi, he believed that a movement based on passive resistance was doomed to failure. Declared Mariátegui: "Revolutionaries of all latitudes must choose between suffering violence or using it." *La Escena Contemporánea*, p. 199.

55. Mariátegui, *El Alma Matinal*, p. 33.

56. Luis Valcárcel, *Tempestad en los Andes* (Lima: Edición Universo, 1972), prologue.

57. Mariátegui, *Ideología y Política*, p. 58. See also Mariátegui's remarks on the Indian situation in his prologue to Ernesto Reyna's *El Amauta Atusparia*, 2d ed. (Lima, 1932).

58. Mariátegui, *Peruanicemos al Perú* (Lima: Empresa Editora Amauta, 1970), p. 122.

59. Mariátegui, *Siete Ensayos*, p. 140.

60. Ibid., p. 141. Valcárcel made his comparison between Christianity and the Inca religion in his work, *De la Vida Incaica* (Lima: Editorial Garcilaso, 1925), p. 99.

61. James Georges Frazer, "Oriental Religions in the West," *Adonis, Attis, Osiris: Studies in the History of Oriental Religion*, 3d ed. (New York: The Macmillan Company, 1935), 1:298-312.

62. Mariátegui, *Siete Ensayos*, pp. 157-58. See also Waldo Frank, *Our America* (New York: AMS Press, 1972).

63. Ibid., pp. 149-53. Mariátegui cites Romero's article, "El Cuzco Católico" in *Amauta* (December, 1927):54.

64. Frazer, "Oriental Religions," pp. 310-312.

65. Mariátegui drew these conclusions directly from Javier Prado's *Estado Social del Perú durante la Dominación Española* (Lima: Imprenta de El Diario Judicial, 1894), p. 95.

66. Mariátegui, *Siete Ensayos*, pp. 97, 153.

67. Ibid., p. 11.

68. Ibid., p. 161.

69. Ibid., p. 164.

70. Ibid., p. 167.

71. Furthermore, as Basadre observed, Mariátegui was primarily a journalist, not a philosopher, who developed his ideas in response to concrete situations as they arose. Basadre, *Historia de la República del Perú*, 13:335.

NOTES TO CHAPTER 6

A Protest Against the Sacred Heart

1. José Carlos Mariátegui, *Ideología y Política* (Lima: Empresa Editora Amauta, 1969), pp. 91-92; *Defensa del Marxismo*, 3d ed. (Lima: Empresa Editora Amauta, 1967), p. 91.

2. For pro-Aprista studies of the movement, see the works by Harry Kantor, *The Ideology and Program of the Peruvian Aprista Movement* (Berkeley and Los Angeles: University of California Press, 1953), and Robert J. Alexander, *Prophets of the Revolution: Profiles of Latin American Leaders* (New York: The Macmillan Company, 1962). Among pro-Aprista Peruvian works, see Felipe Cossío del Pomar's biographies, *Víctor Raúl Haya de la Torre: El Indoamericano* (Lima: Editorial Nuevo Día, 1946), and his revised version, *Víctor Raúl* (Mexico: Editorial Cultura, 1969), and the well-documented political biographies by Luis Alberto Sánchez, *Raúl Haya de la Torre o el Político* (Santiago de Chile: Editorial del Pacífico, 1954). See also Alberto Baeza Flores, *Haya de la Torre y la Revolución Constructura de las Américas* (Buenos Aires: Editorial Claridad, 1962), and the article by Robert McNicoll, "Intellectual Origins of Aprismo," *Hispanic American Historical Review*, 23 (August, 1943), 424–40.

3. Alberto Hidalgo, "Haya de la Torre en su Víspera," *In Radiografía de Haya de la Torre* (Lima: Ediciones "Páginas Libres," 1946), p. 12.

4. Luis Alberto Sánchez, *Haya de la Torre y el Apra*, p. 238.

5. For a review of the literature on the controversial Aprista movement, as well as many of the later revisionist views of the party, see Richard Lee Clinton, "Apra: An Appraisal," *Journal of Inter-American Studies and World Affairs* 12, no. 2 (April, 1970):280–97.

6. Both these views are expressed by Fredrick Pike in *The Modern History of Peru* (New York: Frederick A. Praeger, 1967), pp. 278, 289–90. See also the article by Thomas Davies, Jr., "The *Indigenismo* of the Peruvian Aprista Party: A Reinterpretation," *Hispanic American Historical Review* 51 (November, 1971):626–45, in which the author denies that Apra ever took such key themes in its early program as Indian rights seriously.

7. Three works which study the economic conditions which favored the rise of the Aprista party as well as the social background of party members are Peter Klaren, *Modernization, Dislocation, and Aprismo: Origins of the Peruvian Aprista Party, 1870-1932* (Austin: University of Texas Press, 1973); Grant Hilliker, *The Politics of Reform in Peru: The Aprista and Other Mass Parties of Latin America* (Baltimore: The Johns Hopkins Press, 1971); and Stephen Jay Stein, "Populism and Mass Politics in Peru: The Political Behavior of the Lima Working Classes in the 1931 Presidential Election" (Ph.D. diss., University of Stanford, 1973). Professor Klaren in particular holds the thesis that Apra responded to the resentment of hacienda workers and a displaced middle class in the north against foreign imperialism.

8. Ricardo Martínez de la Torre, *Apristas y Sanchezcerristas* (Lima: Ediciones "Frente," 1934), p. 21. Expressing a somewhat similar view, Professor Pike emphasizes the Apristas' concern over losing middle-class support in the late thirties as a key factor to account for the Apra's alleged shift to the Right. Pike, *Modern History of Peru*, p. 278.

9. Cossío del Pomar, *Víctor Raúl*, pp. 181–82.

10. Emanuel de Kadt, "Paternalism and Populism: Catholicism in Latin America," *Journal of Contemporary History* 2 (October, 1967):89.

11. Sánchez, *Haya de la Torre y el Apra*, p. 17.

12. *El Pueblo*, Arequipa, October 8, 1931, p. 3.

13. Sánchez, *Haya de la Torre y el Apra*, pp. 39–42; Cossío del Pomar, *El Indoamericano*, pp. 76–78.

14. Haya de la Torre, Private Interview, Lima, July 26, 1973.

15. John A. MacKay, *The Other Spanish Christ* (London: Student Christian Movement Press, 1932), p. 194.

16. Ibid. Dr. MacKay was a missionary of the Free Church of Scotland and the first Presbyterian minister in Peru. In 1925 he traveled extensively throughout Latin America as a lecturer under the auspices of the YMCA. In 1932, after sixteen years in Latin America, he became a secretary of the Board of Foreign Missions of the Presbyterian church in the United States. From 1936 until 1959 he was a professor of ecumenics and president of the Princeton Theological Seminary until he retired in 1959. John A. MacKay, *Christianity on the Frontier* (New York: Macmillan Company, 1950), preface.

17. Luis Alberto Sánchez, "John A. MacKay y el Anglo—Peruano," *Leader* 45 (December, 1972):50. *Leader* is the yearbook of Colegio San Andrés in Lima, which is the old Colegio Anglo-Peruano, founded by MacKay.

18. Luis Alberto Sánchez, *Haya de la Torre y el Apra*, pp. 80–81.

19. A chronicle of the activities of the Popular University by Enrique Köster is found in Gabriel del Mazo, *La Reforma Universitaria*, 6 vols. (Buenos Aires: Ediciones del Centro de Estudiantes de Ingeniería, 1941), 2:15-60.

20. Josefina Yarlequé de Marquina, *El Maestro o Democracia en Miniatura* (Lima: Librería J. Alvarez, 1963), p. 39.

21. Ibid., pp. 52, 91. Photographs of the students of the Lima center may be found in *Mundial*, Lima, January 28, 1921, p. 20.

22. Cossío del Pomar, *El Indoamericano*, p. 55.

23. *Claridad*, Lima, July, 1923, p. 20.

24. Félix Anaya, *Bohemia Azul*, Lima, April 13, 1924, p. 22.

25. *El Obrero Textil*, Lima, January 13, 1920, p. 3. For other examples of anticlerical articles, see the editions of December 6, 1919, p. 1, and January 13, 1920, pp. 3-4.

26. *El Obrero Textil*, Lima, October, 1923, p. 4. The article, "Jesús fue Anarquista," was reproduced in *Bohemia Azul*, Lima, January 24, 1924, pp. 16-17, and in *La Puna* of Ayaviri, January 25, 1927, pp. 7-8.

27. *Claridad, Organo de la Juventud Libre del Perú*, Lima, May, 1923, no. 1, p. 8; no. 2, 1923, p. 6.

28. Yarlequé de Marquina, *El Maestro o Democracia en Miniatura*, pp. 61–63. La Sra. Yarlequé, a school teacher in Vitarte who is also an Aprista and a devout Catholic, may have nostalgically superimposed her own sentiments on events which occurred forty years before she composed her history of the Popular University of Vitarte. Nevertheless, it is revealing that nowhere in her work does she mention the anticlericalism of which Apristas were later accused. Private Interview with La Sra. Yarlequé de Marquina, Vitarte, July 27, 1967.

Other examples of the exaltation of religious figures, in this case that of Saint Francis of Assisi, appeared in *Amauta* (October, 1926):3, 41.

29. *La Crónica*, Lima, May 23, 1923, p. 10.

30. *El Amigo del Clero*, Lima, May 1, 1923, pp. 204-5.

31. *Variedades*, Lima, May 12, 1923, p. 1150.

32. *La Crónica*, Lima, May 16, 1923, p. 1.

33. Private Interview with Haya de la Torre, Lima, August 11, 1967.

34. For a detailed account of the background of the May 23 protest movement, see Sánchez, *Haya de la Torre y el Apra*, pp. 116-28.

35. Luis E. Heysen, *El ABC de la Peruanización* (Lima: Editorial Apra, 1931), p. 22.

36. Manuel Seoane, *La Revolución que el Perú Necesita* (Arequipa, 1965), pp. 101-2.

37. Cossío del Pomar, *El Indoamericano*, pp. 88-89.

38. *El Tiempo*, Lima, May 21, 1923, p. 2; *La Crónica*, Lima, May 24, 1923, p. 10.

39. *El Tiempo*, Lima, May 24, 1923, p. 4.

40. *La Crónica*, Lima, May 24, 1923, p. 2; *El Tiempo*, Lima, May 24, 1923, p. 1. Haya's references to Vigil and González Prada were not isolated allusions. An unsigned propaganda flyer emanating from the Popular University stated that from their tombs Vigil, González Prada, Christian Dam, and Lino Urquieta "were crying out against all those who exploit the ignorance of the people." *La Crónica*, Lima, May 24, 1923, p. 10. Dam was an anarchist from Lima and Urquieta a liberal from Arequipa.

41. *El Tiempo*, Lima, May 24, 1923, p. 4. The two demonstrators killed were a student, Manuel Alarcón Vidalón, and a worker, Salomón Ponce.

42. *El Tiempo*, Lima, May 25, 1923, p. 2.

43. Guillermo Thorndike, *El Año de la Barbarie* (Lima: Editorial Nueva América, 1969), pp. 83-84. *El Tiempo*, Lima, May 26, p. 1; *La Crónica*, Lima, May 26, 1923, p. 1.

44. *El Amigo del Clero*, Lima, June 1, 1923, p. 253. The decree was dated May 25, 1923.

45. Ibid., June 1, 1923, p. 1.

46. Along the same lines, in an open letter to Haya, Dora Mayer de Zulen denied that his movement was free of political motivation, because many anti-government elements were involved in it. *La Crónica*, May 29, 1923, pp. 3-4. Haya answered the *indigenista* writer by assuring her that the students were not moved by political ambition but by an ideal, liberty of conscience. *El Tiempo*, Lima, May 30, 1923, p. 3.

47. *La Semana*, Arequipa, May 20, 1923, pp. 6-8.

48. *La Semana*, Arequipa, May 20, 1923, pp. 6-8.

49. Private Interview with Haya de la Torre, Lima, July 25, 1975. In January, 1931, largely because of his close association with the Leguía regime, Lisson stepped down as archbishop and was named titular bishop of "Methymne" in Rome. But he chose to live and do research in Seville, Spain, on the church in Peru instead. The result of his research was a work surveying church documents *La Iglesia de España en el Perú: Colección de Documentos para la Historia de la Iglesia, que se Encuentran en Varios Archivos* (Seville, 1943). From 1941 until his death in 1961 he lived in Valencia. Before stepping down he had incurred a large debt for the archdiocese through bad financial risks. For two apologies of the controversial churchman, see Fausto Linares Málaga, *Monseñor Lisson y sus Derechos al Arzobispado de Lima* (Lima, 1933), and Alfonso Ponte Gonzáles, "Quién es Lisson? " *Con el Perú Adentro* (Lima: Editorial "Thesis," 1965), pp. 281-91.

50. Private Interview with Haya de la Torre, Lima, July 25, 1975. Unfortunately, there is no documentary source to corroborate this interesting claim of Haya.

51. *El Tiempo*, Lima, May 24, 1923, p. 4.

52. Seoane, *La Revolución que el Perú Necesita*, pp. 100-102. Luis Alberto Sánchez adds the detail that in his rush to organize the assembly Haya signed the document without reading it. *Haya de la Torre y el Apra*, p. 123.

53. *El Comercio*, Lima, May 22, 1923, p. 4, and May 26, 1923, p. 3.

54. Haya de la Torre, *Impresiones de la Inglaterra Imperialista y la Rusia Soviética* (Buenos Aires: Colección Claridad "Acción y Crítica," 1932).

55. Haya de la Torre, "What is Apra? " *Labour Monthly* 8 (December, 1926): 756-59.

56. Haya de la Torre, *Por la Emancipación de América Latina* (Buenos Aires: M. Gleizer, 1927).

57. For an example of this early spirit of collaboration, see the article by Mariátegui in which he defended Haya de la Torre's ideas on religion and politics, *Amauta*, no. 11 (October, 1926): 3. In *Nuestros Fines* Manuel Seoane declares that Mariátegui was highly sympathetic to the Apra until about 1927. (Lima: F.Y.E. Rosay, 1931), p. 55.

58. José Carlos Mariátegui, *Siete Ensayos de Interpretación de la Realidad Peruana*, 11th ed. (Lima: Empresa Editora Amauta, 1967), p. 122.

59. The exchange of correspondence between Mariátegui and Haya de la Torre in which they broke off their relationship is found in Ricardo Martínez de la Torre, *Apuntes para una Interpretación Marxista de Historia Social del Perú*, 4 vols. (Lima: Editora Peruana, 1947), 2:296-99.

60. MacKay, *The Other Spanish Christ*, p. 198. See also the extensive comments by MacKay on Haya de la Torre in a later work, *That Other America* (New York: Friendship Press, 1935), pp. 103-16.

NOTES TO CHAPTER 7

Aprismo Alone Will Save Peru!

1. *La Colmena*, Arequipa, August 8, 1931, p. 1.

2. Ibid., September 5, 1931, p. 1.

3. *Verdades*, Lima, October 3, 1931, p. 2. Earlier, *Verdades* had warned Catholics that of all the leftist parties, the "greatest danger which exists in Peru . . . is the Apra." August 15, 1931, p. 2.

4. *El Amigo del Clero*, Lima, July, 1933.

5. *La Opinión*, Lima, August 30, 1931, p. 6.

6. *El Amigo del Clero*, Lima, June, 1933, p. 125.

7. *Verdades*, Lima, August 8, 1931, p. 1.

8. *El Heraldo*, Puno, November 26, 1931, p. 4.

9. *La Tribuna*, Lima, May 23, 1931, p. 2.

10. Ibid., p. 9.

11. Dora Mayer de Zulen, *El Desarrollo de las Ideas Avanzadas en el Perú* (Callao, 1934), pp. 14-18.

12. *Verdades*, Lima, August 8, 1931, p. 2.

13. Mayer de Zulen, *El Desarrollo de las Ideas Avanzades*, p. 16.

14. Private interview with Luis Alberto Sánchez, Lima, August 14, 1974. See also Dr. Sánchez's remarks on the process by which the final party platform was developed, in *Haya de la Torre y el Apra* (Santiago de Chile: Editorial del Pacífico, 1955), pp. 276-77.

15. Víctor Raúl Haya de la Torre, *Política Aprista,* 2d ed. (Lima: Editorial Imprenta Amauta, 1967), p. 11.

16. Manuel Seoane, *Páginas Polémicas* (Lima: Editorial La Tribuna, 1931), pp. 44–45, 82–83. Seoane also expressed his views on the church in *Nuestros Fines* (Lima: F.Y.E. Rosay, 1931), pp. 31–38, and *Comunistas Criollos* 3d ed. (Lima, 1933), p. 42. For statements of other Aprista leaders on the Church and religion, see Luis Heysen, *El ABC de la Peruanización* (Lima: Editorial Apra, 1931), pp. 21–23; Pedro Muñiz and Carlos Showing, *Lo Que es el Aprismo* (Lima: Partido Aprista Peruano, 1932), pp. 144–46; Aprista party's *El Proceso Haya de la Torre,* 2d ed., (Lima: Editorial Imprenta Amauta, 1969), pp. 43–47; and the series of articles by Carlos Alberto Butrón in *Antorcha,* Lima, November 23, 25; November 3, 4, and 6 of 1933.

17. Haya de la Torre, *Política Aprista,* p. 101.

18. *El Heraldo,* Puno, October 15, 1931, p. 2.

19. *El Pueblo,* Arequipa, October 8, 1931, p. 3.

20. *El Pueblo,* Arequipa, October 5, 1931, p. 3.

21. "Una Apostilla a la Conferencia del Señor Víctor Raúl Haya de la Torre," *El Heraldo,* Puno, November 5, 1931, pp. 3–5.

22. Partido Aprista Peruano, *El Proceso Haya de la Torre* 2d ed. (Lima: Editorial-Imprenta Amauta, 1969), pp. 45–46. Another incident which gained notoriety for the party occurred in the small town of Cutervo, Cajamarca. When the local pastor saw the words, "Death to the clergy; long live the Apra! " on the front door of his church, he delivered a tirade against Apra in the middle of the Sacred Heart procession in late June. *La Tribuna,* Lima, June 29, 1931, p. 6. In early August *La Tribuna* complained that "some preachers," particularly "foreign clergymen," were attacking Apra from their pulpits in different parts of Peru. August 12, 1931, p. 1.

23. In his analysis of the election, Jorge Basadre believes that there was no major election fraud as the Apristas claimed at the time. *Historia de la República del Perú,* 6th ed. (Lima: Editorial Universitaria, 1970), 14:169–72. But in another examination of the 1931 elections, Guillermo Thorndike holds that there definitely was an election fraud and that the Apristas probably won the election. *El Año de la Barbarie* (Lima: Editorial Nueva América, 1969), pp. 133–39. Basadre and most other historians do not doubt that after 1931 Apra rapidly became the major popular political movement in Peru until the late fifties.

24. *El Heraldo,* Puno, December 10, 1931, p. 2.

25. *El Amigo del Clero,* Lima, November, 1931, pp. 226–55.

26. Luis Alberto Sánchez, *Aprismo y Religión* (Lima: Editorial Cooperative Aprista "Athaulpa," 1933), pp. 25–27.

27. Ibid., p. 35. For a further development of Sánchez's ideas and the Apra's official stand on the church, see Harry Kantor, *The Ideology and Program of the Peruvian Aprista Movement* (Berkeley and Los Angeles: University of California Press, 1953), pp. 93–97.

28. Rubén Vargas, S.J., *¿Aprista o Católico?* (Lima: Editorial Alfama, 1934), p. 31. Although the pamphlet appeared anonymously, it was well known at the time that Father Vargas was the author. But the Jesuit historian waited until the storm clouds of the thirties and forties had cleared before admitting being the author. Private interview with Father Vargas, Lima, July 6, 1967.

Outside of a few scattered names, little is known of the pro-Aprista priests which all Aprista leaders claim existed. In this regard it is interesting to note a warning to Catholics in the Unión Revolucionaria newspaper, *Acción*, that Apra was about to form an "Aprista clerical cell." *Acción*, Lima, January 1, 1934, p. 7.

29. The signature "Catholic Apristas" is only partially true. Like Father Vargas's work, this pamphlet appeared anonymously. The author was Carlos Rodríguez Pastor, who at the time of writing was an independent deputy from Huancavelica and not an Aprista. Haya de la Torre, who knew Doctor Rodríguez as a fellow law student at San Marcos, asked him to write an answer to Father Vargas's tract, mainly because after San Marcos, Rodríguez had studied at Santo Toribio Seminary for several years. As a favor to an old friend, Rodríguez composed his work. Doctor Rodríguez later served as Minister of Education under President Manuel Odría in 1955. Private interview with Doctor Carlos Rodríguez Pastor, Lima, August 6, 1975.

30. *Catolicismo y Aprismo* (Lima: Imprenta Minerva, 1934), p. 24.

31. *Aprismo-Anticatolicismo* (Lima: Verdades, 1934), p. 18.

32. Whether or not the campaign to expose Apra as antireligious made a significant impact on the elections is at best difficult to determine. One important consideration is that women, who might have been more sensitive to the religious issue, still did not have the right to vote in 1931. *El Pueblo* of Ayacucho reported that a large number of women turned out for a pro-Sánchez Cerro demonstration because "they were told that Apra is an enemy of religion." September 21, 1931, p. 2. But two weeks later the Apristas held their own rally, at which the "Aprista women's cell" was present. *El Pueblo*, Ayacucho, October 9, 1931, p. 2.

In his opinion, Haya de la Torre does not believe that the "religious issue" cost Apra votes in 1931. Conservative Catholics voted for Sánchez Cerro and reform-minded Catholics voted for Haya. Private interview with Haya de la Torre, Lima, July 26, 1972. But the former secretary general of the party and long-time senator from Junín, Ramiro Prialé, believes that the church-state-separation clause definitely lost the party some votes in 1931. Private interview with Ramiro Prialé, Lima, July 25, 1972.

33. During the period of *Clandestinidad*, as the Apristas term the years of underground life, there were no less than five Popular Universities operating secretly in different parts of Lima. Private interview with Orestes Rodríguez, current director of the Popular University in Lima, July 4, 1967. The Apristas' sense of mission and solidarity is illustrated by the Aprista political prisoners on the prison island of San Lorenzo who maintained an informal "Popular University" among themselves from 1942 until May, 1945, when the party was legalized again. Partido Aprista Peruano, *Boletín de las Universidades Populares González Prada*, Lima (April, 1946): 3–4.

34. *Acción Aprista*, Trujillo, May 19, 1934, p. 13.

35. Ibid., May 26, 1934, p. 4. See also the comments of Grant Hilliker on "Aprismo as a Cult" in *The Politics of Reform in Peru: The Aprista and Other Mass Parties of Latin America* (Baltimore: The Johns Hopkins Press, 1971), pp. 106–7.

36. Haya de la Torre, *Política Aprista*, p. 108.

37. Ibid., p. 109.

38. The full truth of the Trujillo massacres, either of the military officers in Fort O'Donovan or of the Apristas in the ruins of Chan Chan, has never been adequately brought to light. The Apristas claim that irresponsible and unknown

parties took the lives of the officers, but anti-Aprista writers blame the Apristas themselves. Both Basadre, *Historia de la República del Perú*, 4:235–36, and Thorndike, *El Año de la Barbarie*, pp. 272–76, accept the Aprista version more or less. The mystery over the number of Apristas killed by Sánchez Cerro was created in great part by the fact that an undetermined number of militants in the uprising were simply executed without a trial, and therefore without record. The government officially admitted having tried and executed forty-four partisans. But in *Haya de la Torre y el Apra*, p. 314, Luis Alberto Sánchez puts the figure of Apristas massacred, tried or otherwise, at 2,000. In his *Manifesto to the Nation* of November, 1933, Haya de la Torre claimed 4,000 (*Política Aprista*, p. 171). But an Aprista in *Acción Aprista* Trujillo, July 28, 1934, p. 21, put the number at 6,000, which has since become the standard figure cited by most Apristas. Undoubtedly, the figure became inflated in direct proportion to the growth of the martyrdom cult within the party. Two revisionist works on the Trujillo uprising which blame Apra for its failure are Rogger Mercado, *La Revolución de Trujillo*, (Lima: Fondo de Cultura, 1932), and Víctor Villanueva, *El Apra en Busca del Poder, 1930–1940* (Lima: Editorial Horizonte, 1975).

39. John A. MacKay, *That Other America* (New York: Friendship Press, 1935), pp. 109–110.

40. Haya de la Torre, *Política Aprista*, pp. 200–201.

41. *Homenaje de Víctor Raúl a los Mártires del 32* (Partido Aprista Peruano, Trujillo, n.d.), p. 4. Haya's speech also appeared in *Antorcha*, Trujillo, December 24, pp. 5–6, and December 25, p. 2, 1933, and *Nor-Perú*, Trujillo, July 7, 1945, pp. 9–12.

42. *Homenaje de Víctor Raúl a los Mártires del 32*, p. 5.

43. Ibid., p. 11.

44. Ibid., p. 12.

45. These character references and biographical data on Carlos Philipps were gathered in private interviews with Sra. Julia Jaramillo Philipps, widow of Doctor Philipps, Caraz, August 9, 1974, and with Father Alfonso Ponte González, June 10, 1975.

46. Isaías Zavaleta Figueroa, *Biografía Sucinta del Dr. Carlos Philipps* (Caraz: Imprenta "Atún Huaylas," 1960), p. 11.

47. *Libertad*, Lima, August, 1933, p. 1.

48. *Libertad*, Lima, September, 1933, p. 2.

49. *Acción Aprista*, Trujillo, July 28, 1934, p. 22.

50. Alberto Hidalgo, *Cantos de la Revolución* (Lima: Editorial Cooperativa Aprista, 1934), p. 28.

51. Carlos Manuel Cox, *Cartas de Haya de la Torre a los Prisioneros Apristas* (Lima: Editorial Nuevo Día, 1946), pp. 67, 69, 70.

52. Lima, National Library.

53. *Libertad*, Lima, September, 1933, p. 2. On one occasion Haya himself denied being another Christ. *La Sierra*, no. 31, 1930, p. 91.

54. Mayer de Zulen, *El Desarrollo de las Ideas Avanzadas en el Peru*, p. 9.

55. *Cartilla Aprista* (Lima, National Library, n.d.), p. 28. Another example of Aprista appropriation of Catholic symbols occurred at a eucharistic congress in Lima in the thirties. Either out of zeal or a sense of humor certain Apristas circulated at the congress a holy card which bore Carlos Philipp's last words—"May Christ save my soul; Apra alone will save Peru! "—on the back. Private interview with Ramiro Prialé, Lima, July 25, 1972.

56. Hidalgo, *Cantos de la Revolución*, p. 47. See also Leandro Caballo and "Gavroche", *Cancionero Aprista* (Lima: Editorial Apra, n.d.) for other examples of the quasi-messianic religious songs and marches of the Aprista movement.

57. Serafín Delmar, *Sol: Están Destruyendo a tus Hijo* (Buenos Aires: Editorial Americale, 1941), pp. 55-58.

58. Serafín Delmar, *El Año Trágico* (Lima: Editorial Cooperativa Aprista Atahualpa, 1933), pp. 15-16. Other works by Delmar are: *El Derecho de Matar*, cowritten with Magda Portal (La Paz: Impresa Continental, 1926); *El Hombre de Estos Años* (Mexico City: Ediciones Apra, 1929); *La Tierra es el Hombre* (Buenos Aires: Editorial Americalee, 1942); and *Los Campesinos y Otros Condenados* (Santiago de Chile: Ediciones Orbe, 1943).

59. Ciro Alegría, *Novelas Completas* (Madrid: Ediciones Aguilar, 1959), pp. 94-107.

60. The prayer to the "Just Judge" was actually recited by bandits in turn-of-the-century Peru, the period in which the story takes place. The prayer is reproduced in José Varallanos, *Bandoleros en el Perú* (Lima: Editorial Altura, 1937), p. 92.

61. Alegria, *Novelas Completas*, p. 586.

62. Ibid., p. 385.

63. Ibid., p. 930. Disillusioned by Apra, which he believed failed to work for the "integral liberation of man," Alegría left the party in 1948. Years later he became a militant supporter of Fernando Belaúnde and he served as an Acción Popular deputy from Lima until his death in 1967.

64. Private interview with Father Augusto Soriano, Huaraz, July 9, 1974. Father Soriano, who currently resides in Huaraz where he served as mayor of the city from 1960 to 1962, was the parish priest of Caraz from 1932 to 1933.

65. *Acción Aprista*, Trujillo, June 7, 1934, p. 21; Zavleta Figueroa, *Biographia Sucinta del Dr. Carlos Philipps*, p. 5.

66. Dora Mayer de Zulen, *La Intangibilidad de las Communidades Indígenas* (Callao, 1936), pp. 64-65.

67. At least this is the opinion of the two priests, Augusto Soriano and Alfonso Ponte, who worked in the Callejón de Huaylas during the Aprista uprising of 1932. Both of these priests had many friends among the Apristas, but both believe that the Apristas failed to attract the Indians in part because of their alleged anticlerical attitudes. Private interviews with Father Alfonso Ponte González, Lima, June 10, 1975, and with Father Augusto Soriano, Huaraz, July 9, 1974.

68. Haya de la Torre, *Política Aprista*, pp. 185-86.

69. Sánchez, *Aprismo y Religión*, p. 30.

70. Private interview with Father Francisco Díaz, Trujillo, August 10, 1972. Father Díaz, a Spanish Claretian priest who was teaching at San Carlos Seminary, Trujillo, in July, 1932, asserts that the Apristas never committed a single act of aggression against the church during the uprising.

71. *El Comercio*, Lima, December 1, 1934, p. 5; *El Estandarte Católico*, Ayacucho, December 11, 1934, p. 2.

72. Private interview with Carlos Rodríguez Pastor, Lima, August 6, 1975. Doctor Rodríguez, who was the deputy from Huancavelica at the time of the assassination of the priest, went to Archbishop Pedro Farfán to request that the bodies of the priest and others killed be taken directly to the cemetery in Lima so as to avoid turning the funeral ceremonies into an anti-Aprista rally, which many enemies of Apra wished to do. The archbishop granted the request.

73. *El Comercio,* Lima, December 3, 1934, p. 1.

74. *Verdades,* Lima, January 13, 1934, pp. 1, 4.

75. Ibid., September 2, 1939, p. 1.

76. *La Tribuna,* Lima, August 9, 1942, p. 4.

77. José Luis Bustamante y Rivero, *Tres Años de Lucha por la Democracia en el Perú* (Buenos Aires, 1949), p. 18.

78. *JAP,* Lima, February 22, 1949, p. 4. *JAP* was the voice of the Aprista youth. For the remarks of one disenchanted former Aprista who found Apra's about face on the church question hypocritical, see Luis Eduardo Enríquez, *La Estafa Política Más Grande de América* (Lima: Ediciones del Pacífico, 1951), pp. 52–57.

79. For additional comments on the possible impact of Apra on the church, see Carlos Astiz, *Pressure Groups and Power Elites in Peruvian Politics* (Ithaca: Cornell University Press, 1969), pp. 178–81.

80. In an excellent study of the interaction between ideology and religion in Latin America, Professor Ivan Vallier speculated that one reason why the "Apristas never got off the ground" was that they did not seek the legitimatizing support of the church. *Catholicism, Social Control, and Modernization in Latin America* (Englewood Cliffs, New Jersey: Prentice-Hall, Inc., 1970), pp. 53–54. The thesis proposed in these pages is just the opposite: the Apra did "get off the ground" without church support because it sought and won religious legitimacy from among lower-class Peruvian Catholics.

81. Haya de la Torre, *Tres Discursos* (Lima: Ediciones del Bloque Antifascista, 1945), p. 24.

NOTES TO CHAPTER 8

Long Live Christ the King!

1. Bustamante's apologia for his three years in office is presented in his work, *Tres Años de Lucha por la Democracia en el Perú* (Buenos Aires: 1949). Other works which cover the political history of Peru in the postwar years are Fredrick B. Pike, *A Modern History of Peru* (New York: Frederick A. Praeger, 1967), Carlos Astiz, *Pressure Groups and Power Elites in Peruvian Politics* (Ithaca, New York: University of Cornell, 1969), and François Bourricaud, *Power and Society in Contemporary Peru,* trans. Paul Stevenson (New York: Frederick A. Praeger, 1970).

2. Two early works by Cornejo Chávez that express the principal points of Christian Democracy are *Nuevos Principios para un Nuevo Perú* (Lima, 1960) and *Qué se Propone la Democracia Cristiana* (Lima, 1962).

3. *El Comercio,* Lima, June 5, 1962, p. 2, and June 10, p. 2.

4. Ibid., June 7, 1962, p. 8.

5. Ibid., June 10, 1962, p. 4.

6. Ibid., June 10, 1962, p. 4.

7. See Father Bolo's first work in which he approves of the support of Communists for his movement, *Cristianismo y Liberación Nacional* (Lima, 1962); see also his later work repudiating communism, *Cristianismo y Marxismo, ¿Son Compatibles?* (Lima, 1973).

8. Héctor Béjar, *Perú 1965: Una Experiencia Guerrillera* (Lima: Ediciones Campodónico, 1969), pp. 99–101.

9. Ibid., p. 96. For similar criticisms of the church and religion in the Andes, see Hugo Neira, *Cuzco: Tierra y Muerte* (Lima: 1964), pp. 88–89, and Hugo Blanco, *Land or Death: The Peasant Struggle in Peru* (New York: Pathfinder Press, 1972), p. 88.

10. A recent work which gathers together essays analyzing most of the major events and reforms of the military government is Abraham Lowenthal, ed., *The Peruvian Experiment: Continuity and Change under Military Rule* (Princeton, New Jersey: Princeton University Press, 1975). For a study of the reforms themselves, see Ernst-J. Kerbusch, ed., *Cambios Estructurales en el Perú 1968–1975* (Lima: Instituto Latinoamericano de Investigaciones Sociales, 1976). See also Henry Pease and Olga Verme, *Perú, 1968–1974: Cronología Política*, 3 vols. (Lima: Desco, 1976); Juan Velasco Alvarado, *Velasco: la Voz de la Revolución*, 2 vols. (Lima: Editorial Ausonia, 1972); Juan Velasco Alvarado, *El Proceso Peruano* (Lima: Instituto Nacional de Investigación y Desarrollo de la Educación, 1974); and, *Ideological Basis of the Peruvian Revolution* (Lima: Oficina Central de Información, 1975).

11. For a Peruvian journalist's account of the men behind the October takeover, see Augusto Zimmermann Zavala, *El Plan Inca, Objetivo: Revolución Peruana* (Lima: Editorial "El Peruano," 1974).

12. See the works of Víctor Villanueva on the background and formation of the military in Peru: especially, *El CAEM y la Revolución de la Fuerza Armada* (Lima: Instituto de Estudios Peruanos, 1972) and *Ejército Peruano: Del Caudillaje Anárquico al Militarismo Reformista* (Lima: Editorial Juan Mejía Baca, 1973).

13. Hugo Pesce, *El Factor Religioso* (Lima: Empresa Editora Amauta, 1972), pp. 107-10.

14. *Expreso*, Lima, October 20, 1968, p. 3.

15. Ibid., October 19, 1970, pp. 1, 4.

16. Many of these observations on the religious background and formation of the military were gathered in interviews with General Ernesto Montagne, prime minister from 1968 to 1973, Lima, September 7, 1976, and with Major Víctor Villanueva, Lima, July 10, 1976.

17. See, for example, General Fernández Maldonado's article, "Fuerza Armada, Cristianismo y Revolución en el Perú," *Participación*, Lima (August, 1973): 4–13.

18. *Ley General de Educación* (Lima: Pontificia Universidad Católica, n.d.), p. 30.

19. Private interview with Father Ricardo Morales, S.J., former president of the superior advisory council of the Ministry of Education, Lima, September 12, 1976. For an overall study of the educational reform in Peru, see the essay by Robert S. Drysdale and Robert G. Myers, "Continuity and Change: Peruvian Education," in *The Peruvian Experiment*, ed. Lowenthal, pp. 254-301.

20. Carlos Delgado, *Revolución y Participación* (Lima: Ediciones del Centro, 1974).

21. *Ideological Basis of the Peruvian Revolución*, pp. 8-15.

22. Many of these editorials as well as Cornejo Chávez's reflections on the military government are found in his work, *Socialcristianismo y Revolución Peruana* (Lima: Ediciones Andinas, 1975). For the ideas of another Christian thinker who influenced many of the military before and after they took power, see the different editorials by Father Romeo Luna Victoria, S.J., in *El*

Comercio, Lima, June 27, p. 2, July 3, 4, p. 2, August 1, 30, p. 2, and September 10, p. 2, 1976.

23. Private interview with Héctor Cornejo Chávez, Lima, September 6, 1976. The Christian Democratic leader's discrepancies with the "First Phase" of the revolution are outlined in *Socialcristianismo y Revolución Peruana,* pp. 242-53.

24. *El Peruano,* Lima, September 3, 1976, pp. 1, 4-5.

25. Secretariado Nacional del Episcopado del Perú, *Familia y Población* (Lima, 1974).

26. Private interviews with Father Juan Julio Wicht, S.J., and Father Enrique Bartra, S.J., advisor to the church's commission on responsible parenthood, Lima, September 11, 1976.

27. For critical analyses of Velasco's regime and Morales' first year in power, see Ismael Frías, *La Revolución Peruana y la Vía Socialista* (Lima: Editorial Horizonte, 1970); Aníbal Quijano, *Nationalism and Capitalism in Peru: A Study in Neo-Imperialism,* trans. Helen R. Lane (New York: Monthly Review Press, 1971); Robert Adams, "Ancient Incas and Modern Revolution," *New York Review of Books,* 32 (March 18, 1976):43-47; and "Peru: Fireside Chat," *Latin America* 10 (April, 1976):116-17.

28. *El Comercio,* Lima, July 29, 1972, p. 4, and July 29, 1975, p. 6.

29. See Jane S. Jacquette, "Belaúnde and Velasco: On the Limits of Ideological Politics," in *The Peruvian Experiment,* ed. Lowenthal, pp. 402-37.

30. Many of these observations on the Peruvian church are influenced by Ivan Vallier's analyses of the Latin American church in general. See, for example, his article, "Radical Priests and the Revolution," in *Changing Latin America: New Interpretations of its Politics and Society,* ed. Douglas A. Chalmers (New York: The Academy of Political Science, 1972); and his book, *Catholicism, Social Control, and Modernization in Latin America* (Englewood Cliffs, New Jersey: Prentice-Hall, 1970). For a review of general tendencies in the modern Latin American Catholic church, see Brian Smith, S.J., "Religion and Social Change: Classical Theories and New Formulations in the Context of Recent Developments in Latin America," *Latin American Research Review* 10 (Summer, 1975):3-34.

31. For studies of the modern Church in Peru, see Carlos Astiz, *Pressure Groups and Power Elites in Peruvian Politics,* pp. 172-88; Astiz's "The Catholic Church in Politics: The Peruvian Case," *Ladoc* (March, 1972):1-13; Fredrick B. Pike, "The Modernized Church in Peru," *The Review of Politics* 26 (July, 1964):307-318; Pike, "Catholic Church and Modernization in Peru and Chile," *Journal of Inter-American Affairs* 20 (1966):272-88; and Pike, "South America's Multifaceted Catholicism: Glimpses of Twentieth-Century Argentina, Chile and Peru," *The Church and Social Change in Latin America,* ed. Henry Landsberger (Notre Dame: University of Notre Dame Press, 1970), pp. 53-75. For a brief history of the church in the twentieth century, see Luis Lituma, "La Iglesia Católica en el Perú durante el Siglo XX," in *Visión del Perú en el Siglo XX,* ed. José Pareja Paz-Soldán (Lima: Ediciones Librería Studium, 1963) 2:473-523.

32. Secretaría General del Episcopado del Perú, *Primera Semana Social del Perú* (Lima, 1959).

33. Secretaría General del Episcopado del Perú, *Carta Pastoral Colectiva del Episcopado Peruano sobre la Actividad Social y Política en la Hora Presente* (Lima, 1963), p. 15.

34. Romeo Luna Victoria, S.J., *Ciencia y Práctica de la Revolución* (Lima: Editorial Studium, 1966).

35. Onis's document and the cardinal's response are found in *Iglesia Latino-americana, ¿Protesta o Profecía?* ed. Juan José Rossi (Avellaneda, Argentina: Ediciones Búsqueda, 1969), pp. 298-99. For a short history of Onis, see Fernando Montes, "How the 'ONIS' Movement Began and Grew," *Ladoc*, no. 24 (February, 1974). See also Michael G. Macaulay, "Ideological Change and Internal Cleavages in the Peruvian Church: Change, Status Quo, and the Priest: The Case of Onis" (Ph.D. diss., University of Notre Dame, 1972).

36. See especially Gustavo Gutiérrez, *A Theology of Liberation*, trans. Sister Caridad Inda and John Eagleson (Maryknoll, New York: Orbis Books, 1973).

37. See the article, "La Derecha en la Iglesia," *Marka* (November 13, 1975): 11-13.

38. Secretariado Nacional del Episcopado, *Iglesia en el Perú* (June, 1974): 11; ibid. (March, 1975):2.

39. Arzobispado de Lima, "Departamento de Estadística," mimeographed, Lima, June 1976. For a study of the foreign missionaries in Peru, see the chapter by Dan C. McCurry, "U.S. Church-Financed Missions in Peru," in *U.S. Foreign Policy and Peru*, ed. Daniel Sharp (Austin: University of Texas Press, 1972), pp. 379-415.

40. Juan Velasco Alvarado, *Velasco, la Voz de la Revolución*, 1:54.

41. *Expreso*, Lima, October 11, 1968, p. 1; *Noticias Aliadas* (Maryknoll), Lima, March 15, 1969, pp. 2-3. For an article emphasizing the compatibility of the church's teachings and the revolutionary government, see Patrick Brady, "Peru: Revolution, Church, Salvation," *The Furrow* 23 (March, 1972):140-52.

42. *Noticias Aliadas*, Lima, November 18, 1972, p. 2.

43. Jaime Ponce, Julián Rojas, and Daniel Roach, *Juli: Actitudes y Estructuras Sociales* (La Paz, Bolivia: Instituto Boliviano de Estudios y Acción Social, 1968), p. 342.

44. William J. McIntire, "Maryknoll and Peruvian Education," *Catholic Mind*, November, 1972, p. 50.

45. *Noticias Aliadas*, October 18, 1972, p. 1.

46. Alfredo Rodríguez, Gustavo Riofrío, and Eileen Welsh, *De Invasores a Invadidos* (Lima: Desco, 1973), p. 110.

47. Interviews with Father Antonio Bach, S.J., and Father Kevin Gallagher, S.J., directors of Fe y Alegría, Lima, September 22, 1976.

48. *Noticias Aliadas*, February 19, 1969, p. 6, March 26, p. 2, and March 29, p. 2.

49. Ibid., February 19, 1972, pp. 7-8.

50. Lowenthal, *The Peruvian Experiment*, p. 130. For an overview of government policy toward Peru's squatter settlements, see David Collier, "Squatter Settlements and Policy Innovation in Peru," in *The Peruvian Experiment*, ed. Lowenthal, pp. 128-78.

51. *Expreso*, Lima, May 2, 1969, p. 1, and May 19, p. 3.

52. *La Prensa*, Lima, May 19, 1969, p. 2.

53. *Expreso*, Lima, May 22, 1969, p. 4.

54. *La Prensa*, Lima, May 24, 1969, p. 2.

55. See, for example, *La Prensa*, Lima, May 26, 1969, p. 2.

56. The archbishop's office published a chronology of these events which appeared in the newspapers. See, for example, *El Correo*, Lima, May 14, 1971,

p. 17, and *El Comercio*, May 14, 1971, p. 10. The chronology was later re-published in a set of documents dealing with the Pamplona affair, *Pamplona: Más Allá de los Hechos* (Lima: Centro de Estudios y Publicaciones, May, 1971), pp. 27-28. Also, many general impressions on the Pamplona affair were gathered in an interview with Bishop Bambarén, Lima, September 1, 1976.

57. *El Correo*, Lima, May 10, 1971, p. 8.

58. Ibid., May 12, 1971, pp. 1, 16-17.

59. Years later Artola attributed his downfall to a Communist conspiracy within the government directed against him. *Equis X*, Lima, January 22, 1976, p. 23.

60. Dirección General de Educación Básica, Universidad Católica, *Diagnóstico Situacional de Villa El Salvador* (Lima, 1973), p. 11.

61. "Los Invasores Piden una Misa," *Páginas* (March, 1976):35-37.

62. Comisión Episcopal de Acción Social, *Participación Popular* (Lima: December, 1975).

63. *Noticias Aliadas*, May 20, 1976, pp. 5-7.

64. Manuel Marzal, S.J., "La Religiosidad Popular en el Perú," *Iglesia en el Perú*, April, 1972, pp. 1-6.

65. "Orientaciones para una Pastoral Popular," *Allpanchis* (journal of the Instituto de Pastoral Andino, Ipa) 5 (1973):200-202. For other discerning analyses of popular religiosity, see Ricardo Antoncich, S.J., "Sociología Religiosa: Reflexiones Pastorales," in *Survey S.J. del Perú*, mimeographed (Lima, 1969), pp. 9-79; Thomas M. Garr, S.J., *Cristianismo y Religión Quechua en la Prelatura de Ayaviri* (Arequipa: Editorial Miranda, 1972); and Raúl Vidales and Tokihiro Kudo, *Práctica Religiosa y Proyecto Histórico: Hipótesis para un Estudio de la Religiosidad Popular en América Latina* (Lima: Centro de Estudios y Publicaciones, 1975).

66. *Estampa* (*Expreso* Sunday Supplement), October 27, 1968, p. 4.

67. *Correo Aprista*, Lima, May-June, 1976, p. 9.

68. *La Crónica*, Lima, June 15, 1976, p. 2.

69. Ibid., May 14, 1976, p. 5.

70. For the Left's view of the president's piety, see *Marka*, Lima, July 1, 1976, pp. 6-7.

BIBLIOGRAPHY OF WORKS CITED AND INTERVIEWS

Primary Sources

Manuscripts (National Library, Lima)

Documentos sobre la Destrucción de Fuerzas del Orden que a las Ordenes de los Subprefectos de las Provincias del "Dos de Mayo" y "Humalíes," Marchaban a Restablecer la Tranquilidad en Aquellas Circunscripciones, Huanuco, Abril 21 de 1895.

Documentos sobre los Graves Sucesos Promovidos por los Indígenas de la Ciudad de Juli, Noviembre 12 de 1896.

Informes Evacuados por el Jefe de la Expedición Pacificadora Enviada a Huánuco a Reestablecer el Orden, Huallanca, Junio 5 de 1895.

Memoria Elevada por el Subprefecto de la Provincia, D. Federico Amat, a la Prefectura del Departamento de Puno, Mayo 25, 1898.

Oficio Dirigido por el Prefecto del Departamento de Ancash, al Ministro de Gobierno, Dándole Cuenta de los Sucesos que Han Tenido Lugar en esa Villa y las Incidencias de la Toma del Pueblo de Yautan, Casma, Marzo 29 de 1885.

Parte Elevada a la Subprefectura de la Provincia de Chucuito por el Comisario de Policía de la Frontera del Perú con Bolivia, Informándole sobre los Sucesos de Ilave, Ilave, Abril 10 de 1897.

Vigil, Francisco de Paula González. "La Religión Natural."

Newspapers and Periodicals (with the years cited)

Acción (Unión Revolucionaria), Lima, 1934.
Acción Aprista, Trujillo, 1934.
Allpanchis, Cuzco, 1973.
Amauta, Lima, 1926-30.
El Amigo del Clero, Lima, 1923, 1931, 1933.
Antorcha (Aprista), Lima, 1933.
El Ateneo, Lima, 1887.
La Autonomía, Lima, 1915.
El Bien Público, Lima, 1885.
Bohemia Azul, Lima, 1924.
El Católico Cristiano, Lima, 1855.
El Censor Eclesiástico, Cuzco, 1825.

Claridad, Lima, 1923.
La Colmena, Arequipa, 1931.
Colónida, Lima, 1916.
El Comercio, Lima, 1866, 1868-69, 1885, 1896, 1915, 1923, 1931, 1934, 1962, 1971-72, 1975-76.
El Constitucional, Lima, 1858.
El Correo, Lima, 1971.
El Correo Aprista, Lima, 1976.
La Crónica, Lima, 1917, 1923, 1976.
El Deber Pro-Indígena, Lima, 1912-17.
El Discreto, Lima, 1827.
Equis X, Lima, 1976.
El Estandarte Católico, Ayacucho, 1934.
Expreso, Lima, 1968-69.
El Fénix, Lima, 1834.
Germinal, Lima, 1899.
El Heraldo, Puno, 1931.
Iglesia en el Perú, Lima, 1972, 1974-75.
La Iglesia Puneña, Puno, 1866, 1868.
La Integridad, Lima, 1889, 1892.
JAP (Aprista), Lima, 1949.
Labour Monthly, London, 1926.
Ladoc, Washington, D.C., 1972, 1974.
Latin America, London, 1975.
Libertad, (Aprista), Lima, 1933.
La Luz Eléctrica, Lima, 1885-86.
La Lucha, Lima, 1914.
Marka, Lima, 1975; 1976.
El Mercurio Peruano, Lima, 1930-31.
Mundial, Lima, 1921, 1923, 1926.
Nor-Perú (Aprista), Trujillo, 1945.
Noticias Aliadas, Lima, 1969, 1972, 1976.
El Obrero de Ancash, Huaraz, 1880.
El Obrero Textil, Lima, 1919-20, 1923.
La Opinión (Unión Revolucionaria), Lima, 1931.
La Opinión Nacional, Lima, 1885.
Páginas, Lima, 1976.
El País, Lima, 1896.
Los Parias, Lima, 1906.
El Perú Católico, Lima, 1867.
El Peruano, Lima, 1826-27, 1976.
La Prensa, Lima, 1914, 1918, 1923, 1931, 1969.
La Protesta, Lima, 1911-26.
El Pueblo, Arequipa, 1931.
El Pueblo, Ayacucho, 1931.
La Puna, Ayaviri, 1927.

El Radical, Lima, 1889.
El Revisor, Lima, 1827.
Revista de Actualidades, Lima, 1917.
La Revista de Lima, Lima, 1859-62.
La Revista Social, Lima, 1885.
La Semana, Arequipa, 1923.
La Sierra, Lima, 1927-30.
El Tiempo, Lima, 1916-17, 1923.
La Tribuna (Aprista), Lima, 1931, 1942.
El Triunfo de la Libertad, Cuzco, 1831.
Variedades, Lima, 1923.
Verdades, Lima, 1931, 1934, 1939.

Published Works (Books, articles, and addresses)

Aguilar, Luis. *Cuestiones Indígenas.* Cuzco: Tipografía de El Comercio, 1921.

Aguirre Morales, Augusto. *El Pueblo del Sol.* Lima: Imprenta Torres Aguirre, 1927.

Ahumada, Pascual, ed. *Recopilación Completa de Todos los Documentos Oficiales, Correspondientes y demás Publicaciones referentes a la Guerra que Ha Dado a Luz la Prensa de Chile, Perú y Bolivia.* Vol. 5. Valparaíso: Imprenta del Progreso, 1884.

Alegría, Ciro. *Novelas Completas.* Madrid: Ediciones Aguilar, 1959.

Amezaga, Mariano. *Los Dogmas Fundamentales del Catolicismo ante la Razón.* Valparaíso, Chile: Tipografía de Justo Fierro, 1873.

Aprismo-Anticatolicismo. Lima: Verdades, 1934.

Aréstegui, Narciso. *El Angel Salvador.* Lima: "El Comercio," 1872.

_____. *El Padre Horán.* 2 vols. Lima: Editorial Universo, n.d.

Béjar, Héctor, *Perú 1965: Una Experiencia Guerrillera.* Lima: Ediciones Campodónico, 1969.

Bilbao, Francisco. *La América en Peligro.* Santiago de Chile: Ediciones Ercilla, 1941.

Blanco, Hugo. *Land or Death: The Peasant Struggle in Peru.* New York: Pathfinder Press, 1972.

Bolo Hidalgo, Salomón. *Cristianismo y Liberación Nacional.* Lima, 1962.

_____. *Cristianismo y Marxismo, ¿Son Compatibles?.* Lima, 1973.

Bustamante, Juan. *Los Indios del Perú.* Lima: Imprenta dirigida por J. M. Monterola, 1867.

Caballo, Leandro, and "Gavroche." *Cancionero Aprista.* Lima: Editorial Apra, n.d.

Cabello de Carbonera, Mercedes. "Una Fiesta Religiosa en un Pueblo del Perú." *El Ateneo de Lima,* 3 (1887):182-87.

_____. *La Religión de la Humanidad: Carta al Señor D. Juan Enrique Lagarrigue.* Lima: Imprenta de Torres Aguirre, 1893.

Camacho, Juan, and Cossío, Juan. *¡Pobre Indio!* Lima: Imprenta Liberal, 1868.

Capelo, Joaquín. *Los Menguados.* Madrid: Librería de Fernando Fé, 1912.

Castro y Luna Victoria. *Relaciones Históricas sobre la Guerra y la Paz en el Perú.* Lima: Imprenta del Universo, 1884.

Castro Pozo, Hildebrando. *Nuestra Comunidad Indígena.* Lima: Editorial "El Lucero," 1924.

_____. *El Yanaconaje en las Haciendas Piuranas.* Lima: Compañía de Impresiones y Publicidad, 1947.

Causa Célebre: Informe del Dr. Sr. Fernando Palacios ante la Excelentísima Corte Suprema de Lima, por la Combustión de la India Llamada Bruja Benigna Huamán en el Pueblo de Bambamarca. n.p., n.d.

Cornejo Chávez, Héctor. *Nuevos Principios para un Nuevo Perú.* Lima, 1960.

_____. *Qué se Propone la Democracia Cristiana.* Lima, 1962.

_____. *Socialcristianismo y Revolución Peruana.* Lima; Ediciones Andinas, 1975.

Cox, Carlos Manuel, ed. *Cartas de Haya de la Torre a los Prisioneros Apristas.* Lima: Editorial Nuevo Día, 1946.

Delgado, Carlos. *Revolución y Participación.* Lima: Ediciones del Centro, 1974.

Delmar, Serafín [Reynaldo Bolaños]. *El Año Trágico.* Lima: Editorial Cooperativa Aprista Atahualpa, 1933.

_____. *Los Campesinos y Otros Condenados.* Santiago de Chile: Ediciones Orbe, 1943.

_____. *El Hombre de Estos Años.* Mexico City: Ediciones Apra, 1929.

_____. *Sol: Están Destruyendo a tus Hijos.* Buenos Aires: Editorial Americalee, 1941.

_____. *La Tierra es el Hombre.* Buenos Aires: Editorial Americalee, 1942.

Delmar, Serafín, and Portal, Magda. *El Derecho de Matar.* La Paz: Impresa Continental, 1926.

Del Valle, Felix. "Nuestros Grandes Prestigios," *Revista de Actualidades* (July 14, 1917):31-34.

Discursos Pronunciados en la Convención Nacional sobre la Cuestión Religiosa en las Sesiones de los Días 2, 3, 4, 5, 6 y 8 de Octobre. Lima: Tipografía del "Heraldo de Lima," 1855.

Fernández Maldonado, Jorge. "Fuerza Armada, Cristianismo y Revolución en el Perú," *Participación* (August, 1973):4-13.

Frisancho, José. *Del Jesuitismo al Indianismo.* Cuzco: Talleres Tipográficos "Imperial," 1931.

Fuentes, Hildebrando. *El Cuzco y sus Ruinas.* Lima, 1905.

Fundamentos en que se Apoya la Resolución Suprema Expedida el 20 del Actual sobre el Enjuiciamiento del Obispo de Puno y su Vicario General. Lima: Imprenta del Estado, 1869.

Garro, J. Eugenio. "La Iglesia y el Estado," *Amauta* (November-December, 1928):31-36.

González Prada, Manuel. *Anarquía.* Santiago de Chile: Editorial Ercilla, 1936.

_____. *Apostolado de la Prensa.* Arequipa: Imprenta La Patria, 1903.

_____. *Bajo el Oprobio*. Paris: Tipografía de Louis Bellenand et Fils, 1933.

_____. *Baladas Peruanas*. Lima: Ediciones de la Biblioteca Universitaria, 1966.

_____. *Exóticas*. Lima: Tipografía de "El Lucero," 1911.

_____. *Grafitos*. Paris: Tipografía de Louis Bellenand et Fils, 1937.

_____. *Horas de Lucha*. Lima: Fondo de Cultura Económica, Ediciones "Futuro," 1964.

_____. *Libertarias*. Paris: Tipografía de Louis Bellenand et Fils, 1938.

_____. *Minúsculas*. Lima: Tipografía de "El Lucero," 1909.

_____. *Nota Informativa acerca de la Biblioteca Nacional*. Lima: Imprenta de la Acción Popular, 1912.

_____. *Nuevas Páginas Libres*. Santiago de Chile: Editorial Ercilla, 1937.

_____. *Pájinas Libres*. 2 vols. Lima: Fondo de Cultura Popular, 1966.

_____. *Poemas Desconocidos*. Lima: Editorial Jurídica, 1973.

_____. *Presbiterianas*. Lima: Imprenta: "El Olimpo, " 1909.

_____. *Propaganda y Ataque*. Buenos Aires: Ediciones Imán, 1939.

_____. *Prosa Menuda*. Buenos Aires: Ediciones Imán, 1941.

_____. *El Tonel de Diógenes*. Mexico City: Fondo de Cultura Económica, 1945.

_____. *Trozos de Vida*. Paris: 1933.

Haya de la Torre, Víctor Raúl. *Homenaje de Víctor Raúl a los Mártires del 32*. Trujillo: Partido Aprista Peruano, n.d.

_____. *Política Aprista*. 2d ed. Lima: Editorial Imprenta Amauta, 1967.

_____. *Tres Discursos*. Lima: Ediciones del Bloque Antifascista, 1945.

Heysen, Luis E. *El ABC de la Peruanización*. Lima: Editorial Apra, 1931.

Hidalgo, Alberto. *Arenga Lírica al Emperador de Alemania*. Arequipa: Quiroz Hnos., 1916.

_____. *Cantos de la Revolución*. Lima: Editorial Cooperativa Aprista, 1934.

_____. *Radiografía de Haya de la Torre*. Lima: Ediciones "Páginas Libres," 1946.

Huerta, Juan Ambrosio. *Cartas del Illmo. y Rmo. Sr. D. D. Juan Ambrosio Huerta, Dignísimo Obispo de Puno al D. D. Francisco de Paula González Vigil, con Motivo del Análisis que éste Hizo de la Nota con que S. S. Illma. Contestó la Circular del Sr. Ministro del Culto sobre Supresión de las Comunidades Religiosas de la República*. Arequipa: Imprenta Seminario, 1873.

_____. *Instrucción Pastoral que, sobre el Syllabus Publicado por Nuestro Santísimo Padre el Sr. Pío IX el 8 de Diciembre de 1864 Dirige a sus Amados Diocesanos el Iltmo. Obispo de la Diócesis*. Puno: Imprenta de D. Mariano C. Martínez, 1874.

Idiological Basis of the Peruvian Revolution. Lima: Oficina Central de Información, 1975.

Irigoyen Pedro. *Inducciones acerca de la Civilización Incaica.* Lima: Imprenta "La Industria," 1909.

Itolararres, José [Juan Torres Lara]. *La Trinidad del Indio o Costumbres del Interior.* Lima: Imprenta "Bolognesi," 1885.

Laso, Benito. *Artículos Editoriales del Correo Peruano Escritos por El S. D. D. Benito Laso.* Lima: National Library, n.d.

_____. *Exposición que Hace Benito Laso Diputado al Congreso por la Provincia de Puno.* Lima: Imprenta Republicana Administrada, 1826.

_____. *El Poder de la Fuerza y el Poder de la Ley.* Lima: Ediciones Hora del Hombre, 1947.

Ley General de Educación. Lima: Pontificia Universidad Católica, n.d.

López Albujar, Enrique. *Cuentos Andinos.* 6th ed. Lima: Editorial Juan Mejía Baca, 1971.

Luna Victoria, Romeo. *Ciencia y Práctica de la Revolución.* Lima: Editorial Studium, 1966.

MacKay, John A. *Christianity on the Frontier.* New York: Macmillan Company, 1950.

_____. *That Other America.* New York: Friendship Press, 1935.

_____. *The Other Spanish Christ.* London: Student Christian Movement Press, 1932.

[Mariátegui, Francisco Javier.] *Defensa Católica del Primer Tomo del "Curso de Derecho Eclesiástico" del Sr. Vidaurre contra las Censuras del Presbítero D. José Mateo Aguilar y del P. F. Vicente Seminario.* Lima: Imprenta de Eusebio Aranda, 1840. This work appeared under the pseudonym of "Marca-Martillas."

_____. *Manual del Regalista, con la Agregación de la Carta Escrita al Sr. D. Francisco de Paula G. Vigil sobre la Infalibilidad y el Entredicho de Puno.* Lima: Imprenta del Universo, 1873. This work appeared under the pseudonym of "Patricio Matamoros."

_____. *Refutación al Papel Titulado Abuso del Poder contra las Libertades de la Iglesia, Escrita por un Verdadero Católico.* Lima: Imprenta de Manuel Corbal, 1831.

_____. *Reseña histórica de los Principales Concordatos Celebrados con Roma.* Lima; Impreso por José María, 1856.

_____. *Vindicación que la Mayoría de los Vocales de la Comisión de Códigos Presenta al Público contra las que se le Hacen por el S. D. D. Manuel Perez de Tudela en la Nota con que Pasó al Ministerio El Proyecto del Código Civil, Escrita por uno de Ellos.* Lima: Imprenta de Eusebio Aranda, 1847.

Mariátegui, José Carlos. *El Alma Matinal y Otras Estaciones del Hombre de Hoy.* 4th ed. Lima: Empresa Editora Amauta, 1972.

_____. *El Artista y la Epoca.* 4th ed. Lima: Empresa Editora Amauta, 1970.

_____. *Cartas de Italia.* 2d ed. Lima: Empresa Editora Amauta, 1972.

_____. *Defensa del Marxismo.* 3d ed. Lima: Empresa Editora Amauta, 1970.

_____. *La Escena Contemporánea*. 4th ed. Lima: Empresa Editora Amauta, 1970.

_____. *Historia de la Crisis Mundial*. Lima: Empresa Editora Amauta, 1959.

_____. *Ideología y Política*. 3d ed. Lima: Empresa Editora Amauta, 1972.

_____. *La Novela y la Vida*. 3d ed. Lima: Empresa Editora Amauta, 1967.

_____. *Peruanicemos al Perú*. Lima: Empesa Editora Amauta, 1970.

_____. *Seven Interpretive Essays on Peruvian Reality*. Translated by Marjory Urquidi. Austin: University of Texas Press, 1971.

_____. *Siete Ensayos de Interpretación de la Realidad Peruana*. 11th ed. Lima: Empresa Editora Amauta, 1967.

_____. *Temas de Educación*. Lima: Empresa Editora Amauta, 1970.

_____. *Temas de Nuestra América*. Lima: Empresa Editoria Amauta, 1960.

Matto de Turner, Clorinda. *Aves sin Nido*. Buenos Aires: Ediciones Solar/Hachette, 1968.

_____. *El Evangelio Según San Lucas en Quechua y Castellano*. 2d ed. Lima: Imprenta El Progreso, 1912.

_____. *Hima-Sumac*. Lima: Imprenta la Equitativa, 1892.

_____. *Herencia*. Lima, 1895.

_____. *Indole*. Lima, 1891.

_____. *Tradiciones Cuzqueñas*. 2 vols. Lima: Imprenta de Torres Aguirre, 1884.

Mayer de Zulen, Dora. *El Desarrollo de las Ideas Avanzadas en el Perú*. Callao, 1934.

_____. *El Indígena Peruano a los Cien Años de República Libre e Independiente*. Lima, 1921.

_____. *La Intangibilidad de las Comunidades Indígenas*. Callao, 1936.

Mejía Xesspe, Toribio. *Algunas Costumbres y Creencias de los Indígenas*. Lima, 1922.

Mendoza Díaz, Vicente. "La Cuestión Religiosa Indígena en el Perú." *La Sierra* no. 29 (1929):30-32.

Moreno, José Ignacio. *Ensayo sobre la Supremacía del Papa, Especialmente con respecto a la Institución de los Obispos*. Lima: Imprenta de José Masías, 1831.

Muñiz, Pedro, and Showing, Carlos. *Lo que es el Aprismo*. Lima: Partido Aprista Peruano, 1932.

Una Ojeada a la Novela 'Aves sin Nido'. Cuzco: Tipografía de Propaganda Católica, 1891.

Olivas Escudero, Fidel. *Curso de Geografía para Escuelas y Colegios de Instrucción Media Arreglado Conforme al Programa Oficial*. 2d ed. Lima: Imprenta Calle del Mascarón, 1889.

_____. *Obras de Monseñor Dr. Fidel Olivas Escudero, Obispo de Ayacucho*. 6 vols. Lima: Imprenta Comercial de Horacio la Rosa, 1911.

Pamplona: Más Allá de los Hechos. Lima: Centro de Estudios y Publicaciones, 1971.

Partido Aprista Peruano. *Boletín de las Universidades Populares González Prada.* Lima, April, 1946.

_____. *Cartilla Aprista.* Lima: National Library, n.d.

_____. *El Proceso Haya de la Torre.* 2d ed. Lima: Editorial Imprenta Amauta, 1969.

Prado y Ugarteche, Javier. *Estado Social del Perú durante la Dominación Española.* Lima: Imprenta de El Diario Judicial, 1894.

El Pueblo de Huanta ante la Opinión Pública. Lima: Private Collection of Rubén Vargas, S.J., n.p., n.d.

La Raza Indígena en los Albores del Siglo XX. Lima: Imprenta Calle de Filipinas, 1902.

Reyna, Ernesto. *El Amauta Atusparia.* 2d ed. Lima, 1932.

[Rodríguez Pastor, Carlos.] *Catolicismo y Aprismo.* Lima: Imprenta Minerva, 1934.

Romero, Emilio. "Las Campanas Religiosas de Ayer y los Tiempos Nuevos." *La Sierra* (January, 1927):27–30.

_____. "El Cuzco Católico." *Amauta* (December, 1927):54.

_____. *3 Ciudades del Perú.* Lima: Imprenta Torres Aguirre, 1929.

Rossi, Juan José, ed. *Iglesia Latinoamericana, ¿Protesta o Profecía?.* Avellaneda, Argentina: Ediciones Búsqueda, 1969.

Sánchez, Luis Alberto. *Aprismo y Religión.* Lima: Editorial Cooperativa Aprista "Atahualpa," 1933.

Secretaría General del Episcopado del Perú. *Carta Pastoral Colectiva del Episcopado Peruano sobre la Actividad Social y Política en la Hora Presente.* Lima, 1963.

_____. *Familia y Población.* Lima, 1974.

_____. *Primera Semana Social del Perú.* Lima, 1959.

Seoane, Manuel. *Comunistas Criollos.* 3d ed. Lima, 1933.

_____. *Nuestros Fines.* Lima: F.Y.E. Rosay, 1931.

_____. *Páginas Polémicas.* Lima: Editorial La Tribuna, 1931.

_____. *La Revolución que el Perú Necesita.* Arequipa, 1965.

Uriel García, José. *El Nuevo Indio.* Lima: Editorial Universo, 1973.

Valcárcel, Luis, Valega, José M., Larco Herrera, Rafael, Antúnez de Mayolo, Santiago. *Hacia el Despertar del Alma India.* Lima: Southwell, 1929.

Valcárcel, Luis. *Kon, Pachacamac, Viracocha.* Cuzco: Imprenta de "El Trabajo," 1912.

_____. *Mirador Indio.* Lima, 1937.

_____. *Tempestad en Los Andes.* Lima: Editorial Universo, 1972.

_____. *De la Vida Incaica.* Lima: Editorial Garcilaso, 1925.

Vargas, Rubén. *¿Aprista o Católico?* Lima: Editorial Alfama, 1934.

Velasco Alvarado, Juan. *El Proceso Peruano.* Lima: Instituto Nacional de Investigación y Desarrollo de la Educación, 1974.

_____. *Velasco: la Voz de la Revolución.* 2 vols. Lima: Editorial Ausonia, 1972.

Vidaurre, Manuel Lorenzo de. *Cartas Americanas, Políticas y Morales.* 2 vols. Philadelphia: Juan F. Hurtel, 1823.

_____. *Escritos Políticos.* Lima: Imprenta del Estado por J. González, n.d.

_____. *Plan del Perú.* Philadelphia: Juan Francisco Hurtel, 1823.

_____. *Proyecto del Código Civil Peruano.* 3 vols. Lima: 1834–1836.

_____. *Proyecto del Código Eclesiástico.* Paris: Imprenta de Julio Didot, 1830.

_____. *Proyecto de un Código Penal.* Boston: Hiram Tuper, 1828.

_____. *Proyecto de Reforma de la Constitución Peruana.* Lima: Imprenta de J. M. Masías, 1833.

_____. *Vidaurre contra Vidaurre.* Lima: Imprenta del Comercio, 1839.

Vigil, Francisco de Paula González. *Cartas al Papa Pío IX con Varios Documentos al Caso.* Lima: Imprenta de "El Comercio," 1871.

_____. *Catecismo Patriótico para el Uso de las Escuelas Municipales de la Ciudad del Callao.* Callao: Imprenta de Estéban Danino, 1859.

_____. *Diálogos sobre la Existencia de Dios y de la Vida Futura.* Lima: Imprenta del "Pueblo," 1863.

_____. *Defensa de la Autoridad de los Gobiernos y de los Obispos contra las Pretensiones de la Curia Romana.* 6 vols. Lima: Imprenta José Huidobro Molina, 1848–49.

_____. *Importancia de las Asociaciones; Importancia de la Educación Popular.* Edited by Alberto Tauro. Lima: Ediciones Hora del Hombre, 1948.

_____. *Los Jesuitas Presentados en Cuadros Históricos.* 4 vols. Lima: Imprenta de Manuel Reyes, 1863.

_____. *De la Libertad de Cultos sin Religión del Estado.* Tacna: Imprenta de "El Porvenir" por José Huidobro Molina, 1861.

_____. *Manual de Derecho Público-Eclesiástico para el Uso de la Juventud Americana.* Lima: Imprenta del "Pueblo," 1863.

_____. *Opúsculos Sociales y Políticos Dedicados a la Juventud Americana.* Lima: Tipografía de Guillermo Guerrero, 1862.

_____. *Roma: Opúsculo sobre el Principado Político del Romano Pontífice.* Lima: Imprenta de "El Comercio" por J. R. Sánchez, 1871.

Yarlequé de Marquina, Josefina. *El Maestro o Democracia en Miniatura.* Lima: Librería J. Alvarez, 1963.

Secondary Sources (Books and Articles).

Adams, Robert. "Ancient Incas and Modern Revolution." *New York Review of Books* 32 (March 18, 1976):43–47.

Aguirre, Manuel. *El Abate de Pradt en la Emancipación Hispanoamericana (1800–1830).* Analecta Gregoriana. Vol. 25. Rome: Typis Pontificiae Universitatis Gregoriannae, 1941.

Alayza y Paz Soldán, Alejandro. *Breve Historia de la Francmasonería Peruana y del Pacto Celebrado entre la Gran Logio del Perú y el Supremo Consejo del Grado 33 del Rito Escocés.* Lima: Ediciones Revista Masónica del Perú, n.d.

Alexander, Robert J. *Prophets of the Revolution: Profiles of Latin American Leaders.* New York: The Macmillan Company, 1962.

Alvarez Brun, Felix. *Ancash: Una Historia Regional Peruana.* Lima, 1970.

Angeles Figueroa, Artemio. *Yungay, Tierra Mía.* Lima, 1963.

Antoncich, Ricardo. "Sociología Religiosa: Reflexiones Pastorales." *Survey S.J. del Perú.* Mimeographed. Lima, 1969.

Antúnez de Mayolo, Santiago. "La Sublevación de los Indios del Callejón de Huaylas." Lima: Ediciones de la Revista El Luzuriaguino, 1957.

Astiz, Carlos. *Pressure Groups and Power Elites in Peruvian Politics.* Ithaca, New York: University of Cornell, 1969.

Baeza Flores, Alberto. *Haya de la Torre y la Revolución Constructiva de las Américas.* Buenos Aires: Editorial Claridad, 1962.

Basadre, Jorge. *Historia de la República del Perú, 1822-1933.* 16 vols. 6th ed. Lima: Editorial Universitaria, 1970.

_____. *La Multitud, la Ciudad y el Campo en la Historia del Perú.* 2d ed. Lima: Editorial Huascarán, 1947.

_____. *Perú: Problema y Posibilidad.* Lima: Casa Editorial E. Rosay, 1931.

Barreda, Felipe. *Vida Intelectual del Virreinato del Perú.* 3d ed. Lima: Universidad Nacional Mayor de San Marcos, 1964.

Bazán, Armando. *Mariátegui y su Tiempo.* Lima: Empresa Editora Amauta, 1969.

Belaúnde, Víctor Andrés. *La Realidad Nacional.* 3d ed. Lima, 1963.

Bergson, Henri. *Oeuvres.* Edited by André Robinet and Henri Gouhier. Paris: Presses Universitaires de France, 1962.

Blanco Fombona, Rufino. *Crítica de la Obra de González Prada.* Lima: Fondo de Cultura Popular, 1966.

Bourricaud, François. *Power and Society in Contemporary Peru.* Translated by Paul Stevenson. New York: Frederick A. Praeger, 1970.

Brady, Patrick. "Peru: Revolution, Church, Salvation." *The Furrow* 23 (March, 1972):140-52.

Bustamante y Rivero, José Luis. *Tres Años de Lucha por la Democracia en el Perú.* Buenos Aires, 1949.

Cabello, Pedro. *Guía Política, Eclesiástica y Militar del Perú.* Lima: Imprenta del Estado, 1873.

Castro Arenas, Mario. *La Novela Peruana y la Evolución Social.* 2d ed. Lima: José Godard, Editor, n.d.

_____. *La Rebelión de Juan Santos Atahualpa.* Lima: Imprenta Editora Atlántida, 1973.

Carreño, Juan Manuel. *La Anarquía en el Perú.* Callao, 1915.

Cavero, Luis. *Monografía de la Provincia de Huanta.* 2 vols. Lima: Empreso Editorial Rimac, 1953.

Censo General de la República del Perú Formado en 1876. 7 vols. Lima: Imprenta del Teatro, 1878.

Clinton, Richard Lee. "Apra: An Appraisal." *Journal of Inter-American Studies and World Affairs.* 12, no. 2 (April, 1970):280-97.

Cossío del Pomar, Felipe. *Víctor Raúl.* Mexico: Editorial Cultura, 1969.

_____. *Víctor Raúl Haya de la Torre: El Indoamericano.* Lima: Editorial Nuevo Día, 1946.

Chang-Rodríguez, Eugenio. *El Pensamiento Político de González Prada, Mariátegui and Haya de la Torre.* Mexico City: Ediciones Andrea, 1957.

Chavarría, Jesús. "The Intellectuals and the Crisis of Modern Peruvian Nationalism." *Hispanic American Historical Review.* 50 (May, 1970): 257-78.

_____. "José Carlos Mariátegui, Revolutionary Nationalist: The Origins and Crisis of Modern Peruvian Nationalism, 1870-1930." Ph.D. dissertation, University of California, Los Angeles, 1967.

Davies, Thomas M., Jr. *Indian Integration in Peru: A Half Century of Experience, 1900-1948.* Lincoln: University of Nebraska, 1970.

_____. "The *Indigenismo* of the Peruvian Aprista Party: A Reinterpretation." *Hispanic American Historical Review* 51 (November, 1971): 626-45.

Del Mazo, Gabriel. *La Reforma Universitaria.* 6 vols. Buenos Aires: Ediciones del Centro de Estudiantes de Ingeniería, 1941.

Diagnóstico Situacional de Villa El Salvador. Lima: Dirección General de Educación Básica, Universidad Católica, 1973.

Díaz, Alida. *El Censo General de 1876 en el Perú.* Lima: Seminario de Historia Rural Andina, 1974.

Elvira Romero, María. "El Protestantismo Anglosajón en el Perú, 1822-1915." Ph.D. dissertation, Catholic University, Lima, 1974.

Enríquez, Luis Eduardo. *La Estafa Política Más Grande de América.* Lima: Ediciones del Pacífico, 1951.

Ferrero, Raúl. *El Liberalismo Peruano: Contribución a una Historia de las Ideas.* Lima: Biblioteca de Escritores Peruanos, 1958.

Frank, Waldo. *Our America.* New York: AMS Press, 1972.

Ford, Thomas R. *Man and Land in Peru.* Gainesville: University of Florida Press, 1955.

Frazer, James Georges. *The Golden Bough.* 12 vols. 3d ed. New York: The Macmillan Company, 1935.

Frías, Ismael, *La Revolución Peruana y la Vía Socialista.* Lima: Editorial Horizonte, 1970.

Fuenzalida, Fernando, Mayer Enrique, et. al. *El Indio y el Poder en el Perú.* Lima: Moncloa-Campódonico, Editores Asociados, 1970.

Garr, Thomas M., S.J. *Cristianismo y Religión Quechua en la Prelatura de Ayaviri.* Arequipa: Editorial Miranda, 1972.

González Marín, Alberto. *Francisco de Paula González Vigil, El Precursor, El Justo, El Maestro.* Lima, 1961.

González Prada, Adriana. *Mi Manuel.* Lima: Editorial Antártica, 1947.

Gutiérrez, Gustavo. *A Theology of Liberation.* Translated by Sister Caridad Inda and John Eagleson. Maryknoll, New York: Orbis Books, 1973.

Haya de la Torre, Víctor Raúl. *El Antiimperialismo y el Apra*. Santiago de
Chile: Ediciones Ercilla, 1936.

_____. *Construyendo el Aprismo*. Buenos Aires: Colección Claridad
"Ciencias Políticas," 1933.

_____. *¿A Dónde Va Indoamerica?* Santiago de Chile: Ediciones
Ercilla, 1935.

_____. *Impresiones de la Inglatera Imperialista y la Rusia Soviética*.
Buenos Aires: Colección Claridad "Acción y Crítica," 1932.

_____. *Pensamiento Político de Haya de la Torre*. Edited by Luis
Rodríguez Vildosola, et al. 5 vols. Lima: Ediciones Pueblo, 1961.

_____. *Por la Emancipación de la América Latina*. Buenos Aires: M.
Gleizer, 1927.

_____. *Teoría y Táctica del Aprismo*. Lima: "La Cultura Peruana,"
1933.

_____. "What is A.P.R.A.? " *Labour Monthly* (London) 8 (December, 1926):756-59.

Haya de la Torre, Víctor Raúl, and Ingenieros, José. *Teoría y Táctica de la
Acción Renovadora y Antiimperialista de la Juventud en América Latina*.
Buenos Aires: Publicaciones "Centro Estudiantes de Ciencias Económicas,"
1928.

Herr, Richard. *The Eighteenth Century Revolution in Spain*. Princeton, New
Jersey: Princeton University Press, 1969.

Hilliker, Grant. *The Politics of Reform in Peru: The Aprista and Other Mass
Parties of Latin America*. Baltimore: The Johns Hopkins Press, 1971.

Kadt, Emanuel de. "Paternalism and Populism: Catholicism in Latin America."
Journal of Contemporary History 2 (October, 1967):89-106.

Kantor, Harry. *Ideology and Program of the Peruvian Aprista Movement*.
Berkeley and Los Angeles: University of California, 1953.

Keith, Robert, et al. *La Hacienda, la Comunidad y el Campesino en el
Perú*. Lima: Moncloa-Campodónico, Editores Asociados, 1970.

Kerbusch, Ernst-J., ed. *Cambios Estructurales en el Perú, 1968-1975*. Lima:
Instituto Latinoamericano de Investigaciones Sociales, 1976.

Klarén, Peter. *Modernization, Dislocation, and Aprismo: Origins of the
Peruvian Aprista Party, 1870-1932*. Austin: University of Texas, 1973.

Leguía, Jorge Guillermo. *Estudios Históricos*. Santiago de Chile: Ediciones
Ercilla, 1939.

_____. *Manuel Lorenzo de Vidaurre: Contribución a un Ensayo de
Interpretación Sicológica*. Lima, 1935.

Lewin, Boleslao. *La Rebelión de Tupac Amaru y los Orígenes de la Independencia de Hispanoamérica*. 3d ed. Buenos Aires: Sociedad Editora
Latinoamericana, 1967.

Linares Málaga, Fausto. *Monseñor Lisson y sus Derechos al Arzobispado de
Lima*. Lima, 1933.

Lisson, Emilio. *La Iglesia de España en el Perú: Colección de Documentos
para la Historia de la Iglesia, que se Encuentran en Varios Archivos*.
Seville, Spain, 1943.

Lituma, Luis. "La Iglesia Católica en el Perú durante el Siglo XX." In *Visión del Perú en el Siglo XX*, edited by José Pareja Paz-Soldán, 2:473-523. Lima: Ediciones Librería Studium, 1963.

Lowenthal, Abraham, ed. *The Peruvian Experiment: Continuity and Change under Military Rule*. Princeton, New Jersey: Princeton University Press, 1975.

Macaulay, Michael G. "Ideological Change and Internal Cleavages in the Peruvian Church: Change, Status Quo, and the Priest: The Case of *Onis*." Ph.D. dissertation, University of Notre Dame, 1972.

McCurry, Dan C. "U.S. Church-Financed Missions in Peru." In *U.S. Foreign Policy and Peru*, edited by Daniel Sharp, Austin: University of Texas Press, 1972.

McIntire, William J. "Maryknoll and Peruvian Education." *Catholic Mind*, (November, 1972):48-54.

McNicoll, Robert Edwards. "Intellectual Origins of Aprismo." *Hispanic American Historical Review* 23 (August, 1943):424-40.

Mahon, Leo T. "Machismo and Christianity." *Catholic Mind*, (February, 1965): 4-11.

Mannheim, Karl. *Ideology and Utopia: An Introduction to the Sociology of Knowledge*. Translated by Louis Wirth and Edward Shils. New York: Harvest Books, Harcourt, Brace and World, Inc., n.d.

Martín, Luis. *The Kingdom of the Sun*. New York: Charles Scribner's Sons, 1974.

Martínez de la Torre, Ricardo. *Apuntes para una Interpretación Marxista de Historia Social del Perú*. 4 vols. Lima: Editora Peruana, 1947.

Marzal, Manuel. "Investigación e Hipótesis sobre la Religiosidad Popular," *Pastoral y Lenguaje, Colección del Instituto Pastoral Latinoamericano* 18, Bogotá: IndoAmerican Press Service, 1973, 20-22.

_____. *El Mundo Religioso de Urcos*. Cuzco: Instituto de Pastoral Andina, 1971.

_____. "La Religiosidad Popular en el Perú." *Iglesia en el Perú* (April, 1972):1-6.

Mason, J. Alden. *The Ancient Civilizations of Peru*. Baltimore: Penguin Books, 1957.

Melis, Antonio, Dessau, Adalbert, and Kossok, Manfred. *Mariátegui: Tres Estudios*. Lima: Empresa Amauta, 1971.

Mercado, Rogger. *La Revolución de Trujillo*. Lima: Fondo de Cultura, 1932.

Meseguer, Diego. *José Carlos Mariátegui y su Pensamiento Revolucionario*. Lima: Instituto de Estudios Peruanos, 1974.

Molina, Alfronso, ed. *Cuentos Revolucionarios del Perú*. Lima: Ediciones América Latina, 1967.

Montes, Fernando. "How the 'ONIS' Movement Began and Grew." *Ladoc* (February, 1974) Article 24.

Neira, Hugo. *Cuzco: Tierra y Muerte*. Lima, 1964.

Olivas Escudero, Fidel. *Apuntes para la Historia de Huamanga o Ayacucho, con Motivo del Primer Centenario de la Batalla, 1824-1924*. Ayacucho: Imprenta Diocesana, n.d.

Palma, Ricardo. *Tradiciones Peruanas.* Vol. 5. Lima: Editorial Cultura Antártica, 1951.

Paris, Robert. "El Marxismo de Mariátegui." *Aportes,* no. 17 (July, 1970):7-30.

Payne, Robert L. *Labor and Politics in Peru.* New Haven: Yale University Press, 1965.

Pease, Henry, and Verme, Olga. *Perú, 1968-1974: Cronología Política.* 3 vols. Lima: Desco, 1976.

Pesce, Hugo. *El Factor Religioso.* Lima: Empresa Editora Amauta, 1972.

Pike, Fredrick B. "Catholic Church and Modernization in Peru and Chile." *Journal of Inter-American Affairs* 20 (1966):272-88.

_____. "Heresy, Real and Alleged in Peru: An Aspect of the Conservative-Liberal Struggle, 1830-1875." *Hispanic American Historical Review* 47 (February, 1967):50-74.

_____. *A Modern History of Peru.* New York: Frederick A.Praeger, 1967.

_____. "The Modernized Church in Peru." *The Review of Politics* 26 (July, 1964):307-18.

_____. "The Problem of Identity and National Destiny in Peru and Argentina." In *Latin American History: Select Problems,* edited by Fredrick B. Pike, pp. 174-204. New York: Harcourt, Brace and World, Inc., 1969.

_____. "South America's Multifaceted Catholicism: Glimpses of Twentieth-Century Argentina, Chile and Peru." In *The Church and Social Change in Latin America,* edited by Henry Landsberger, pp. 53-75. Notre Dame: University of Notre Dame Press, 1970.

Pino, Juan José. *Las Sublevaciones Indígenas de Huanta.* Lima: Centro de Estudios Históricos y Militares, n.d.

Ponte González, Alfonso. *Con el Perú Adentro.* Lima: Editorial "Thesis," 1965.

_____. *Por la Senda.* Lima: Imprenta Gráfica "Stylo," 1943.

Quijano, Aníbal. *Nationalism and Capitalism in Peru: A Study in Neo-Imperialism.* Translated by Helen R. Lane. New York: Monthly Review Press, 1971.

Raimondi, Antonio. *El Departamento de Ancash y sus Riquezas Minerales.* Lima: Imprenta de "El Nacional," 1873.

Reina Loli, Manuel. "Causas del Movimiento Campesino de 1885." Mimeographed. Lima, 1969.

_____. "Monseñor Fidel Olivas Escudero." In *Justitia et Pax: En Memoria de Mons. Fidel Olivas Escudero,* pp. 235-57. Lima, 1971.

Reyna, Ernesto. *Fitzcarrald, el Rey del Caucho.* Lima: P. Barrantes, Castro, 1942.

_____. *Los Tesoros de Huarmey.* Lima: Editorial Perú Actual, 1936.

Richardson, Miles, Pardo, Marta Eugenia, and Bode, Barbara. "The Image of Christ in Spanish America as a Model for Suffering." *Journal of Inter-American Studies and World Affairs* 13 (April, 1971):246-57.

Rodríguez, Alfredo, Riofrío, Gustavo, and Welsh, Eileen. *De Invasores a Invadidos.* Lima: Desco, 1973.

Romero, Emilio. *Historia Económica del Perú.* Buenos Aires: Editorial Sudamericana, 1949.

Rouillón, Guillermo. *Biobibliografía de José Carlos Mariátegui.* Lima: University of San Marcos Press, 1963.

_____. *La Creación Heroica de José Carlos Mariátegui.* 2 vols. Lima: Editorial Arica, 1975.

Saenz, Moisés. *Sobre el Indio Peruano y su Incorporación al Medio Nacional.* Mexico City: Publicaciones de la Secretaría de Educación Pública, 1933.

Salazar Bondy, Augusto. *Historia de las Ideas en el Perú Contemporáneo.* 2 vols. Lima: Francisco Moncloa, Editores, 1965.

Salvatecci García, Hugo. *El Anarquismo Frente al Marxismo y el Perú.* Lima: Mosca Azul Editores, 1972.

_____. *El Pensamiento de González Prada.* Lima: Editorial Arica, 1972.

San Cristóbal-Sebastián, Antonio. *Economía, Educación y Marxismo en Mariátegui.* Lima: Ediciones Studium, 1960.

Sánchez, Luis Alberto. *Antología del Pensamiento Democrático Americano: Manuel González Prada.* Mexico: Imprenta Universitaria, 1945.

_____. *Don Manuel.* 4th ed. Lima: Populibros, n.d.

_____. *Haya de la Torre y el Apra.* Santiago de Chile: Editorial del Pacífico, 1954.

_____. "John A. MacKay y el Anglo-Peruano." *Leader* 45 (December, 1972):50–53.

_____. *La Literatura Peruana.* 3 vols. Lima: Ediciones de Ediventas, 1965.

_____. *Testimonio Personal.* 3 vols. Lima: Ediciones Villasán, 1969.

Sarrailh, Jean. *La España Ilustrada de la Segunda Mitad del Siglo XVII.* Translated from the French by Antonio Alatorre. Mexico City: Fondo de Cultura Económica, 1957.

Smith, Brian, S.J. "Religion and Social Change: Classical Theories and New Formulations in the Context of Recent Developments in Latin America." *Latin American Research Review* 10 (Summer, 1975):3–34.

Sorel, Georges. *Les Illusions de progrès.* 3d ed. Paris: Marcel Riviére, 1921.

_____. *Introductión a l'économie moderne.* Paris: Marcel Riviére, 1922.

_____. *Matériaux d'une Théorie du Prolétariat.* Paris: Riviére, 1921.

_____. *Réflexions sur la violence.* 3d ed. Paris: Marcel Riviére, 1912.

_____. *La Ruine du monde antique.* 2d ed. Paris: Marcel Riviére, 1925.

_____. *De l'utilité de pragmatisme.* Paris: Marcel Riviére, 1921.

Stabb, Martin S. *In Quest of Identity: Patterns in the Spanish American Essay of Ideas, 1890–1960.* Chapel Hill, North Carolina: University of North Carolina Press, 1967.

Stanger, Francis Merriam. "Church and State in Peru." *Hispanic American Historical Review* 7 (November, 1927):410–37.

Stein, Stephen Jay. "Populism and Mass Politics in Peru: The Political Behavior of the Lima Working Classes in the 1931 Presidential Election." Ph.D. dissertation, University of Stanford, 1973.

Stiglich, Fernando. *Relaciones Estado-Iglesia en el Perú.* Lima, 1969.

Tamayo Vargas, Augusto. *Literatura Peruana.* 2 vols. Lima: Imprenta de la Universidad Nacional Mayor de San Marcos, 1954.

Tauro, Alberto. *Diccionario Enciclopédico del Perú.* 3 vols. Lima: Editorial Mejía Baca, 1966-67.

Thorndike, Guillermo. *El Año de la Barbarie.* Lima: Editorial Nueva América, 1969.

Tibesar, Antonine, O.F.M. "The Peruvian Church at the Time of Independence in the Light of Vatican II." *The Americas* 26 (April, 1970):349-75.

Torres Luna, Alfonso. *Biografía de Juan Bustamante.* Lima: Imprenta "Lux," 1941.

Valcárcel, Daniel. *La Rebelión de Tupac Amaru.* 2d ed. Mexico City: Fondo de Cultura Popular, 1973.

_____. *Rebeliones Indígenas.* Lima: Editorial P.T.C.M., 1946.

Valdez de la Torre, Carlos. *Evolución de las Comunidades de Indígenas.* Lima: Editorial Euforión, 1921.

Vallier, Ivan. *Catholicism, Social Control, and Modernization in Latin America.* Englewood Cliffs, New Jersey: Prentice-Hall, Inc., 1970.

_____. "Radical Priests and the Revolution." In *Changing Latin America: New Interpretations of its Politics and Society,* edited by Douglas A. Chalmers, pp. 15-26. New York: The Academy of Political Science, 1972.

Vanden, Harry. *Mariátegui: Influencias en su Formación Ideológica.* Lima: Empresa Editora Amauta, 1975.

Varallanos, José. *Bandoleros en el Perú.* Lima: Editorial Altura, 1937.

_____. *Historia de Huánuco.* Buenos Aires: Imprenta López, 1959.

_____. *Legislación Indiana Republicana.* Lima, 1947.

Vargas, Rubén. *Historia de la Iglesia en el Perú.* 5 vols. Burgos, Spain: Imprenta Aldecoa, 1962.

_____. *Historia del Santo Cristo de los Milagros.* 3d ed. Lima, 1966.

Vidales, Raúl, and Kudo, Tokihiro. *Práctica Religiosa y Proyecto Histórico: Hipótesis para un Estudio de la Religiosidad Popular en América Latina.* Lima: Centro de Estudios y Publicaciones, 1975.

Villanueva, Víctor, *El Apra en Busca del Poder, 1930-1940.* Lima: Editorial Horizonte, 1975.

_____. *El CAEM y la Revolución de la Fuerza Armada.* Lima: Instituto de Estudios Peruanos, 1972.

_____. *Ejército Peruano: Del Caudillaje Anárquico al Militarismo Reformista.* Lima: Editorial Juan Mejía Baca, 1973.

Wiesse, María. *José Carlos Mariátegui, Etapas de su Vida.* 3d ed. Lima: Empresa Editora Amauta, 1971.

Zavaleta Figueroa, Isaías. *Biografía Sucinta del Dr. Carlos Philipps.* Caraz, 1960.

Zimmermann, Augusto. *El Plan Inca, Objetivo: Revolución Peruana.* Lima: Editorial "El Peruano," 1974.

Interviews

Bach, Antonio, S.J., and Gallagher, Kevin, S.J., directors of Fe y Alegría of Peru. Interview held in Lima, September 22, 1976.

Bambarén, Luis, auxiliary bishop of Lima y president of the bishops' commission on social justice. Interview held in Lima, September 1, 1976.

Bartra, Enrique, S.J., advisor to the bishops' committee on responsible parenthood. Interview held in Lima, September 11, 1976.

Cornejo Chávez, Héctor, leader of the Christian Democratic party. Interview held in Lima, September 6, 1976.

Cox, Carlos Manuel, an editor of *Amauta;* a principal founder of Apra; and long-time senator from La Libertad. Interview held in Lima, July 31, 1975.

Haya de la Torre, Víctor Raúl, founder of the Popular Universities and the Peruvian Aprista party. Interviews held in Lima, July 26, 1972; July 25, 1975; August 7, 1975; August 6, 1976.

Heysen, Luis, early collaborator in the Popular Universities; a principal founder of Apra; and long-time senator from Lambayeque. Interview held in Lima, July 26, 1975.

Montagne, Ernesto, army general and prime minister of Peru from 1968–1973. Interview held in Lima, September 7, 1976.

Morales, Ricardo, S.J., president of the superior advisory council of the Ministry of Education. Interview held in Lima, September 12, 1976.

Philipps, Julia Jaramillo, widow of Carlos Philipps, the Aprista leader of Huaraz in 1932. Interview held in Caraz, August 9, 1974.

Ponte González, Alfonso, diocesan priest from Ancash; rector of the seminary of Huaraz in the late twenties and early thrities; and currently director of the cathedral library in Lima. Interview held in Lima, June 10, 1975.

Prialé, Ramiro, Secretary General of the Aprista party on many occasions and long-time senator from Junín. Interview held in Lima, July 25, 19 1972.

Reina Loli, Manuel, nephew of Ernesto Reyna and student of Ancash history. Interview held in Lima, August 15, 1974.

Rodríguez Pastor, Carlos, former deputy from Huancavelica and one-time minister of education. Interview held in Lima, August 6, 1975.

Sabroso Montoya, Arturo, founder and co-editor of *El Obrero Textil* and long-time head of the Confederation of Peruvian Workers. Interview held in Lima, August 8, 1967.

Sánchez, Luis Alberto, former rector of San Marcos University; president of the Peruvian Senate; leading Aprista ideologist. Interview held in Lima, August 14, 1974.

Soriano, Augusto, a priest from Huaraz; former pastor of Caraz; and one-time mayor of Huaraz. Interview held in Huaraz, July 9, 1974.

Townsend Ezcurra, Andrés, leading Aprista senator. Interview held in Lima, June 27, 1974.

Vargas, Rubén, S.J., Jesuit historian. Interview held in Lima, July 6, 1967.

Villanueva, Víctor, retired army major and historian. Interview held in Lima, July 10, 1976.

Wicht, Juan Julio, S.J., staff member of the National Planning Institute. Interview held in Lima, September 11, 1976.

Yarlequé de Marquina, Josefa, former student of the Popular University
of Vitarte. Interview held in Vitarte, July 27, 1967.

INDEX